What P

MW01610962

"This book is the ULTIMATE guide for celiacs! LynnRae Ries has done the homework for us. Solutions and guidelines to the confrontations of being gluten-free when away from home are presented in a simple, understandable format that all will understand."
> —Connie Sarros, Speaker and Author of *Wheat-free Gluten-free Recipes for Special Diets*

"People with food sensitivities will find this book a wonderful resource that is filled with practical information about shopping, traveling and dining out".
> —Shelley Case, RD, Dietitian, Speaker and Author of *Gluten-Free Diet: A Comprehensive Resource Guide*

"I wish this book had been available when I was newly diagnosed. It would have let me know there was a wonderful, new world waiting for me, rather than feeling alone."
> —Marie D., Diagnosed 2001

"LynnRae Ries is clearly an expert in the field of living the celiac life. Her work in the gluten-free and allergen-free community is commendable. Whether she is giving a cooking class, delivering educational presentations to our health care and dietetic students, or helping a newly diagnosed person, she does so with professionalism and the passion to help others. I have learned a great deal from LynnRae. Her most recent book, *Waiter, Is there Wheat in My Soup?* is an excellent resource for dietitians and people on gluten-free and medically prescribed special diets.
> —Lori Anonsen, MS, RD Paradise Valley Community College Dietetic Technology Program Director

"Food allergies don't have to spoil the fun of dining out, shopping and traveling. *Waiter, Is there Wheat in My Soup* is like a safe-dining and lifestyle dictionary. It will lower your stress and change the way you shop, travel, eat and look at food in a positive way."

—Rachel Albert-Matesz, food and health writer

"*Waiter, Is there Wheat in My Soup?* is the first guide ever to help our daughter with dietary restrictions and to help the rest of us next to it understand various foods in restaurants and how to safely order them. My hope is that with this book as a guide, restaurants and other facilities will submit their names and commit to working harder to provide special menu items so people on medically prescribed special diets, their family and friends can dine out together, successfully."

—Sarah, mother and sister to gluten-free family members

Waiter, Is there Wheat in My Soup?

Also by LynnRae Ries

What? No Wheat? A primer to living the gluten-free wheat-free life
Delicious Gluten-Free Wheat-Free Breads
No Cook No Bake Gluten-Free Appetizers, Snacks and Finger Food

Waiter, Is there Wheat in My Soup?

The official guide to dining out,
shopping and traveling
gluten-free and allergen-free

LynnRae Ries

Published by What No Wheat Publishing Company
4757 East Greenway Road, Suite 107B - #91
Phoenix, Arizona 85032
602.485.8751

Visit our website at www.whatnowheat.com or www.lynnrae.com for more information on this book, updates, and other publications.

Interior design by Lisa Liddy, The Printed Page
www.theprintedpage.com

Cover design by LynnRae Ries and Lisa Liddy, The Printed Page
www.theprintedpage.com

Ries, LynnRae
Waiter, Is there Wheat in My Soup? the official guide to dining out, shopping and traveling gluten-free and allergen-free

By LynnRae Ries 1st ed.

ISBN 0-9724154-2-4

1. Special Diets   2. Health   3. Travel   4.Gluten intolerance
5. Allergies

Dedication

*To Vern Lang
the love of my life*

Acknowledgments

My sincere appreciation and thanks to everyone who contributed to this book.

Gaye Lloyd-Fisher and Jeanne Basye for their truly generous time and assistance; Sue Clayton, Suzie Eckard, Jennifer Fabiano, Marilee and Liisa for their input and efforts; Jennifer Vredenburg, Hannah and Hillary Day for their administrative help, Sarah Day and Joanne Battershall for listening to me talk about the book for months on end; Barbara Hicks and Melonie Katz for their contributions on the internet to help others; and book designer Lisa Liddy for her patience while *Waiter, Is there Wheat in My Soup?* kept growing and pushing out the completion date. When I received Lisa's first design draft of this book, her creativity with fonts and style made it easy to see that the work of many is worth the effort.

Cynthia Kupper RD, Shelley Case RD, Theresa Cornelius RD, Elaine Monarch, Chef Aaron, Chef Chuck, Mary Schluckebier, Chef Stephanie Green RD, Mireille Normand, Don Matesz, Barbara Strudwick, Janet Rinehart, Betty Barfield, and many others who contributed information.

Many support group members around the country and in Canada contributed to the success of this book, to help their own members as well as others beyond their every day reach. In the next issue, we will keep track of all of the support groups that helped so they can be individually recognized. I can honestly say that each time a support group said they were asking their members to contribute, it touched my heart—as I know this information will touch the lives of many others.

A special thanks to Cynthia Kupper, RD; the Gluten-Free Restaurant Awareness Program™, support groups and individuals who have worked with restaurants across the country so they may reap the benefits of serving their food-sensitive guests in a safer manner."

To all those mentioned, and more, "Thank you for sharing. May your kindness be returned to you ten-fold."

LynnRae Ries

Sponsor Acknowledgments

The following sponsors helped to make
this book possible in a variety of ways

Please support them with your
business and recommendations

Amazing Grains (Montina)
Amy's Kitchen, Inc.
Aspire Markets, Inc.
Authentic Foods
Biaggi's Ristorante Italiano
Bob's Red Mill Natural Foods, Inc
Bumble Bar
'Cause You're Special!
Chebe Bread Products
Chef Aaron, Inc.
Dietary Specialties
Dowd and Rogers, Inc.
EcoNatural Solutions, Inc.
Edward & Sons Trading Co. Inc.
Ener-G Foods, Inc.
Enjoy Life Foods
Everybody Eats, Inc.
Food for Life, Inc.
Fresh & Natural Foods
Gluten-Free Baking and More
Gluten-Free Cooking School
Gluten-Free Consulting Services
Gluten-Free Living Magazine
Gluten-Free Mall, The
Gluten-Free Pantry
Gluten Solutions

Grainaissance, Inc.
Grassroots Baking Company
Madwoman Foods
Manna from Anna
Marlene's Mixes
Masuya (USA) Inc.
Matter of Flax, LLC
Miss Roben's, Inc.
Namaste Foods
Nature's Hilights, Inc.
Nu-World Amaranth, Inc.
Nutrition Studios
P.F. Chang's China Bistro
Pam's Celiac Kitchen
Pamela's Products, Inc.
Pei Wei Asian Diner
Rizopia Food Products
Saz's BBQ Products
Sylvan Border Farm
Thaifoon Restaurants
Trigone, Inc.
U.S. Mills, Inc.
Van's International Foods
Water To Go Diet &
Nutrition Centers
Z'Tejas Southwestern Grill

For contact information, products and services,
refer to the Sponsor section of this book.

IMPORTANT: Read This First

Read this entire section before reading any part of *Waiter, Is there Wheat in My Soup?*

The purpose of this book is to help shed light on the complex area of dining out and traveling with dietary restrictions such as food allergies and intolerances. Due to the complexity of the subject, the information contained within is not all inclusive.

Different allergens or intolerances affect people in different ways. Some people are extremely sensitive while others seldom incur a reaction. A person with gluten-intolerance may suffer reactions immediately after eating a single crumb of bread, while others feel no apparent symptoms after digesting the same amount—or more.

One country may consider a food item to be gluten-free, while another country does not. Some countries do not have a clear definition of 'gluten-free,' or whether a cooking oil, once processed, is free of a particular allergen. Manufacturers have the freedom to change ingredients, formulas and product names. Some foods are being genetically modified, raising questions of purity. Foods may come in contact with allergen foods at points along the food chain, in the packaging and in the kitchen.

The good news is, laws have been passed in the USA and more are being introduced that will require labeling of foods to be more specific and identify the top food allergens. And while recent laws are not all-inclusive, clearer labeling of ingredients is critical in assisting restaurants, and their patrons, to be aware of allergen items.

The livelihood of a restaurant relies on offering memorable food, keeping abreast of the trends, and great customer service while building a reliable reputation and a base of repeat customers—all within budgetary confines. To achieve this goal, restaurants may be bought and sold, change vendors, rework the menu or change recipe ingredients.

For all of these reasons, and more, this book is not a complete source for information on all food ingredients, food components, cooking techniques, restaurant services, dining out services or food labeling. The book itself, its writer and publisher have no control for example, over issues of cross-contact, cross-contamination, human error, mislabeling or sources of differing opinions between medical communities, support communities or individuals.

This book is not intended to give any type of medical or nutritional advice. It is also not intended to take the place of your health care professional. Do not start a totally gluten-free or allergen-free diet without first seeking professional medical advice.

The publisher and author are not responsible for any errors, typographical errors, omissions or mis-statements that may exist within this publication. Nor are they responsible for any quotes or statements made by contributors. This publication is not to be construed as the whole or entire information on the subject of dining out, ingredients, processes or any of the medical conditions or personal choices associated with any specialty diet, whether free of wheat, gluten or common food allergens.

The decisions regarding dining out, menu choices, shopping or traveling is the sole responsibility of the diner or his/her guardian. When making food choices and preparation, the diner and restaurant must act responsibly and use common sense.

Some people with specialty diets will choose to never dine at a restaurant.

For those who do choose to venture out, this book is a great beginning to successful dining, shopping and traveling, gluten-free and allergen-free.

Contents

Contents

Contents

Foreword

Once thought to be a 'rare' disease, current research now shows that celiac disease, this genetically determined autoimmune disorder affects 1:133 individuals, or 1 percent of the population worldwide. Just a tip of the iceberg of those estimated to have celiac disease have been diagnosed.

Gluten to a celiac is more a poison to the system than sensitivity. There is no cure for celiac disease and there is no 'time off.' It is present every moment of every day. The only recourse to avoid the symptoms is to eliminate any and all foods containing gluten.

The gluten-free diet is not a fad diet, nor should it be used as a 'do it yourself' diagnosis or treatment. Many of the symptoms of celiac disease can also occur in other disorders and the gluten-free diet should not be started unless a physician prescribes it. There is no scientific evidence that the gluten-free diet is of any help in conditions other than celiac disease and dermatitis herpetiformis.

The gluten-free diet means a major lifestyle change, one in which the wonderful pleasure of eating turns into a chore. Food shopping, cooking, and dining out becomes a series of questions.

That is why *Waiter, Is there Wheat in My Soup?* is so welcome and so needed.

Thanks to the dedication of LynnRae Ries this book provides the tools to easily stock a pantry and comfortably travel and eat away from home—gluten-free.

Here's wishing you good food, good fun, and good friends! GF—gluten-free!

Elaine Monarch, Executive Director
Celiac Disease Foundation, www.celiac.org

Food is More Than a Four Letter Word

For many people on medically prescribed diets, the word 'food' becomes a fearsome four letter word when it relates to dining away from home.

In reality, food is more than simple **sustenance**.

It evokes **images and feelings** that go well beyond the calming of hunger pains.

Food, and all that surrounds it, adds quality and depth to our lives and the lives of those we love.

Families gather around the dinner table in a spirit of **love**.

Soup lines are charitable means of **giving** to each other.

Dining with friends is **bonding**.

Family vacations mean stopping at roadside stands for something new and **fun** to eat.

Our mother's coffeecake or grandmother's rolls become a family **tradition**.

Food is brought to new neighbors as welcome **gifts**.

People offer **condolences** at a funeral with food in hand.

A box of candy is an **offering** to make amends.

Food is served in **honor** of guests and provides an avenue for mingling at parties.

Potlucks at work foster **teamwork**.

Business **networking** frequently involves lunch.

In school, food is used as a **positive reinforcement** and a way of saying **thank you.**

Food stories are conversation ice breakers.

For the traveler or gourmet diner, food becomes **entertainment** for the senses.

Dining establishments provide a **welcome** environment perfect for large and small groups.

They also allow a person to dine alone with his/her thoughts, while still being in the company of others.

Food is **romance** as couples meet in coffee shops, break rooms, cafeterias and industrial kitchens.

Symbolism is found in food—think church communion hosts and cookies for Santa.

Ads display food as **sensual**.

Dining out is an **escape** from grocery shopping and dishes.

Chicken soup is **healing**.

Food we were brought up on is **comfort**.

Being able to dine out in an informed manner translates to **freedom**.

May this book help you experience the joys of dining out and traveling in a more comfortable fashion.

Bon Appétit—LynnRae

General Overview of the Gluten-Free Diet

Gluten-Free Diet

Theresa Cornelius, MS, RD, CLC, LND, a registered dietitian licensed to practice in Tennessee. Her private on-line practice (www.Changing-Lifestyles.com) specializes in celiac disease, allergies, diabetes and weight management.

Shelley Case, RD, a registered dietitian specializing in nutrition counseling for celiac disease, food allergies and intolerances, heart disease and diabetes. Shelley is a frequent guest speaker on television and radio. She is the co-author of the Celiac Disease section in the *Manual of Clinical Dietetics* (American Dietetic Association and Dietitians of Canada) and sections of the Canadian Celiac Association's *Celiac Disease Needs a Diet for Life Handbook* and *A Guide for the Celiac Diabetic*. She is author of the national best seller, *Gluten-Free Diet, A Comprehensive Resource Guide*. www.glutenfreediet.ca

Gluten Intolerant Medical Conditions

Gluten Intolerant Diseases (Celiac Disease, Gluten Intolerance, and Dermatitis Herpetiformis) are one of the most frequently missed and under diagnosed disorders in the world. All three have similar etiology and treatment.

Celiac Disease (CD) is characterized by malabsorption as a result of an inflammatory injury to the small intestine. This occurs after the ingestion of the gluten (protein found in wheat, rye, and barley) in genetically susceptible individuals. Long-term effects of untreated CD results in nutritional deficiencies, development of autoimmune disorders such as Type I Diabetes Mellitus and thyroid disease, and an increased risk of cancerous lesions. CD has a wide-spectrum of clinical manifestations which includes fatigue, diarrhea, chronic bloating, constipation, weight loss or gain, anemia, skin lesions, osteoporosis, miscarriages, and infertility, to name a few. No matter what symptoms an individual has, the cornerstone of treatment is a strict life-long gluten-free diet.

Gluten is present in most processed foods, where wheat flour is widely used as a thickener in many commercial products. Also, cross contamination can occur at the following food processing areas:

1. Farms where the grains are grown and harvested.

2. Mills where the grains are processed into flours.

3. Food processing lines where one line produces gluten-free foods and the next one produces foods that contain gluten.

4. Open storage of food such as:
   a. Bulk food bins
   b. Salad bars

5. Food preparation sites where gluten and gluten-free foods are prepared side by side.

By keeping these facts in mind and by reading labels religiously, gluten can be almost eliminated from the diet.

Nutritional deficiencies and additional food intolerance allergies are common among individuals with celiac disease and gluten intolerance. Therefore, they need to be evaluated and followed by health care professionals (MD *and* dietitian) to individualize their dietary regimen.

See reference in Bibliography and Reference section: Theresa Cornelius, MS, RD, CLC, LND

The Gluten-Free Diet and Ingredients to be Avoided

Gluten is the general name for the storage proteins (prolamins) in wheat, rye and barley. These specific prolamins damage the small intestine in people with celiac disease and dermatitis herpetiformis. The actual names of the toxic prolamins are gliadin in wheat, secalin in rye and hordein in barley.

Up until 1996, the avenin prolamin in oats was considered to be toxic, however new research indicates that avenin in oats*** is not harmful. Although corn contains zein prolamin and rice contains orzenin prolamin, these prolamins do not have the toxic effect on the intestine of persons with celiac disease.

Gluten is the substance in flour responsible for forming the structure of dough, holding products together and leavening. While the presence of gluten is evident in baked goods (e.g., breads, cookies and cakes) and pasta, it is often a 'hidden ingredient' in many other items such as sauces, seasonings, soups, salads dressings, candy, as well as some vitamins and pharmaceuticals. The challenge for individuals on a gluten-free diet is to avoid these hidden sources.

Gluten-containing ingredients to be avoided

Barley	Bulgur	Cereal Binding
Couscous	Durum*	Einkorn*
Emmer*	Filler	Farro*
Graham Flour	Kamut*	Malt**
Malt Extract **	Malt Flavoring**	Malt Syrup**
Oat Bran***	Oats***	Oat Syrup***
Rye	Semolina	Spelt (Dinkel)*
Triticale	Wheat	Wheat Bran
Wheat Germ	Wheat Starch	

* types of wheat
** derived from barley
*** Many recent studies have demonstrated that consumption of oats (25-60 g/day) is safe for children and adults with celiac disease. However, further studies are needed to determine the long-term safety of oat consumption. Also, the issue of cross contamination of oats with wheat and/or barley remains a concern in North America, therefore, oats are NOT recommended by celiac organizations in Canada or the USA.

Ingredients to Question

Hydrolyzed Plant or Vegetable Protein (HPP/HVP)

Seasonings	Flavorings
Starch	Modified Food Starch
Dextrin	Maltodextrin

For specific labeling regulations in USA and Canada for these ingredients see *Gluten-Free Diet – A Comprehensive Resource Guide*, Shelley Case 2004

Gluten-Free Additives and Ingredients

This is not an all-inclusive list

Additives

Acetic Acid

Benzoic Acid

BHT

Calcium Disodium EDTA

Lactic Acid

Polysorbate 60; 80

Sodium Benzoate

Sodium Nitrate

Sodium Sulphite

Tartaric Acid

Titanium Dioxide

Adipic Acid

BHA

Carboxymethyl cellulose

Fumaric Acid

Malic Acid

Propylene Glycol

Sodium Metabisulphite

Sodium Nitrite

Stearic Acid

Tartrazine

Flavoring Agents

Maltol

MSG

Vanillan

Aspartame

Corn Syrup/Solids

Fructose

Invert Sugar

Mannitol

Sorbitol

Sucrose

Ethyl Maltol

Vanilla Extract

Sugars/Sweeteners

Brown Sugar

Dextrose

Glucose

Lactose

Molasses

Sucralose

White Sugar   Xylitol

Vegetable Gums

Acacia Gum (Gum Arabic)

Carageenan

Cellulose

Karaya Gum

Tragacanth

Algin (Alginic Acid)

Carol Ban (Locust Bean)

Guar Gm

Methylcellulose

Xanthan Gum

Miscellaneous

Annatto

Beta Carotene

Cream of Tartar

Lecithin

Pectin

Baking Yeast

Brewers Yeast

Gelatin

Papain

Psyllium

Reprinted with permission from: *Gluten-Free Diet, A Comprehensive Resource Guide* by Shelley Case RD, Case Nutritional Consulting 2004; www.glutenfreediet.ca

Special Note:

Gluten Intolerance as it relates to celiac disease is not the same as a food allergy.

They are separate and distinctly different from each other.

To be diagnosed with one does not mean a person will automatically have another.

Before eliminating any food or food category from your diet, consult with your physician or dietician.

General Overview of the Top 8 Food Allergens

⫻ **Ingredients to be Avoided For Allergies to Eggs, Fish, Milk, Peanuts, Shellfish, Soy, Tree Nuts or Wheat**

By Chef Stephanie Green, RD

Stephanie Green is a registered dietitian and culinary chef. She received her BS in Clinical Dietetics from the University of Texas Southwestern Medical Center School Of Allied Health Sciences and she's a graduate of the Culinary Arts program at Scottsdale Community College.

Stephanie is the owner of Nutrition Studio, a nutritionally focused consulting business. She is also a Culinary Nutrition instructor at the Arizona Culinary Institute. Stephanie has worked in the clinical environment and as a Chief Research Nutritionist at the Hospital of the University of Pennsylvania General Clinical Research Center. She was the consulting dietitian and assistant chef for *Heartfelt Cuisine,* which was written with chef Eddie Matney. www.nutritionstudio.com.

The Top 8 Food Allergens

Approximately 11 million people are affected by food allergies. The top eight allergenic foods are milk, egg, wheat, soy, tree nuts, peanuts, fish and shellfish which account for 90% of all adverse reactions. Unfortunately, there is no cure and complete avoidance is the only option.

A food allergy involves the immune system and the body views that food as a harmful substance. Once alerted, the body launches an attack against this 'harmful' substance by releasing chemicals like histamine that affects many different systems in the body such as respiratory and the gastrointestinal tract. Serious food allergies may cause an anaphylactic reaction. People with these types of life threatening allergies tend to be proactive and carry an antihistamine or EpiPen at all times.

Categories of Food Allergens and Ingredients to be Avoided

Eggs:

Egg-containing ingredients to be avoided
(*This is not a complete list*)

albumin

consomme

egg drop soup

eggnog

globulin

livetin

lysozyme

mayonnaise

meringue (meringue powder) ovalbumin

ovomucin

ovomucoid

ovoviellin

simplesse

surimi

Egg Beaters™

egg (dried, powdered, solids, white, yolk)

The following *may* indicate the presence of egg protein

baking mixes

breads

commercial ice creams

cakes

glazed nuts

instant oatmeal

instant cream of wheat

lecithin

quick breads

macaroni

marzipan

meatballs

nougat

pasta

processed meats

salad dressings

sausages

sauces made with egg, such as hollandaise

confectioneries containing egg

coquettes made with egg

flavoring (including natural and artificial)

Fish:

Fish-containing ingredients to be avoided
(*This is not a complete list*)

all species of fish	roe
caviar	surimi
fish oils	Caesar salad with anchovy

May **indicate the presence of fish** (*This is not a complete list*)

egg rolls	sushi
sashini	tempura
Thai, Chinese and Satay recipes	

Milk:

Milk-containing ingredients to be avoided
(*This is not a complete list*)

artificial butter flavor	butter, butterfat, butter oil
buttermilk	casein (casein hydrolysate)
caseinates (in all forms)	cheese
cream	cottage cheese
curds	custard
ghee	half & half
ice cream	lactoferrin
lactulose	milk
lactalbumin, lactalbumin phosphate	

(in all forms including condensed, derivative, dry, evaporated, goat's milk and milk from other animals, low-fat, malted milk fat, non-fat, powder, protein, skimmed, solids, whole)

nougat	pudding
rennet casein	sour milk solids
whey (in all forms)	yogurt
sour cream, sour cream solids	
sugar substitutes containing lactose	

Milk, continued

May indicate the presences of milk protein:
(*This is not a complete list*)

caramel candies
chocolate
instant potatoes
lactose
non-dairy products
luncheon meat, hotdogs, sausages

creamed soups
high protein flour
lactic acid starter culture
margarine
sauces

Peanuts:

Peanut-containing ingredients to be avoided
(*This is not a complete list*)

artificial nuts
goobers
hydrolyzed peanut protein
mixed nuts
nutmeat
peanuts
peanut flour
cold pressed or expelled or extruded peanut oil

beer nuts
ground nuts
mandelonas
monkey nuts
nut pieces
peanut butter
peanut oil

May indicate the presence of peanut protein:
(*This is not a complete list*)

African, Chinese, Indian, Indonesian, Thai, and Vietnamese
and Mexican dishes
baked goods (pastries, cookies, etc.)

baking mixes
Chinese dishes
cookies
confectioneries
egg rolls
hydrogenated vegetable oil
marzipan

cheese foods
chili
chocolate bars and ice cream
dried soup mixes
enchilada sauce
margarine
nougat

Peanuts, continued

prepared soups	ready to eat cereals
satay sauces	salad dressings
seasoning packets	vegetable oil and shortening
vegetarian burgers	

commercial or homemade baked goods
fish canned in undisclosed oils
candy (including chocolate candy)
flavoring (including natural and artificial)

Allergic individuals to peanuts should also avoid tree nuts. Sunflower seeds are often produced on equipment shared with peanuts.

Shellfish:

Shellfish-containing ingredients to be avoided:
(*This is not a complete list*)

abalone	calamari
crab	crawfish
crustaceans	mollusks
mussels	octopus
oysters	prawns
quahog	scallops
scampi	shrimp (crevette)
snails (escargot)	squid (calamari)
whelk	winkle

clams (cherrystone, littleneck, pismo, quahog)
lobster (langouste, langoustine, scampo, coral, tomalley)

The following *may* indicate the presence of shellfish protein:
(*This is not a complete list*)

bouillabaisse	congee
fish balls	fish sauce
fish soup	fish stock
flavoring	oyster sauce
prawn chips	sashimi

Shellfish, continued

satay sauce
shrimp balls
shrimp salad roll
sushi
seafood flavoring (such as crab or clam extract)

shrimp noodles
shrimp chips
surimi

Soy:

Soy-containing ingredients to be avoided:
(*This is not a complete list*)

edamame
kyodofu (freeze-dried tofu)
natto
shoyu sauce
soya
soy sauce
supro
taro cake
tofu
yuba

hydrolyzed soy protein
miso
okara (soy pulp)
soy cheese
soybean (curd, granules)
soy sprouts
tamari
tempeh
textured vegetable protein (TVP)
soy protein (concentrate, isolate)

soy (soy albumin, soy fiber, soy flour,
soy grits, soymilk, soy nuts, soy sprouts)

May indicate the presence of soy protein:
(*This is not a complete list*)

Asian cuisine
bouillon cubes
cake icing
chocolate bars
cookies and candies
English muffins
granola
infant cereals
marzipan

bean spouts
breads containing soy
chocolate
commercial soups
emulsifiers
flavoring
hydrolyzed plant protein (HPP)
margarine
meat products

Soy, continued

lecithin
seasoning packets
sprouts
stuffings
vegetable broth
vegetable oils & sprays
vegetable protein
vegetable starch

salad dressings that list 'oil'
soy oil
stabilizers
tuna and other fish canned in oil
vegetable gum
vegetable paste
vegetable shortening
vegetarian meat replacers

commercial canned fruit products
commercial vegetable products
hydrolyzed vegetable protein (HVP)
monosodium glutamate (MSG)
sauces containing soy like barbeque, oriental, soy tamari,
Worcestershire

Tree Nuts:

Tree Nut-containing ingredients to be avoided:
(*This is not a complete list*)

almonds
Brazil nuts
cashews
filbert/hazelnuts
macadamia nuts
marzipan/almond paste
nougat
nut meal
nut oil
nut pieces
pesto
praline

artificial nuts
caponata
chestnuts
hickory nuts
mandelonas
nan-gai nuts
nut butters (i.e., cashew butter)
nutmeat
nut paste (i.e., almond paste)
pecans (Mashuga Nuts ®)
pistachios
walnuts

gianduja (nut mixture found in some chocolates)
natural nut extract (i.e., almond, walnut)
pine nuts (also referred to as Indian, pinon, pignoli)
If you are allergic to tree nuts you should also avoid peanuts.

Wheat:

Wheat-containing ingredients to be avoided:
(This is not a complete list)

bagels	breaded
breads	bread crumbs
bulgur	cakes
commercial pie fillings	couscous
croissants	cracker meal
durum	farina

flour (all purpose, bread, cake, durum, enriched, graham, high gluten, high protein, instant, pastry, self-rising, soft wheat, steel ground, stone ground, whole wheat)

gluten	graham crackers
kamut	matzoh, (matzoh meal or matzo)
pasta	seitan
semolina	spelt
triticale	vital gluten
wheat grass	whole wheat berries

wheat (bran, germ, gluten, malt, sprouts)
breakfast cereals (wheat containing)

For more information on *common food allergens*, contact The Food Allergy & Anaphylaxis Network at 800.929.4040. www.faan.org. Reference September 2004

Note: These lists are not all inclusive. Read all ingredient labels carefully due to the many variations in food manufacturing and processing. Consult with your doctor for a complete listing of foods, food additives and ingredients you should avoid based on your own personal dietary needs.

General Overview of the Gluten-free Casein-free Diet

What is a Gluten-Casein Free (GFCF) Diet?
By Theresa Cornelius, RD

Theresa Cornelius, MS, RD, CLC, LND, a registered dietitian licensed to practice in Tennessee. Her private on-line practice (www.Changing-Lifestyles.com) specializes in celiac disease, allergies, diabetes and weight management.

Gluten-Casein Free Diet

The Gluten-Casein Free (GFCF) Diet

The GFCF diet is the removal of all gluten and casein products from the diet. Individuals with autism as well as those who are intolerant to both gluten and casein are typically on this diet. It is an unproven treatment for autism. However, some studies have found the diet to be helpful in some autistic children who were diagnosed before the age of three.

This is a major lifestyle modification and if the child is eased into it, it will be much easier for them to make it a permanent lifestyle change. According to the Autism Research Unit of the University of Sunderland (Great Britain), initially there may be some negative effects. These include: upset stomach, anxiety, clinginess, and slight ill-temper. These are good signs and precursors of a positive response. They recommend a trial period of about 1 year before determining the child's response to this dietary regimen. The GFCF diet is not a cure for autism, but research has found that it can improve brain function as well as the child's quality of life.

Nutritional deficiencies and additional food intolerances or allergies are common in these children. Therefore, they need to be evaluated and followed by health care professionals (MD *and* dietitian) to individualize their dietary regimen. Since the gluten-free diet is covered in another section, this section focuses on foods containing casein. Please see Figure 1.

References in Bibliography and References section of this book.

Figure 1. Dietary Guidelines for a Casein-Free Diet

Casein-Containing Foods To Be Avoided.
All dairy products from <u>any</u> animal in <u>any</u> form.
- **Products** (milk, butter, yogurt, cream, sour cream, whipping cream, ice cream, cream cheese, cheese, cottage cheese, pudding, custard, ice milk, sherbet, half and half, etc.....)
- **Forms** (derivative, powder, protein, solids, malted, condensed, evaporated, dry, whole, low-fat, milk fat, nonfat, and skimmed)

Casein-Containing Ingredients
- Non dairy creamers
- Hydrolysates (casein, milk protein, protein, whey, whey protein)
- Curds
- Nougat
- Quark (European cheese)
- Ghee
- Rennet casein
- Sour cream solids, sour milk solids
- Artificial butter flavor
- Whey (in all forms including sweet, delactosed, protein concentrate)
- Butter fat
- Butter flavored oil
- Lactoglobulin
- Lactalbumin, lactalbumin phosphate

Foods to Question
- Soy products (soy milk, soy cheese, soy cream cheese, etc...)
- Hot dogs, sausage, and luncheon meats
- Artificial and natural flavoring
- High-protein flour
- Margarine
- Simplesse
- Lactic acid (starter culture may contain milk)

Ingredients that do not indicate casein

■ Calcium lactate	■ Oleoresin
■ Lactylate	■ Sodium lactate
■ Cocoa butter	■ Sodium stearoyl lactylate
■ Cream of tartar	■ Lactate
■ Calcium stearoyl	

Dining Out Is Always a Choice

Dining Out is a Choice

Realities of Dining Out for Those Who Are Gluten-Free or Have Food Allergies

Dining out can be a challenge when you have food allergies, intolerances or need to follow a specialized diet. The thought of an evening meal in a restaurant with friends is terrifying to some people. In fact, some people with special dietary needs are so afraid; they have refused to venture into public eating establishments.

This need not be your life. As a person who travels regularly and is forced to dine out on business trips, I can tell you it is very do-able. As a person with celiac disease and sensitive to ingestion of gluten – I am very careful. Yet in all my travels and dining in various types of restaurants, rarely have I been ill because of my food choices. Here are some tips for making dining out enjoyable and safe.

Attitude is everything!

It can be easy to dine out or a challenge. Your attitude is everything to your success in dining out. If you choose to be a victim, frightened, or negative, I can guarantee that your dining experiences will be less than enjoyable.

My motto is, "I can eat anywhere." OK—I may not always eat well, but I can eat. Think about the dining experience as a time to be with friends and share good company. If you focus the dining experience on something more than food, you can see the experience in a new light. It is not about what you are going to eat, but about the company you share. For example:

I have a business meeting. The restaurant chosen is Italian.
Rather than focus on the fact that I will have fewer choices,
I focus on the people I am with and the business at hand.
So what if I eat a nice salad instead of pasta?

I am the first to admit that it is not always easy to have a positive approach to dining out. When you use a positive, redirected approach to dining out, it is easier to have a good time and enjoy your experience.

Know how things are made to ask the right questions

If you don't know how to cook, it's time to watch the cooking shows on television, read cook books, or take some specialized cooking classes.

Knowing where different foods come from and how dishes are made, makes life so much easier when dining out. Know the terms used in food preparation. *Waiter, Is there Wheat in My Soup?* is an excellent resource for this information.

If you know that a roux is almost always flour-based, you know it must be avoided. Teriyaki is made with soy sauce. Non-fat products, such as low-fat sour cream may have starch stabilizers added to provide the consistency we like. Vinaigrette dressings, being clear or opaque will not have a wheat-based thickener, but flavored vinaigrette or ranch dressing could. Pan frying or plank-roasting are safer cooking methods than fried or grilled (usually done on a flat cooking surface shared by many items). However, grilling might also be done on a barbecue-like surface. Once you have an understanding of the cooking methods, you can look over a menu, select items that you believe might be safe, and then ask questions.

Remember this:

1. Always be polite, ask for the restaurant's help and explain briefly what you need.

   a. There is a saying that you can catch more flies with honey… it is true. When you are polite, you will get much more cooperation than if you become demanding and unpleasant.

   b. Ask for the staff's help—everyone likes being needed. When you ask for their help in a polite way, you often get better service and much more cooperation.

   c. Be brief—if you go into a lengthy explanation about things, you will loose the attention of the staff person. Explain quickly what you need, ask your questions with the idea that their quick answer will let you decide if that menu item is something you want to pursue.

2. The food industry defines gluten differently than the medical industry.

   a. Asking if a product is gluten-free is NEVER the question to ask. Instead ask about cooking methods, ingredients that are in the product, and how it is served.

3. Most waitpersons today are of the Y-generation and according to national food trends, know very little about cooking, where food comes from, or how food is prepared.

   a. Don't rely on their knowledge.

   b. Ask specific questions that the chef could answer. I often will say "Would you please ask the chef…."

4. The food industry DOES understand 'allergies'—it is perfectly acceptable to briefly state that you follow a very specialized diet and must avoid certain foods, and that you have some questions about your menu choices. When asking questions, ask things like:

   a. What is in the sauce on the fish? Based on your knowledge of what you must avoid and your intolerances, you can then decide if you need more information or will eliminate that food choice.

   b. What comes on the plate with that item? Different regions have different ways of serving food. Toast points (triangle pieces of toast) may be used in the mid-west while tomato slices are used on the east coast. The garnish (decoration) may be fried onion rings or battered fried vegetables.

   c. Are the steamed vegetables seasoned? If the waitperson indicates a seasoning mix is used, you might be prompted to make a choice between (i) asking for the vegetables to be steamed without seasonings or made with just salt and pepper; or (ii) ask if the waitperson would be kind enough to check with the chef to see if the seasoning mix has 'flour' or 'wheat' in it. Note that I am being very specific about what I wanted to know. This information is enough for me to make a decision about the vegetables.

Dining out is ALWAYS A CHOICE. There is no reason to avoid dining out. With the right questions you too can eat in any situation without carrying a lot of supplies along. As much as I travel I only carry enough snacks to get me through the plane trips. Even in the smallest airports, I can find food. It is not always what I want or healthy, but it is food. Because I choose not to carry a lot of food supplies for a trip, my attitude toward food is, "Food is energy for my body and while I like eating healthy, sometimes it is not possible for a meal or two and that is okay."

Ultimately your choice in eating in a restaurant is your responsibility. The restaurant industry, for the most part, will bend over backwards to keep your business. Your attitude and approach to the dining experience determines their response to you and your needs. When you have had a good experience and the staff has been helpful, be sure to show your appreciation with a nice tip and thank you note to the manager.

Cynthia Kupper, RD, CD
Executive Director
Gluten Intolerance Group of NA
15110 10th Ave SW, Ste A
Seattle, WA 98166-1820
206.246.6652

Six Tips for Staying Gluten-Free

1. **Selecting a place to eat:** Your success at gluten-free dining will be determined by a number of factors, including the type of restaurant you choose. Be careful of restaurants where language may be a communication barrier. Food service workers may not easily understand your dietary restrictions. Allow extra time to discuss your needs for a gluten-free meal. Fast food, quick service restaurants, and those with a standard menu may have little time to thoroughly check ingredients. Finer dining establishments offer a less harried atmosphere and usually have more time to meet your needs. Calling the restaurant ahead of your arrival may be helpful. Speak to the chef to discuss your meal options. This will increase the quality of your dining experience. The chefs in finer dining establishments are generally aware of gluten and can be very helpful.

2. **Dine early or late:** Time your meal earlier or later than the busiest meal time. You will have more time and easier access to the people who can help you. Even the most cooperative server may not have the time you need during 'rush hour'.

3. **Ask specific questions:** The only person who really knows what went into a dish is the person who made it! Be very specific in your questions about each item. Below are the potential problems involved with them:

a. *Salads:* The possibility of contamination lies in the cleanliness of the boards used to chop ingredients and the addition of croutons or salad dressings containing unsafe ingredients. Ask for dressing to be served on the side. No croutons or other bread products. Ask that a Caesar salad be made in a clean bowl.

b. *Salad Dressings and Marinades:* Salad dressings and marinades may contain thickeners or other unsafe ingredients. Vinegar and oil dressings are the safest options or lemon wedges.

c. *Soups and Sauces:* Bases are often used as a foundation for soups and sauces. Bases contain ingredients comparable to bouillon or broth, and should be carefully checked. Roux (pronounced 'roo') is the thickener for most sauces and is a combination of butter and flour. Canned sauces may also be used in restaurants, so you may be able to check the ingredient listing. Soup base will sometimes appear in sauces.

d. *Prime Rib and Other Meats:* If prime rib is too rare for the customer's taste, the cook may 'cook' it in a pot of au jus until it reaches the desired doneness. Au jus may come from a can or mix and contain unacceptable ingredients. Seasoning is often used in preparing meats; their ingredients should be verified. Self-basting turkeys and imitation bacon bits need to be checked for safety before using.

e. *Fried Foods:* The oil used to deep-fry foods may be used for both breaded and non-breaded items, in which case they should be avoided. (Also true for allergens). In large restaurants where French fries are cooked in separate fryers, there is less chance of contamination.

f. *Rice, Starches, and Hash Browns:* Many hash browns are frozen and pre-packaged with starch added. Ask what other ingredients have been added while cooking them. Many rice pilafs may have added ingredients that you may need to avoid. Plain rice, cooked in water, baked or steamed rice are good choices.

g. *Dairy Products:* Non-dairy products are sometimes used instead of dairy products in restaurants. The three most frequently used non-dairy products are non-dairy creamer, non-dairy 'sour cream' topping, and non-dairy whipped topping. Verify if the ingredients in the non-dairy substitute are okay.

4. **Have your food prepared on a clean cooking surface, with clean utensils:** Choose a cooking method, such as poaching, pan-frying or baking, that are less likely to have a problem with cross-contamination. Suggest using foil to cook on if this is a problem.

5. **Confirm your order before eating:** Is it the 'special' meal you ordered? Were your instructions followed?

6. **Thank your food server:** Leave a generous tip for good service. Patronize the establishment again!

Revised from the Gluten Intolerance Group® Restaurant Dining Tips. Used with permission.

Interview with Chef Chuck

Chef Chuck, you have been involved in the food industry for many years as an exclusive personal chef, Chef de Cuisine, baker and manager. What motivated you to join the restaurant business?

As the grandson of a Greek immigrant, I grew up in a family restaurant in Phoenix. At home the television wasn't the focal point of the gathering, it was always the kitchen. My grandmother made sure at an early age that all of the grandchildren had a hand in cooking. Although the family probably recognized it long before I did, I had a passion for food, not only its consumption, but in the preparation. It wasn't until I was 39 years old that I enrolled at the Scottsdale Culinary Institute where I graduated with honors and a rounded education not only in preparation, but the theories of food science. All of this coupled with the challenge of creativity, a somewhat 'off-center' approach to sharing my knowledge, and the contributions of some truly talented folks along the way, I have realized my passion in many ways.

We are looking for help in understanding the routine of a restaurant kitchen. For instance, would you say it is an easy or difficult task for a chef to use a clean pan and utensils for a person's meal when they have a food allergy or intolerance?

Most of my commercial experience is in Thai, and the majority of Thai food is made to order. The use of clean pans every time is doable. Besides, that's pretty much a basic health concern in general. The industry as a whole has to be educated regarding food allergies. As more and more comes out in the media the more you will see a change. I feel, and it's only my thought, education starts when the staff is hired and is the responsibility of the establishment. The staff should know the consequences of cutting corners, but I also feel the FDA needs to help fight the fight of education in food workers.

If a person with food concerns came into your restaurant, would you prefer they speak to you directly as the chef, or would you prefer they direct their question to their server.

Tough question. Ideally, it would be great if the chef could step away from the stove when there is a question on the floor. Practically, the majority of the time that isn't going to happen. When a chef is calling the orders, his or her absence can slow or stop the progression of preparation. Start your specific questions with your server. If you don't feel you have been given the proper consideration, ask for management or the floor supervisor. These people do have direct access to the chef and can request their help on the floor. If the staff has been properly trained, special requests can be forwarded with the order.

If you are not convinced you have gotten the proper attention, by all means ask to speak with the chef, but be aware this person may take a few minutes to get to your table. In an industry where competition is so harsh, everyone is vying for the public's food dollar. Not only is there a concern to serve the best fare by the safest and healthiest means, but it also must be done in the timeliest manner for **all** who patronize the establishment.

Do restaurants give the chef and his/her assistant the authority to substitute ingredients in a dish if the kitchen is out of the item, without informing the customer, for instance a sauce or broth?

This would be on the chef. When establishing a menu as a Chef de Cuisine, I insisted on the listed ingredients in the dish. My feelings are this, if a particular item in the dish is out of stock, the item should be 86'd (removed) from the menu or a substitution could be offered to the guest only if they insist on the dish. But under no circumstances should the dish be served other than stated in the menu. Not only do you risk a reaction by a guest, but also the integrity of the dish is compromised. Not every restaurant maintains as strict a rule.

In your experience and in discussions with others, do a lot of people with food concerns dine out?

In my experience, people with food concerns do dine out. What I find though, is they are very loyal to particular restaurants where they feel safe. Give the industry time to come around. Establishments are beginning to tailor to special needs as once again competition brings change. This is a learning experience for all involved. Ask questions. You should be able to dine out with the same trust as you impose on your doctor or dentist to know what it is they're doing!

Is it always possible for a restaurant to meet every customer's dietary needs?

No. Perhaps the recipes contain items that cannot be substituted. In my case, I have allergies to MSG. Although a restaurant may not use MSG directly, some items contain the make-up of MSG naturally. If I don't feel that I can communicate my needs, I dine elsewhere. It should be a red flag if for a moment you feel that you have become a burden to the restaurant or the staff. There are many other places to spend your time and money.

Research shows that arguments and activities go on between servers, busboys and other kitchen staff that may affect the service to the customers. Is there a behind the scenes saga that goes on in all the restaurants?

The restaurant industry is in no way without its claim to the drama and trauma of everyday life. When members of the kitchen and wait staff are hired in, efforts are made to find that mature individual that can work the shift and leave the garbage outside the door. Theoretically. This unfortunately, like any other business, can have its ups and downs. With servers, it can be the cranky customer and busboys. With the kitchen, it can be the cranky servers. And, heaven forbid the chef should have a flat tire on the way to work. The difference between a mediocre and a good establishment is simple; you should NEVER see this on the floor. A restaurant with a management team worth their salt won't let this happen. Mistakes happen, it's human nature. But it's human nature that provides the creativity and the drive to excel and be the best in the business. If you see unprofessional behavior, pass it along.

Can you suggest how we, as customers, can help to make sure our order is placed correctly and arrives correctly?

I can. When you enter a restaurant for the first time, scope it out. Maybe the first time in a new restaurant, the dinner rush isn't the appropriate time to get your questions answered. Spot your floor manager. Indicate your needs to this person and allow them to offer suggestions.

Ask them to seat you with a server who 'knows the menu inside out.' (This is really no different than waiting for your favorite server when you go out). If you arrive before the 'rush' you are more apt to have the chef available for questions as well. When your server comes to the table, make sure he or she is truly interested in your needs and not standing with eyes searching for the next table needing attention.

Be aware, in order to do the volume necessary for a successful business, a great many restaurants still use the 'turn 'em' and 'burn 'em' attitude for moving people along. This often time puts strain on the servers to keep moving. Be diligent when checking your delivered entrée. Be sure to thank the server for their special attention and they will remember you. It is always a good idea to refresh the server's memory when you visit. Call ahead and make sure your server is working, this does two things: It will bring you to the front of the server's mind and truly, there is nothing better for a server than to have 'call tables' going into a shift, especially in the summer months.

Finally,

In an industry that is as competitive as ours, being aware of trends and needs can make or break an operation. It is the responsibility of the chef on down to the server to educate themselves on food sensitivity, health and safety. Until it becomes the 'perfect' restaurant world, be diligent but enjoy those special times. We don't know it all and often we need some encouragement. It wasn't so long ago a lady in one of my cooking classes sent me scrambling to learn more about 'gluten-free!' My thanks to you, LynnRae.

—Chef Chuck of www.chefchuckcooks.com

Interview with Chef Aaron Flores

Chef Aaron, how did you become involved in helping those on a gluten-free diet?

For over two years ago I was a Sous Chef at a famous resort hotel in Anaheim, Ca. While working in one of the restaurants I was approached by a little girl. She handed me a restaurant card and told me "these things make my tummy hurt and I don't want my tummy to hurt. Can you help me?" We went back to her table and with the help of her grandmother I was able to provide a meal for her. We talked for awhile and they informed me about celiac disease and the gluten-free diet. This was something I had never heard of in any cookbook or class, so I was compelled to learn more. After they had left the restaurant I went to my computer and searched the word 'Gluten-free.' During my research I came across a conference announcement from *Gluten-Free Living Magazine.* It was to be held in San Diego, Ca. What luck! It was just a stones throw away from Anaheim. So I signed up.

On the day of the conference I came to the hotel ready to learn, still in my chef's jacket after a morning on the line. Over the course of the conference, I met many wonderful people within the celiac community, and learned a lot about the needs of those with gluten-free diets. The rest is as we say in my business; history!

Do you have any hints on how to make the chef your ally when dining out?

- Ask the chef if the kitchen performs from 'scratch cooking' and pick from these items.

- Ask the kitchen staff to use separate pans to cook your food.

- Always ask to check ingredient lists or package labels in regards to questionable items.

- Be patient, courteous and friendly while dealing with restaurant staff.

- Make dining selections with the chef and you should be able to receive a safer and tastier meal in most restaurants.

What advice do you have for the restaurant chefs when catering to guests with special dietary needs?

When catering to guests with special dietary needs, the most important thing to remember is to have an open mind.

- Listen to your guest very carefully.

- Repeat what is being asked of you for clarification.

- When preparing the meal make sure you are using clean and sanitized knives, cutting boards and utensils.

- Always cook food products in separate sauté pans to avoid cross contamination from the item your guest is allergic or intolerant to.

- If time permits ask your guest questions regarding their allergy or intolerance. Just think you might learn something new. Isn't that what being a Chef is all about? It is for me.

—*Chef Aaron, Executive Chef /Owner of Chef Aaron, Inc. www.chefaaron.biz*

Help the Chef to Help You

Suggestions from chefs and customers of various restaurants across the country.

1. Prior to dining out, take a personal assessment of how you are feeling. If you are not feeling well, are newly diagnosed and still recovering, or if you are super sensitive, you may want to consult with your doctor prior to dining out.

2. Take a moment to do a mood check. Are you open to new dining experiences, confident and willing to take the time to ask appropriate questions? Will you be satisfied with a plain chicken breast and steamed vegetables if you cannot find anything else on the menu?

3. Familiarize yourself with the restaurant's menu before going to dinner, either by calling them, driving by and picking up a menu or by visiting their web page.

4. Understand menu terminology and how it relates to your specific diet

5. Upon arriving, ask to speak to the chef, the manager or the sous chef.

6. When talking to your server or the chef, be precise as to what you cannot eat. Tell them up front, not when the meal arrives at your table. Be specific. Don't say

'gluten' or 'dairy'; state specifically what you mean, since many servers will not know the depth of the terms. Chefs too, when they are busy, need to know exactly which ingredients you cannot have, rather than guessing.

7. Consider giving the chef examples of what you are willing, could or would eat. For instance, ask if you could have a fresh piece of tuna, grilled on a piece of aluminum foil with pepper and two thin slices of lemon atop the tuna. Or ask if their stove top has room for a chicken breast poached in a clean pan of water or wine, Italian spices and about ¼ cup of onions. A freshly made salad in a clean salad bowl, a baked potato uncut with real butter on the side (if not allergic) and a side of fresh fruit instead of pasta.

8. Another approach is to give the server or chef two different options from the menu that look the most friendly or easily adjustable to your diet, and ask them to prepare you the one that is gluten-free or free of your dietary concerns.

9. Or use the General Overview technique. As soon as you are seated and the server asks for drinks, ask a couple of general questions: *Is there an English speaking chef on duty? Is most of your chicken marinated? Do you have any steaks that are not prepackaged, but are delivered fresh?* You will be surprised at how quickly the answers will streamline your menu choices.

10. When making a reservation for a large specialty diet group, make certain the chef who knows how to handle your food is on duty and can accommodate a large group.

11. Remember not all ingredients are listed on a menu. State up front what you cannot have—even if it is not shown on the menu—as an ingredient.

12. Let the server and chef know how much you appreciate the service. This feedback benefits everyone.

Prepare For Success

Prepare yourself for successful restaurant experiences. A knowledgeable customer becomes familiar with ingredients likely to be used in a recipe and preparation methods commonly used in restaurants. Learn the basic terminology for sauces and main dishes.

A knowledgeable customer becomes familiar with the restaurant and its fare, its staff and reputation.

A knowledgeable customer asks specific questions about ingredients and preparation to clarify whether a dish will be free of WHEAT, BARLEY, RYE and OATS (WBRO).

A knowledgeable customer recognizes risks and asks questions to assess those risks and then orders accordingly. A careful diner continually assesses the situation before, during, and after being served.

Prepare to dine relaxed, confident and armed with humor. A diner well-served gains much by sharing expressions of gratitude. The best way to express gratitude is by returning often to the establishments whose staff takes your dining needs seriously.

Celiacs Helping Celiacs

Mary Schluckebier
Executive Director
Celiac Sprue Association®
PO Box 31700
Omaha, NE 68131-0700
Toll free 877-CSA-4-CSA
www.csaceliacs.org   celiacs@csaceliacs.org

There's More to a Menu than Meets the Eye

🍴 Mini Cooking Course
Cooking Terms
More Terms
Basic Sauces

A Mini Cooking Course

Throughout *Waiter, Is there Wheat in My Soup?* people have commented on how much easier it is to dine out if you have a basic understanding of cooking.

This mini cooking course is presented as a joint project by the author, the illustrious Chef Stephanie Green RD and renowned Chef Aaron Flores.

- Take the time to review the terms.

- Be positive.

- Highlight the intolerances or allergies that pertain to you.

- Circle your chosen methods of preparation.

- Underline key phrases or words as a reminder of what to ask the chef.

- Personalize this listing by adding your discovery of ingredients, foods or methods that suit your lifestyle.

And always remember:

If all meals were prepared the same,
there would be no reason for Chefs
—Chef Chuck

Italicized words indicate they are described within this section.
For more word descriptions, see International Cuisines.

Cooking Terms

Not all inclusive

Barbeque   To cook with dry heat over hot coals or wood. Food items may be *marinated*, rubbed with spices or *basted* during the cooking process. Ribs are frequently *boiled* prior to barbequing.

Baste   To brush food as it cooks with a *fat*, meat drippings or another *liquid* such as a *stock* or a *sauce* before and during cooking.

Blackened   Meat or fish cooked in a cast-iron skillet that's extremely hot. Food is rubbed with a Cajun spice mix prior to cooking. Flour may be added to the spice mixture.

Blanch   Food is briefly cooked in water however, other *liquids* may be used. Many restaurants use this method to briefly cook vegetables that are then immediately put in an ice water bath to stop the cooking process and set the color. This process is sometimes performed in sauté station using the same water as for pasta dishes. If gluten-free or allergic to wheat, ask for vegetables to be cooked in commercial steamer.

Boil   Cook in a *liquid* that is bubbling rapidly. It is reserved for more durable vegetables and starches. The liquid may contain *seasonings* or be made from a *base*.

Braise   To cook in a small amount of *liquid* after *browning* the food. This is a combination cooking method because the product is first *browned* which would typically involve flour and then *liquid* is added. This method applies to meat and vegetables.

Broast   A registered process that builds pressure in the pot while sealing in the chickens natural juices. Broaster and Broasted are registered trademarks of the Broaster Co. in Beloit, Wisc since 1954. It is the process of *marinating* and frying chickens under pressure.

Broil   To cook with radiant heat from above. It is a rapid high heat method reserved for tender cuts of meats, poultry, fish, and some vegetables. Foods may be slightly *marinated*, brushed with *oil* or rubbed with *seasonings* or a '*rub mix*' prior to broiling.

Brown   To cook over a high heat to retain the moisture of the food. Can be done on the stove or under the broiler. Liquid smoke, butter or flour may be added to enhance the color.

Coat   To cover food with an outer coating. Flour, egg, milk, nuts, seeds, breadcrumbs or mayonnaise are commonly used as well as cornstarch or tapioca starch could be used.

Deep-Fried   Foods are cooked by submerging in hot *oil*. Foods may be dipped in a *breading* or *batter* before frying. The same oil may be continuously used throughout the day, or for weeks, for various foods. Some deep fat fryers are cleaned daily to remove particles. Others are cleaned less often.

Deglaze   To add *liquid* to a pan to dissolve the food particles remaining on the bottom. A method used to gather natural flavors as base for a *sauce* or *gravy*.

En papillote   Food is wrapped in paper or foil and then cooked. The food is steamed in its own moisture. Butter may be added for flavor as well as *seasonings*.

Grilled   The food is placed on an open grid over a heat source that may be charcoal, an electric element or a gas-heated element. Foods may be *marinated*, rubbed with spices and *basted* before, during or after the process. For high sensitivities or intolerances, ask for the grill to be scraped, or ask for your food to be pan grilled or *broiled* without any prohibited ingredients or foods.

Griddled   Food items are cooked on a solid surface with or without small amounts of *fat* to prevent sticking. Many different foods are cooked on a griddle. For high sensitivities or intolerance, ask to have the griddle cleaned or to griddle item in a clean sauté pan.

Marinade, marinate
A mixture of ingredients used to add flavor to meat, poultry, fish or vegetables by soaking over a period of time. Ingredients usually include an acid such as vinegar, lemon, wine or lime and may contain *soy sauce*, *Worcestershire sauce*, cornstarch, herbs and *oil*. Marinades may be made from scratch or be created from a packet or bottle that may contain a food allergen or intolerance.

Pan-broil
Food which may be *seasoned* is placed in a sauté pan or skillet. Excess fat from the food is poured off. Typically no *liquid* is added in the cooking process. Check if a *fat* is used.

Pan-Fry
Food is cooked in a moderate amount of *oil*. It is similar to sautéing except more *fat* is used and it is over a lower heat for a longer period of time.

Poach
To cook in a small amount of *liquid*. Used to cook delicate foods such as fish and eggs but also to partially cook foods or to eliminate undesirable flavors and to firm up the product. A series of suitable questions may be, "do you poach the fish before grilling?" If yes, "In what type of liquid? Is anything else poached in the same liquid?"

Reduction
Liquid that is cooked down by simmering or boiling until the volume is decreased to concentrate flavors. Purchased reductions may include wheat, soy or other allergens/intolerances.

Roast   Cooking food in the oven in an uncovered pan. *Seasoning* may be added, but typically a *liquid* is not. Some foods may be *marinated* or *browned* in a pan using flour prior to roasting. This can be referred to as *Braising*. If the food is *browned* prior to roasting, *oil* or flour may be used. Always ask if a specific allergen was used in the recipe.

Sauteé   Food is cooked quickly in a small amount of *fat*. Food could be *breaded,* floured or *seasoned* and then cooked. Restaurants may use the same pan or *fat* for a number of dishes.

Sear   To *brown* the surface of a food using a high temperature. Technique is used to assist in maintaining moisture within a food product. Ask if any *seasonings* or *marinades* are used or *coatings* applied prior to searing.

Simmer   To keep a *liquid* on low boil. Ideal for soups and *sauces.* This technique can also be used to *braise* or *poach* fish or meat dishes.

Steamed   Food items are cooked by exposing them directly to steam. In commercial kitchens they may use special steam cookers. Steaming can also be done by placing food items above simmering water, *broth* or *stock.* However, some items are referred to as steamed when they are actually in the water. *Seasonings* may be added to the steamed item itself, or the *liquid* may be used for other foods. For instance, the same water used for pasta dishes may be used for the steam water.

Stewed	To simmer food in a small amount of *liquid* with or without *seasonings*. Meat or vegetables may be *browned* prior to placing them in the stew.
Stir Fry	A method of quick frying over a high heat using a wok or large pan. Soybean or peanut *oil* is used, garlic and perhaps *soy sauce* or a commercially prepared *stir-fry sauce* that usually contains wheat. *Fish sauce, oyster sauce, hoisin sauce* or *teriyaki sauce* may be used. *Breaded* items and seafood may be fried in the same wok. The same *oil* may be used repeatedly. Ask for a clean wok or fry pan, oil and utensils if needed.
Sweat	To cook slowly in *oil* without browning the food items. *Seasonings* may or may not be added.

More Terms

Au jus	The natural juices from meat. The juice may contain water or may be combined with a *stock* or *base* for added flavor. A thickener such as cornstarch or wheat flour may be used. The au jus may contain non-gluten-free seasonings or may be pre prepared using a number of allergens. Some meats may be 'refreshed' or 'held' in an au jus after cooking while waiting to be served.

Base   In a commercial kitchen, a Base (a compound of flavors) is either made from scratch (see broth, bouillon, stock) or used from a package. Most prepackaged bases include wheat and some may contain soy, fish or other allergen.

Batter   Usually a *seasoned* mixture of flour, eggs and milk used to *coat* an item for frying in *oil* or to make pancakes, waffles, cakes or cookies. Cornstarch, potato starch or rice flour may be used instead of flour.

Bouillon   Any *broth* made by cooking vegetables, poultry, meat or fish in water. The *liquid* is strained off and used as a *base* for soups and *sauces*. Packaged bouillon may contain wheat stabilizers, soy or other allergens/ intolerances.

Bouillon cubes may contain wheat or soy. They are dissolved in a *liquid* to make bouillon

Broth   A *liquid* obtained from cooking vegetables, meat or fish in water. It may be *seasoned*. This term is also used interchangeably with *bouillon* and *stock*. Broth may be started from 'scratch', from a 'starter or *base*,' pastes, *bouillon cubes*, granules or packets. Broth may also be used from a can or other pre-made sources. Check ingredients. Food servers or cooks may consider using a starter or base as 'cooking from scratch'. To help determine if broths are made from scratch, ask if stocks are prepared with bones and not *bases*.

Clarified Stock

A cloudy *stock* that has been made clear with the use of egg whites.

Compound Butter

Butter with spices and herbs added, depending on the recipe. Pre made steak butter may include flour. Steaks may be served with the steak butter on top without notation on the menu.

Cross Contact

Or cross contamination. Not cooking terms, but important when choosing foods and preparation methods. When one food that may be free of allergen or intolerance comes in contact with a food or ingredient that is not free of allergen or intolerance.

Consommé

Clear *bouillon* made from meat, fish or vegetables; served hot or cold. A cloudy consommé is made clear by adding an egg white.

Crispy

To 'provide a crunch or snap'. Raw vegetables, crackers and fried foods may be 'crispy'. Foods that have been *deep fried* in *oil* are usually defined as 'crispy'. Flour, coconut, crackers, panko Japanese bread crumbs, cornstarch, rice flour, nuts, seeds, cereal, egg or a flour/cornmeal based *batter* may all be used to provide a crunch or 'crispy' texture.

Demi glace   Meat, fish or chicken *stock* that is reduced to a concentrated form. Purchased demi glace may contain wheat, soy or other allergens.

Dry Rub   Seasonings rubbed onto meat or poultry prior to cooking. Many rubs contain wheat, soy or other allergens/intolerances.

Fats/oil   Fats in cooking add texture, shine, and flavor. A fat may be sprayed on an item prior to serving for a delectable looking presentation. Forms of fats that could be used in a restaurant: Lard, butter, margarines, shortening, bacon fat, nut oil, seed oil, rapeseed oil, peanut oil, vegetable oils, porcini or other mushroom oil, corn oil, soybean oil, canola oil, and olive oil. Seasoned oils may contain allergens.

Glaze   A thin glossy *sauce* made from a meat *stock* or aspic. Also could refer to a sweet glaze made from melted jelly or chocolate. Purchased glazes may contain wheat, soy or other allergens.

Gravy   A thickened *liquid* that can be made from the beef, chicken, fish or pork served with the meal. Water, milk, cream, wine, vegetable juice, fruit juice, *broth*, butter, *stock* or a *reduction* may be used as the liquid. Flour, cornstarch, arrowroot, cheese, pureed vegetables, fruits, nuts, onions or a flour roux or slurry may be used as the gravy *thickening* agent. Gravy seasonings or the gravy itself may be made from a packet, paste, jar or from scratch. The words sauce and gravy are sometimes used interchangeably. See also *sauce*.

Kryovac/ kryovak   Not a cooking term, but one that affects the dining public. It is a method of preserving the life and flavor of a food through the process of packaging. Many items in this packaging are already *seasoned* or *marinated*.

Liquid   A liquid may come from many sources. Common ones are fresh water, water used to cook potatoes, water to cook pasta, *broth*, *bouillon*, *stock*, vegetable juices, fruit juices, coconut milk, milk, creams and more.

Miso   Also called bean paste, a Japanese product. It comes in three basic categories: barley miso, rice miso and soybean miso. Most use aged soybeans as a base. Miso is used in sauces, soups, marinades, dips, main dishes and salad dressings.

Oils   See *fat*.

Sauces   See *Sauces* listing at the end of this section.

Seasonings   Herbs and spices may be fresh or dry. Commercially packaged may contain wheat, soy or other allergens or intolerances.

Special of the day/ Chef's Special   Some daily or Chef's Specials are created specifically for that day with fresh ingredients. Other Specials are reliant on the creativity of the chef as they use food that was not served the prior day and turn it into a palate pleasing dish.

Stock   When made from scratch, a strained liquid that is the result of cooking mire poix, poultry, meat or fish bones and a bouquet garni in water or another *liquid*.

Mire Poix Coarsely chopped onions, celery and carrots used to start a stock.

Bouquet Garni Parsley and thyme stems with bay leaves and leeks wrapped in cheesecloth and place as a flavor enhancer in stock.

A stock from a bottle, jar or can may contain wheat, soy or other additives. See *Broth* and *Clarified Stock*.

Thickener   Sauces, soups, gravies, and many more items may be thickened by creating a *roux, slurry*, a modified food starch, onions, eggs, creams, wheat, nuts, seeds, pastes, mushrooms, gums and more. Inquire how the item is thickened.

Basic Sauces

Adobo Sauce   Made from ground chilies, herbs and vinegar. It can be used as a marinade. Chipotle peppers are sold in a can of adobo sauces.

Aioli   A sauce prepared with eggs similar to a garlic mayonnaise. Commercially prepared sauces may include allergen ingredients such as wheat stabilizers.

Barbeque Sauce

May include *Worcestershire sauce*, *teriyaki sauce*, wheat, *soy sauce*, or anchovies. Request an ingredient listing.

Béarnaise Sauce

French sauce made with vinegar, wine, tarragon, shallots, eggs and butter. Commercially prepared sauces may contain wheat stabilizers.

Béchamel

A white sauce made with milk, butter and flour. It is the *base* for many other types of sauces. May be referred to as a cream sauce.

Bercy Sauce

Can be made with *fish stock*, flour, cream and *seasonings*.

Beurre Blanc

Butter based sauce made from a reduction of dry white wine, vinegar, and shallots. Classically no flour is used to thicken this sauce. Check for modifications with the Chef.

Beurre Manie

Butter mixed with an equal amount of flour; used to thicken sauces.

Beurre noir

Butter cooked over a low heat until dark brown and seasoned with vinegar, lemon juice, capers and parsley.

Brown Sauce

Also referred to as Espagnole sauce. It is made from a brown *stock*, vegetables, flour, and herbs. Many restaurants use a prepared sauce or a base for making the sauce.

Basic Sauces, continued

Chili Sauce   As a seasoning, it is a thin liquid created with a blend of spices, chiles or chili powder, onions, peppers, vinegar, sugar and spices. If the sauce is thick, ask for ingredients.

Coulis   Any thick puree or sauce. It can be animal protein based, fruit or vegetable.

Fish Sauce   Made from fish. Many brands of Vietnamese fish sauce contain wheat. Check the label.

Hoisin Sauce   Also called Peking sauce. It is a mixture of soybeans, garlic, chile peppers and various spices. Wheat is a common ingredient. Commercial preparations may contain allergen/intolerance. There is gluten-free hoisin sauce on the market.

Hollandaise Sauce   A yellow sauce made from egg yolks, butter and lemon juice. Commercial preparations may contain wheat stabilizers, soy or other allergens.

Oyster Sauce   A dark brown sauce made with oysters, brine and soy sauce. There is a gluten-free oyster sauce on the market.

Ponzu Sauce   A Japanese sauce made with lemon juice or rice vinegar, soy sauce, mirin (rice wine) and or sake, Kombu (seaweed) and dried bonito (tuna) flakes.

Basic Sauces, continued

Roux
A mixture of flour and butter that is cooked in an oven and used to thicken *liquids*.

Slurry
A paste of water and cornstarch used to thicken liquids. Flour may also be used.

Soy Sauce
Made from fermented boiled soybeans and roasted wheat or barley. True tamari is a Japanese soy sauce that does not contain wheat. Not all tamari sauces are wheat-free. There are wheat-free gluten-free soy sauces on the market.

Stir Fry Sauce
A commonly pre-prepared sauce used when stir frying. *Soy Sauce* and *fish sauce* may be used.

Teriyaki Sauce
Ingredients frequently include *soy sauce*, sake, sugar and ginger. There are gluten-free wheat-free teriyaki sauces on the market. Other allergens/intolerances may still be present.

Worcestershire Sauce
A flavoring sauce for cooking and used as a condiment. May contain wheat, soy, anchovies, molasses and vinegar.

International Cuisines

Life extends beyond hamburgers, salads, steaks, and potatoes. The following are general overviews and term descriptions to help you dine out in restaurants with international flavors.

Remember, each restaurant will cook a little differently and even combine diverse flavors for a totally different taste.

- Chinese Cuisine

- Indian Cuisine

- Italian Cuisine

- Japanese Sushi Cuisine

- Mexican Cuisine

- Persian (Iran) Cuisine

- Thailand Cuisine

- Vietnamese Cuisine

Action: If you would like to know more about a particular cuisine not included here, please complete and send us the Submittal Form on page 357 so all may enjoy the benefits in the next edition.

Chinese Cuisine

Cantonese * Mandarin * Shanghai * Szechwan * Dim Sum

China is a vast land with a wide variety of cooking techniques and ingredients. While the diversity of this land makes it difficult to provide a general description of the food, certain characteristics help us understand what to expect when ordering a meal. Of course, any of the cooking styles may be represented in a restaurant. In the United States, ingredients are usually altered to American preferences.

Cantonese or southern Chinese cooking is characterized by fresh ingredients served in delicious *sauces* made with cornstarch and *stock*, *oyster sauce* (usually made from fermented oysters and *soy sauce*), ginger, plenty of vegetables, very little meat and lots of rice. This was the first style of Chinese cooking in the United States.

Mandarin or Peking is northern Chinese cooking. It usually centers on wheat, millet, barley, wheat noodles and steamed buns, in lieu of rice. *Soy sauce*, sweet and sour sauces, *hoisin sauce* and wine based cooking *stock* is popular. Lamb is frequently used and Peking Duck is northern China's culinary achievement. Hotpots and barbeques have a Mongolian influence.

Shanghai, eastern Chinese meals are frequently prepared with sugar along with rice wines to give the sweet-and-sour dishes. Seafood is popular along with bean

Italicized words further explained in "A Mini Cooking Course" section beginning on page 47.

pastes and bean curd from soybeans. Some bean sauces contain flour. Slow braising in soy sauce is a favored cooking technique. This braising sauce is used in many of their master sauces and recipes.

Szechwan, western Chinese cooking gives us spicy dishes seasoned with the Szechwan peppercorn. Other traditional ingredients include cashews and walnuts combined with chicken and mushrooms. Hot and Sour Soup is a favorite dish.

Major allergens and intolerances:

Wheat, gluten, fish, shellfish and soy are used in many meals. Commercial pre-packaged sauces and pastes may contain wheat, or other allergen/intolerances.

Hoisin Sauce, Oyster Sauce, Soy Sauce and perhaps *fish sauce* are used as a *base* in many dishes. This presents a challenge for people who cannot have wheat or gluten. P.F. Chang's Chinese Cuisine, a national chain of restaurants, accommodates its gluten-free patrons via a gluten-free menu. Look for other restaurants that will share this open mindedness. For instance, some restaurants will allow you to bring in your own soy sauce. Wheat and gluten-free hoisin sauce, fish and oyster sauce are available on market shelves.

Cooking and ingredient information

A wok is the most frequently used item in Chinese cooking. It is used for stir frying, a method of cooking usually with soy sauce and rice wine. The wok is also used for deep frying. Woks are seldom washed thoroughly between different foods since the same ingredients are used in a number of different ways.

Many dishes are prepared with a fish or chicken *stock* that may be made from scratch or out of a bottle or can. If the stock is freshly made, ask about the ingredients and *seasonings*. If not, ask to see the 'stock starter' or 'base' ingredients. They are usually in a round tub.

Soy sauce is frequently used as an ingredient to enhance flavor. Some restaurants may use a vegetarian soy sauce that still contains wheat but no animal protein.

As a preparation technique, scallops or shrimp may be rubbed with *oil* or a cornstarch to remove the fishy smell. Chicken may also be *coated* and left to *marinate* in a mixture of cornstarch, sugar, wine and oil. They may also be marinated in soy sauce.

When ordering at a Chinese restaurant, ask if the chicken or meat has a reddish tint. If so, it is usually referred to as 'red-cooked,' meaning the item has been slowly *simmered* in *soy sauce* or a grain mash until all the sauce evaporates.

Dim Sum, or lunch, consists of choosing from bite-sized morsels of filled steamed dumplings made of wheat flour, baked or fried pastries, noodles with slices of meat or other delicacies. Carts filled with dim sum are rolled along the restaurant aisle and the patron chooses morsels as the tray rolls past. A few dim sum appetizers are made with rice paper. The fillings may contain seafood, nuts, *soy sauce* or *hoisin sauce*. Egg whites or flour may be used to seal the wrappers closed.

Rice Noodle Rolls are a dim sum favorite. Hand made rice noodles may include flour or wheat starch. Soy sauce, hoisin sauce, oyster sauce or fish may be in the filling. Rice paper may also be used as the roll. Most rice papers do not contain wheat.

Turnip Cake is a popular dim sum item. It is usually made with rice flour, shrimp and no soy or hoisin or oyster sauce. Verify ingredients.

Sauces

The names of sauces and ingredients are not always clear in Chinese cuisine, as well as in other cuisines. All of the sauces used may be purchased already prepared and may originate outside the USA.

Dipping Sauces may contain Worcestershire sauce, hoisin sauce, soy sauce, and broth.

Stir Fry Sauces start with a broth, soy sauce, oil and spices. Spicier sauces may add a garlic sauce or hot sauce—if either comes pre-prepared, check the ingredients.

Hoisin Sauce is used in many of the dishes. Some restaurants use it in place of sweet bean paste.

Sweet and Sour Sauce may contain sugar, soy sauce, vinegar, tomato sauce or ketchup, pickles and oil. Cornstarch may be the thickener, or flour. Sweet and Sour Pork is usually pork breaded in cornstarch (or flour) with egg and fried in perhaps a soy-based oil in the wok. Once done, it is combined with the Sweet and Sour Sauce.

Yellow Bean and Black Bean Sauces are frequently made from soy beans and may be mixed with soy sauce.

Make certain your sauce is made to order. Some restaurants may use an old technique of reusing a sauce many times over to increase and deepen the flavor. Do not attempt to determine any sauce contents by how it looks.

Fortune Cookie Lovers, if egg, wheat or gluten are a concern, skip the cookie but enjoy the good fortune.

Please remember this is not an all-inclusive listing of ingredients, processes, foods or techniques. Do not rely upon this listing as your only source of information. Read labels, ask questions and add your own notes to this section to suit your special dietary need.

Chinese Restaurants Questionnaire

The following questions were asked managers, owners, or chefs of Chinese restaurants randomly chosen from phone books.

Is it possible for you to prepare a dish without soy sauce?

Yes: 80% of all questioned said yes
No: 20% of all questioned said no

Does your plum sauce contain flour/wheat?

Yes: 60%
No: 30%
N/A: 10% said they do not offer plum sauce

Are oyster and hoisin sauces used in many of the dishes?

Yes: 40%
No: 60%

What liquid do you use to cook your rice?

Water: 70%
Fish stock or water flavored with fish sauce: 10%
Chicken broth: 20%

Indian Cuisine

Indian food is filled with intriguing aromas and inviting, spicy flavors. It is a fascinating diversity of foods that can be enjoyed by many people with dietary concerns.

India is a country of over 1500 dialects, vast differences in geographical areas, religious influences, and social status. Because of this, Indian food is considered a multicultural cuisine and the same dish may be prepared in different ways between different restaurants.

Loosely speaking, northern cuisine is mildly spiced. The more south, the hotter the spices and the more rice appears on the menu. Northern Indian cuisine is found in most U.S.A. restaurants, however southern influence is growing.

Foods originating from southern and central will focus on vegetarian with beans being the major source of protein. The east is known for its seafood and the west for its use of vinegar. While this is an overgeneralization, it gives us an idea of what to expect when an Indian restaurant says it serves cuisine from a particular area. You can also expect foods unique to a restaurant as they cultivate their own specialties.

There are commonalities in most Indian restaurants that help us read the menu and know what to ask. For instance, curry, long grain rice, yogurt, cream, coconut milk, chutneys, ghee, paneer, chickpeas, lentils, mung beans, soybeans, tamarind and noodles are prevalent in an Indian kitchen. Some brief definitions are at the end of this section.

Italicized words further explained in "A Mini Cooking Course" section beginning on page 47.

Sweet spices (nutmeg, cloves, cardamom, cinnamon and black pepper) and herbs (mint, coriander/cilantro/Chinese parsley and fenugreek) are the beginnings of a delicate balance at each meal

Many Indian restaurants will ask if you want your meal spiced mild, medium or hot. If they don't ask, you mention it.

Main Allergens or Intolerance:

Milk, casein and nuts are used in many of the meal items. Shellfish and fish may be on the menu, but are not a major cooking component. Commercial pre-packaged curries, sauces and pastes may contain wheat, or other allergen/intolerances.

Dining Ideas:

If not allergic to milk or avoiding casein. Always verify ingredients and cooking methods

Chicken Tikka is a traditional menu item. Generally, the chicken may be marinated in lemon, garlic, ginger, garam masala (see next page), spices, yogurt and oil and then baked in a tandoori (an Indian clay oven) or in the oven. The chicken will be red due to a tandoori food coloring or red food coloring mixed with tomato paste.

Chicken Tikka Masala is Chicken Tikka (see above) served in a Masala Sauce made with spices and tomatoes.

Paneer is homemade or purchased cottage cheese combined with lemon juice, cream, spices, perhaps an egg and chickpea flour. Verify the flour. Peas or spinach or a curry *sauce* may be added. Tofu may also be used for paneer.

Papadam are wafers usually made with lentil or bean flour. They may be fried or baked.

If you have never eaten Indian food before, and you can tolerate yogurt, order a **Raita**, a salad-type side dish with a smooth yogurt base. It refreshes and cools the warm temperature of a meal.

Ingredients and Methods

Garam masala is a combination of spices that add warmth, but not fire to a dish. Some restaurants will create their own garam masala using 7–20 different spices. Others will purchase a pre-packaged garam masala combination. During our research we looked at 7 different brands of packaged garam masala and none contained wheat or soy—but that does not mean they all do not contain wheat or soy.

Masala sauce means spices combined with *stock*, cream, milk or coconut milk and perhaps ground nuts to form a smooth and flavorful curry sauce. This sauce may be served over chicken, vegetables, rice or shrimp.

A basic **Curry (sauce)** may include garlic, ginger, onions, tomatoes, cilantro, peppers, spices, garam masala, turmeric, water or *stock*, yogurt and oil.

Dum is a cooking technique of browning the meat or vegetables in *oil* or butter and completed by steaming. Sometimes an item previously *braised* may be finished using the dum technique.

Korma is a braising technique using a sauce of yogurt, cream, purees or *stock*. The Korma sauce may be purchased premade.

Any of the following items may be made from scratch, but may be from commercial pastes or packages (pre-made) that may or may not contain wheat, oils, nuts, and dairy or other food concerns:

Garam Masala Paste, Tamarind Paste, Fried Onion Paste, Curry Paste, Marinades, curry sauce, *stock, broth, sauces,* and breading mixes

Marinade: Meats, chicken or seafood may be marinated in spices, lime juice, yogurt, soy bean or milk curd.

Breading: Batters for deep frying may contain besan, lentil bean flour/chickpea flour and/or wheat flour. Besan is a gram flour, a member of the chickpea family—not to be confused with graham flour which is <u>not</u> wheat or gluten-free. Ask specifically which flour(s) is used.

Rice noodles/rice sticks/chaaval ke sev may be found in some of the dishes, or available as a substitute.

A few common words to help you read the menu. Words may be spelled different ways due to language dialects. Always verify the ingredients with the chef and ask questions.

Akhroot	Walnut
Anda	Egg
Asafoetida	Powder or resin gum from a fennel-like plant. Wheat often in packaging
Ata, Atta, Chupatti flour	Are wheat flours
Badam	Almond
Badaami	Meat or chicken with ground almonds
Besan	Chickpea or lentil bean flour
Bhaji or Bhajee	Means a vegetable dish without a sauce.

Bhajia	A deep fried fritter. Made with wheat or bean flours or both.
Bhona	Fried
Biriani or biriyani	A traditional rice dish with meat, chicken or lamb filling
Bombay duck or bombil	Small transparent fish. May be in (seafood) curry
Brinji	Aubergine, a vegetable like an eggplant
Chana	A type of lentil pea
Chapatti	Wheat flour
Chilgoze or Nioze	Nuts
Chupatti	Unleavened wheat bread
Curry	Sauce. May or may not be spicy
Curry powder	Mixed spices
Dal	Lentils, beans or peas
Dahi	Yogurt, yoghurt
Doodh	Milk
Dosa or Dosai	Pancake from the south of India made from rice or lentil flour.
Firni	Rice flour pudding with almonds and milk

Ghee	Usually clarified butter—purchased may have oil or wheat added
Idli	Rice and lentil flour cake from southern India. Verify flours
Jinga	Prawns
Kadhi	Yogurt soup—may include chickpea flour dumplings
Kekada	Crab
Kofta	Minced meat or vegetable balls, deep fried. May contain wheat or other allergens.
Kajoo	Cashews
Korma	Oftentimes means a sauce (may be bottled) with cream, yogurt, nuts, spices
Macchi or macchli	Fish
Makhan	Butter
Makkee	Cornflour
Malai	Cream
Matar	Chickpeas or peas
Mollee	Fish cooked in a sauce
Murgh	Chicken
Naan	Wheat flour leavened bread

Oil	Peanut, soy, canola, vegetable, Indian oil—read the bottle labels
Patia	Seafood curry
Payasam	Southern India pudding made with beans, peas and coconut milk
Rabadi	Milk sauce
Rasam	Spicy lentil sauce
Rice	May be soaked in a liquid. Some chefs fry in an oil to keep rice separate
Tala, Talna	Deep fry
Tari	Gravy
Tamarind	Date-like fruit used in chutneys and for cooking

Please remember this is not an all-inclusive listing of ingredients, processes, foods or techniques. Do not rely upon this listing as your only source of information. Read labels, ask questions and add your own notes to this section to suit your special dietary need.

Italian Cuisine

The history of Italian cuisine is brimming with simplicity influenced by its peasant heritage as well as the elaborate banquets of the Roman Empire and the Renaissance. Up until 1861, Italy was divided into separate kingdoms, states and regions under the control of Spanish, Austrian, French and sometimes Arab powers that influenced the country and cuisine.

Most Italian restaurants in the United States seldom refer to the differences in Italian cooking. Many have 'Americanized' the dishes with more meat and commercially prepared stocks and sauces. Some restaurants have replaced the traditional olive oil or butter with vegetable oils. However, there are wonderful restaurants in the United States that thrive on the old fashioned quality of ingredients and home-made sauces. These are the restaurants to look for as they are the ones equipped to accommodate specialty diets.

Major Allergens and Intolerances:

Wheat and wheat-gluten in the pastas, pizza crust and breads. Milk, cheese and egg in some sauces. Soy if using a soy based oil. Commercially packaged sauces and pastes may contain wheat, soy or other allergen/intolerances.

Italicized words further explained in "A Mini Cooking Course" section beginning on page 47.

Dining Ideas—after asking appropriate questions

Even if some of these items are not on the menu, ask if the ingredients are in the kitchen. A 'friendly' restaurant may prepare it for you if they are not busy.

Antipasto platter:	Slices of Provolone or aged Italian cheeses, olives, vegetables either fresh or marinated in olive oil, salami, Prosciutto or other sliced meats, capers, or perhaps anchovies. Request a vegetable dip (Pinzimoni) of olive oil, lemon juice and salt. Ask if your food allergen may be omitted or exchanged for more of what you can eat and that bread not be put on the plate. Verify all ingredients.
Prosciutto e melone	Slices of cantaloupe served with thin slices of prosciutto (Italian word for ham). Enjoy together for a salty, sweet taste.
Insalata Caprese	Thick slices of fresh mozzarella, tomatoes and fresh basil enhanced with extra-virgin olive oil.
Minestrone	Soup made with *oil*, onion, tomatoes, vegetables, *stock* or water, beans perhaps, and cheese. Minestrone alla Milanese may include pasta. All soups may be commercially prepared and contain wheat or other allergen/intolerances.

Carpaccio	Unmarinated raw beef sliced paper thin served with arugula (a type of lettuce) with olive oil, lemon, capers and shavings of fresh Parmesan rolled and put on the top.
Pasta	Dine at restaurants that offer gluten-free pasta or will prepare the special diet pasta you provide in a clean pot of fresh water.
Chicken or Veal Marsala	Many restaurants prepare this without first *dredging* or flouring the meat. Instead of the flouring, Marsala is often prepared by sprinkling the cutlets with salt and pepper and cooking them in a large skillet with butter or *oil* until brown. Shallots, onions, mushrooms and garlic may be added. When almost cooked through, Marsala (a famous Italian wine) is added to the pan. A bit of butter may be added to the sauce just prior to removing from the pan and serving.
Veal Scallopino al Marsala	Ask if this dish can be made without *dredging* the veal in flour. The veal is cooked in butter, chicken *broth*, Marsala wine, salt and pepper. Verify the veal is fresh and is not already breaded and frozen.
Veal in Lemon and Wine Sauce	Ask if veal can be served without the flour dredging. This is a simple dish that includes veal, butter, salt, white wine, parsley. Fresh lemon is served for you to squeeze onto the veal.

Saltim Bocca	Veal Cutlets with Prosciutto, seasoned with sage leaves, salted and cooked in butter and ground pepper. Verify fresh veal and no *dredging*.
Grilled Chicken with Pesto Sauce	A chicken breast that has not be marinated, grilled in a pan with a small amount of olive *oil* until done, then served with a Pesto Sauce (if freshly made with verified ingredients).
Polenta	Cornmeal and water. Prepared polenta is available in a tube. It can be baked or fried and used as a base for a tomato topping or Marina Sauce, or in lieu of pasta.
Pizza	Pizza crust is primarily made from wheat and perhaps eggs. There are restaurants serving gluten-free pizza crusts as evidenced in this book. If your restaurant does not serve a pizza crust you can eat, consider other options as the crust (after you have verified the sauce and other items fit your dietary needs). Polenta, baked or mashed potatoes, rice, vegetables, French fries or bring in your own crackers and use the pizza sauce as a dip.
Risotto	A dish made with Italian rice—like Arborio. Oil or butter is placed in a fry pan along with, perhaps onions and then the rice is added to the pot and stirred. Wine or *stock* is added to produce creamy rice. Other *seasonings* or *base* may be added. Commercially prepared risotto is available.

| Gnocchi | A potato pasta that is ordinarily made with flour and perhaps eggs. It is possible you could come across a restaurant that uses potato flakes or potato flour instead of wheat flour. |

Steaks that are not marinated, or Broiled Fish with vegetables grilled in olive oil are usually available.

Sauces and Ingredients in Italian Cooking:

| Alfredo Sauce | When made from scratch it may include cream, butter and Parmesan cheese. Some include an egg. There are many recipes for Alfredo Sauce. Many restaurants thicken with flour or use commercially prepared sauces that may contain wheat or other allergen/ intolerances. |

| Marinara Sauce | A basic tomato sauce that usually does not contain meat. Ingredients may include tomato sauce, garlic, wine, basil, oregano, sugar, Tabasco, tomatoes or tomato paste, onions, *stock* or a multitude of other ingredients, as per the chef. Sauce may be thin or thick. Flour may be used or a commercially prepared sauce may contain wheat or other allergen/intolerances. Marinara Sauce may be used as a pizza sauce. |

Pesto Sauce	There are many varieties. One of the most common is spinach with *oil*, lemon juice, salt, and pepper and Parmesan cheese. Many restaurants prepare this sauce from scratch.
Beans	Cannellini, fava, broad and lentils.
Cheeses	Asiago, Parmesan, Parmigiano Reggiano, Provolone, Mozzarella, Ricotta and many more.
Meats	Cured meats like Pancetta or Lardo (bacons), Sausages and Salamis. Processed meats may contain cheese, wheat, soy or other allergens or intolerances.
Anchovy Fillets	May be added to sauces or salads for extra flavor.
Capers	The small buds of a low growing bush. They have a bitter taste that enhances the flavor of other ingredients.
Salad	No dusting.

Please remember this is not an all-inclusive list of ingredients, components, processes, foods or techniques. Do not rely upon this listing as your only source of information. Read other sections of this book for more information. Read labels, ask questions and add your own notes to this section to suit your special dietary needs.

Italian and Pizza Restaurant Questionnaire

The following are questions asked managers, owners, or chefs of Italian restaurants randomly chosen from phone books.

Pasta Sauces:

Do any of your red pasta sauces contain wheat/flour—whether made from scratch or from a bottle?
> Yes: 10% said all of their red sauces contain wheat
> No: 90% said none of their red sauces contain wheat

Do your white or Alfredo sauces contain wheat/flour?
> Yes: 50%
> No: 40%
> Other: 10% said their Alfredo sauce can be made special order without flour

Marinated items:

Do you marinate your chicken?
> Yes: 30% marinate chicken in olive oil and herbs
> Yes: 20% marinate chicken in canola oil, mustard and herbs
> No: 50% do not marinate the chicken

Do you marinate the beef or shrimp?
> Yes: 10% marinate the shrimp in a sauce
> No: 80% do not marinate the shrimp
> N/A: 10% do not offer shellfish
> No: 100% do not marinate the beef

Noodles:

Would your restaurant allow a customer to bring in an unopened package of gluten-free or allergen-free pasta during non-rush hour for your kitchen to prepare in a fresh pot of water?

    Yes: 70%
    No: 30%

Pizzas:

Would your restaurant allow a customer to bring in an unopened package of gluten-free or allergen-free pizza crust during non-rush hour for your kitchen staff to use in place of your crust?

    Yes: 40%
    No: 50%

If a family dined at your pizza restaurant on an average of twice a month, would you keep pre-made gluten-free pizza crusts on hand?

    Yes: 20%
    No: 60%
    Possibility: 20%

Japanese Sushi Bars

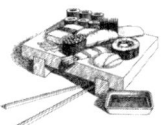

In most Japanese restaurants you will find quality of ingredients over quantity. Simplicity and elegance prevail in every dish. The food is usually prepared meticulously and the arrangement and presentation of the food is considered an important part of each nutritious meal.

Plenty of vegetarian meals are usually on the menu, along with noodles, miso soup, rice, tofu, seafood, chicken, beef and vinegar side dishes.

Sushi Bars specialize in serving an abbreviated menu of sushi, rice and side dishes. Sushi rolls are usually made of a layer of sushi rice wrapped around vegetables or fish and rolled up using a wrapper. Soy sauce is not usually added to the roll itself but may be part of an ingredient wrapped within the roll.

Main Food Allergens or Intolerances:

Fish, shellfish, and soy are mainly used in the meals. Very little dairy, egg or nuts are used in Japanese dishes. Wheat is common in soy sauce, a major ingredient used in cooking.

Commercially prepared sauces and pastes may contain wheat, or other allergen/intolerances.

Italicized words further explained in "A Mini Cooking Course" section beginning on page 47.

Dining Ideas:

*If not allergic to soy or fish—**after asking appropriate questions***

Edamame	Steamed fresh whole soy beans. Remove from pod prior to eating.
Miso soup	see Miso below
Cucumber Salad	Thinly sliced cucumbers and onions in vinegar and perhaps soy sauce or fish sauce.
Sushi	Vegetables or seafood wrapped in rice and seaweed. (See the Sushi Questionnaire at end of this section)

Cooking Techniques and Ingredients:

The main cooking techniques include simmering in a flavored stock, steaming, grilling on a grill or in a pan with a sauce and deep frying.

Imitation crab	Usually contains Pollock fish and wheat starch.
Mirin	A sweet wine made from rice. Ordinarily Mirin does not contain wheat. There is always an exception to the rule. While researching this book, we saw a bottle labeled 'Sweet Cooking Seasoning Mirin' that contained wheat.
Miso	A thick seasoning paste made from soybeans an important ingredient in miso soup. Some misos are made from barley. Miso may be used in sauces, entrees, dressings or miso

soup. Miso soup may be made with dashi (soup base made with bonita (tuna) flakes), tofu, miso, onions and mushrooms.

Noodles   Popular in Japanese dishes.

- Soba noodles are usually made from a combination of buckwheat and wheat flour.

- Udon and Somen noodles are made from wheat.

- Bifun are clear noodles made from rice flour and potato starch.

- Saifun are clear noodles made from mung bean starch. They are also known as cellophane noodles.

- Kuzu kiri are a light colored noodle made with sweet potato starch. Bifun, Saifun and kuzu kiri may be substituted for the wheat noodles in most dishes.

Panko   Japanese (wheat) bread crumbs that may be used to coat or batter shrimp, fish, chicken or crab. Often times they are not listed on the menu as part of the dish preparation process.

Ponzu sauce   For dipping tempura or crab or on salads, can be made with wheat soy sauce, mirin, bonita (tuna) flakes and rice vinegar.

Rice	The mainstay in a Japanese meal.

- White, red, brown or black rice is usually steamed or simmered in water or *stock*.

- Rice may be seasoned. Some rice seasonings include salmon, shellfish, *soy sauce*, or wheat.

- Sushi rice is sweetened with rice vinegar and sugar or honey. It is possible that a restaurant may use rice syrup. Many rice syrups contain barley.

Seaweed	Highly nutritious and used in many dishes, either as a wrapping (nori), a flavoring (kombu), as a vegetable (wakame) or garnish.
Shoya (soy sauce)	A soy sauce made with soybean extracts, wheat, salt and water. Ask if they have wheat-free tamari in the kitchen to substitute for the shoya. The tamari must say wheat-free on the bottle. An **alternative** is to use an equal measurement of barley-free miso and thin the miso with water
Stock	May be made entirely from kombu and water. Additional *stock* seasonings may be bonita (tuna) flakes, mushrooms and perhaps *soy sauce*. The *stock* may also be started from a concentrate or powdered form. Stock is the *base* for soups and may be used in any of the sauces or at the chef's discretion.

Tempura	A batter made with eggs and wheat flour. Fish, chicken or vegetables are dipped in the batter and then deep fried. It is a popular method of cooking. You may find some restaurants that use cornstarch.
Teriyaki sauce	Often referred to as a sweet soy sauce contains rice wine, sugar and usually wheat soy sauce. Teriyaki may be used as a *marinade* or accent seasoning. There are brands of teriyaki sauce that are wheat-gluten-free. An *alternative* may be a mixture of wheat-free *fish sauce* or barley-free miso mixed with rice wine and sugar.
Tofu	A pressed soybean curd.
Umeboshi	A paste or liquid made from salt-pickled Japanese plums. The pink color comes from sisho leaves that are brined along with the plums for flavor and color. Umeboshi is both salty and tart and may be used as a seasoning as well as a condiment.
Wasabi	A hot green Japanese horseradish. It is ordinarily a paste or pure powder reconstituted with water. Some restaurants may add flour or other ingredients to temper the heat.

Please remember this is not an all-inclusive list of ingredients, processes, foods or techniques. Do not rely upon this listing as your only source of information. Read labels, ask questions and add your own notes to this section to suit your special dietary need.

See the Sushi Questionnaire on the next page for more information.

Japanese Sushi Restaurants Questionnaire

The following are questions asked of sushi or executive chefs of Japanese and Sushi restaurants randomly chosen from phone books.

Do you use malt vinegar, fish sauce or soy sauce in your cucumber salad?

Malt vinegar: 100% said "No" they do not it

Fish sauce: 40% said "Yes", they do use fish sauce

Soy sauce: 40% said "Yes"

Note: Some restaurants included both fish sauce and soy sauce in cucumber salad

Do you marinate eel in soy sauce, fish sauce or teriyaki sauce before putting in a roll?

No: 1% said No

Yes: 99% said the eel is marinated in a sauce, usually soy sauce.

Other fish: 99% said they do not marinate fresh fish or seafood in soy sauce, fish sauce or teriyaki sauce.

Do you add flour to your wasabi powder while preparing it?

Yes: 30% said Yes, they add flour to wasabi powder

No: 60% said they do not add flour to their wasabi powder

Other: 10% said they use real wasabi and grind it fresh

Note: Not all wasabi powders or pre-prepared mixes are wheat and gluten-free. Ask for ingredients.

What ingredients do you commonly use when making your sushi rice?

Stock – 10% start the rice with stock, either fresh or commercially prepared

Water – 90% start the rice with just water

Any of the following may be added, some add more than one ingredient

Barley miso – 10%
Bonita flakes – 20%
Soy sauce – 10%
Fish sauce – 10%
Malt vinegar – 0%
Seasonings – 10%
Rice vinegar – 50%

Does your fish roe have flour in it?
Yes: 30% said Flying Fish Roe contains wheat
No: 50% said none of the fish roe contain wheat
20% said it depended upon their source

Mexican Cuisine

When the Spanish landed in northern Mexico in 1590 the "Spanish expedition described the Aztec food in detail, reporting corn tortillas…tamales with a multitude of fillings, a dozen kind of beans…Corn, avocados, tomatoes, chiles and cacti."

The Spanish added wheat, rice, cheese, dairy and pork and turkey to the menu. This Mexican 'Moveable Feast', excerpts from *The Border Cookbook* Jamison & Jamison, traveled up the California border, across Arizona into Texas and into New Mexico.

Mexican food became known as the Cal-Mex, Tex-Mex, and Southwestern cuisine.

As borders were drawn, the Mexican food influence remained and still thrives today. The food has made a few changes over the years, becoming lighter in nature, healthier and more creative. Proving that the 'snacks and street foods' of Mexico—the enchiladas, tamales and tacos are here to stay.

Major allergens and intolerances:

Milk, wheat and eggs are the most common ingredients. Shellfish and fish are on menus but are not usually used as flavorings or bases for other dishes. Peanuts are in some moles. Commercially packaged items may contain food allergens or intolerances such as wheat and soy. Always verify ingredients.

Italicized words further explained in "A Mini Cooking Course" section beginning on page 47.

Ingredients and Entree Information:

Note: Almost all items may be purchased commercially rather than made from scratch. The more items a Mexican restaurant prepares from scratch, the closer you will be to a meal that meets your dietary needs.

Arroz con Pollo
Rice with chicken is a *simmered* dish that is a traditional favorite. Ask if the chicken is *marinated* or if it is *dredged* in flour before *browning*. Also, be sure that the chef does not add toasted pasta noodles to the rice. If so, it is likely they cannot be omitted.

Black beans (Frijoles Negros)
Served whole after cooking with bacon or other fat, jalapeno and onion—topped with Pico de Gallo and cheese. Vegetarian version has no bacon.

Burrito, Burro
Soft flour tortilla folded and rolled around a bean and cheese or meat filling. Corn tortilla substitutions will be smaller in size.

Carne Asada
Seasoned *broiled* or *roasted* beef often served as an entrée with chile sauce or used as a meat filling for tacos. Chicken prepared the same way is Pollo Asado.

Chalupa
Fried corn (or sometimes flour) tortillas with a cup of meat, beans or guacamole on top and garnished with lettuce, diced tomatoes, cheese and olives. This is what most Americanized restaurants call a tostada. Some restaurants call a 'chalupa' a crispy fried bread-like taco shell with fillings.

Mexican

Cheese Crisp A purely Americanized appetizer: A flour tortilla is lightly crisped (fried or broiled) and covered with melted cheese and peppers, along with meat or vegetables and served 'pizza-style.' Sometimes called a **Quesadilla**.

Chilaquiles Soggy corn tortilla chips seasoned with taco sauce and used as a base for some egg dishes. Sometimes cream and cheese is added.

Chile Con Carne This is not 'chili' with ground beef and beans. It is actually cubes or beef round steak that have been *browned* and then *simmered* with chili powder and spices to create its own *gravy/sauce*.

Chile Relleno Mild green chiles stuffed with a filling then dipped in a batter of flour and egg, then fried, deep fried or baked. They can be filled with *seasoned* or *stewed* meats, seafood, vegetables or cheeses.

Chimichanga Basically a deep-fried burrito.

Chorizo Mexican sausage that may contain soy, cheese or wheat.

Enchilada A corn tortilla is lightly fried in *oil* and then rolled around any number of fillings and covered with a *sauce*. Sonoran-style Enchiladas are flat and stacked instead of rolled. Sour cream enchiladas are baked after they are rolled.

Enchilada sauces, including red, green and sour cream varieties may contain wheat flour. If commercially prepared, may contain soy as well. See questionnaire at end of this section.

Guacamole (aguacate salsa) Thick sauce or dip made with mashed avocado, onion, tomato, lemon juice and spices. A thinner version is used as a dressing.

Huaraches Thick masa patties fried in oil, ordinarily made with all corn. Corn cakes may have wheat or egg in the batter.

Huevos Rancheros 'Ranch eggs' are traditionally cooked to order, served on oil-dipped corn tortillas and covered with a thin sauce of simmered tomatoes, onions and green chiles. It is becoming trendy to serve with flour tortillas, so ask to be sure. Sour cream usually served on top. Egg-eating vegetarians should ask about the presence of beef in the ranchero sauce.

Flan Traditional vanilla custard made with milk and eggs and served with caramel sauce.

Flautas Traditionally, flour tortillas rolled around a seasoned meat filling into the shape of a flute (hence the name) and deep fried until crispy. Increasingly, the name flauta is being used interchangeably with taquito to describe both the corn and flour tortilla items.

Machaca, Carne Machaca, Carne Seca	Beef that has been *stewed* and separated into strings of meat, blended with chile, onion and stewed tomatoes. It can be served as an entrée with tortillas for wrapping, used as a filling for tacos or scrambled with eggs.
Manteca	Pork lard, used in traditional Mexican cooking for meaty flavor.
Masa	Corn dough used for making tortillas, enchiladas and tamales. Fried patties are called huaraches. Should not contain flour, however some 'American-ized' restaurants have added wheat flour for lighter texture.
Menudo:	Spicy stew of tripe (stomach lining), chiles and hominy. This traditional hang-over cure is usually gluten-free, with a long cooking time naturally thickening the broth to the proper consistency. Can also be served 'with hoof' for meatier taste. Ask for corn tortillas on the side. Verify ingredients.
Mole	There are many varieties depending on region or origin and personal tastes. This thick sauce usually accompanies chicken and turkey, sometimes pork and fish. They are labor-intensive to create and have complicated recipes; so many restaurants choose the commercially prepared moles that are available in powdered or paste form that is reconstituted with water or *broth*. Common ingredients are: chile, tomatoes, nuts, coriander (cilantro), cumin, cinnamon, chocolate,

onion, ground seeds and clove. Bread is often added to add more body to the sauce. Moles tend to be heavy and slowly-digested, so even after thoroughly checking ingredients for wheat-gluten, there may be some digestive issues following a large, enjoyable mole dish!

Nopales   Flat cactus leaves used in dishes as a vegetable. Ask about softening or cooking techniques.

Pico de Gallo salsa bandera   Diced tomatoes, minced onions and minced jalapeno peppers, mixed together and served as a garnish.

Pollo Fundido   Chicken, cheese and sour cream rolled in a flour tortilla and fried to a golden brown. This is a very Americanized version of a traditional dish, available on many Mexican restaurant menus...and clearly not appropriate for anyone with wheat or milk sensitivities. See **Queso Fundido** for a description of the traditional dish.

Pozole   Hearty soup with many ingredients, including (but not limited to) hominy (white corn), chopped pork, chopped chicken, chicken *broth*, onion, garlic, avocado, tomatoes, jalapenos, lime juice and spices like oregano, cilantro and bay leaf. The meats may be *marinated*, the soup may be *thickened* and the *broth* may contain allergens or intolerances.

Quesadilla	This traditional dish has become as mainstream as the grilled cheese sandwich! A flour tortilla is warmed on a griddle, and then filled with cheese, and sometimes meat and vegetables, and folded into a large semicircle and grilled until the cheese is melted. Instead of folding, some restaurants will make a round sandwich of two tortillas. If asked, a restaurant will often substitute corn tortillas for flour, making adjustments in quantity to compensate for the smaller size. Be aware that some restaurants call a **Cheese Crisp** (see above) a **Quesadilla**.
Queso Fundido cheese fondue	Baked melted cheese served with flour tortillas for wrapping and dipping. Traditional Pollo Fundido adds chicken to the dish. Corn tortillas or tortilla chips may be substituted for the flour tortillas. Ask about *thickeners* and if chicken is in a *marinade*!
Queso Dips (Espinaca con Queso, Chile con Queso)	Cheese dip. Most restaurant dips contain flour to thicken the cheese dip and keep it from separating.
Refried beans	Frijoles (red kidney beans) are cooked then crushed and reheated, refried, with Manteca (lard) cheese and spice. Vegetarian versions do not contain lard. Refried beans are often served topped with cheese.

Rice	Mexican rice is cooked in a *liquid* and may be seasoned. Verify the liquid and the *seasoning*.
Salsa (**salsa roja**)	Combines tomatoes, onions, jalapenos and spices, and other ingredients as taste dictates. Salsa verde substitutes tomatillos or other green tomatoes for the red tomatoes. (See Mexican Questionnaire at the end of this section.)
Sauces	Commercially packaged sauces and pastes may contain wheat, or other allergen/intolerances. Look for restaurants that create their sauces from scratch.
Taco	Fresh made or commercially packaged meat filling may be inserted into a folded corn tortilla and served soft, or deep-fried to a crunchy texture after filling. Sour cream may be a topping. Verify sour cream ingredients. If the restaurant uses crunchy ready-made corn taco shells, ask for ingredients. Many restaurants use flour tortillas as their "soft tacos" and may substitute corn asked. See **Tortillas, corn**.
Tamales	Corn masa filled with pork or beef that may have been *marinated* or mild green chiles, corn and cheese. Most often wrapped in corn husks, but can also be wrapped in plantain leaves, parchment paper or served unwrapped with sauce. Order without sauce if red sauce contains wheat. See **Masa**.

Taquito	Literally, a 'little taco,' this is often a corn tortilla rolled around a *seasoned* meat filling and deep fried into a crispy tube and served with sour cream and guacamole as a garnish. Some restaurants use a flour tortilla and call it a 'taquito,' too. See **Flauta** for more information
Tortilla Chips	Chips and salsa may be placed on the table. Chips may be corn or flour. They may be purchased or deep fried on location in oil used for other items.
Tortillas (corn)	Usually 100% made from corn, but you may want to verify. Used in common dishes such as enchiladas, chalupa/tostada, huevos rancheros, tacos. Corn tortillas are frequently dipped in oil used for other purposes to soften them. Ask if this step can be avoided.
Tortillas (flour, wheat, whole wheat, flavored)	Clearly wheat-based. Used in popular dishes such as burritos, chimichangas, quesadillas and as table bread. Substitute corn tortillas when appropriate, or choose another entrée.
Tostada	See **Chalupa**

Please remember this is not an all-inclusive listing of ingredients, processes, foods or techniques. Do not rely upon this listing as your only source of information. Read labels, ask questions and add your own notes to this section to suit your special dietary need.

Mexican Restaurant Questionnaire

The following are questions asked chefs and managers of Mexican restaurants randomly chosen from phone books.

Is there flour in the red enchilada sauce?
    Yes: 70% said Yes; there is flour in their red sauce
    No: 30% said No; there is no flour in their red sauce

Is your red enchilada sauce made fresh?
    Yes: 80%
    No: 20%

Is there flour in your green sauce?
    Yes: 90%
    No: 10%

Is your green enchilada sauce made fresh?
    Yes: 80%
    No: 20%

Is there flour in the salsa?
    Yes: 20%
    No: 80%

Is the salsa sauce made from scratch?
    Yes: 80%
    No: 20%

Are the corn tortillas dipped in oil before presenting to the customer?

    Yes: 80%, almost half of them said they would avoid this step if requested

    No: 20%

Do you marinate your chicken?

Yes: 50% said fajita chicken marinated in soy sauce

No: 50% do not marinate chicken

Do you marinate the beef?

Yes: 50% said fajita beef marinated in soy sauce

No: 50%

Persian (Iran) Cuisine

A Taste of Middle Eastern Cuisine

Persia has one of the richest and oldest cultures in the world. Under Cyrus the Great, it became the center of the world's first empire.

The country is usually know by its people as Iran (land of the Aryans), and as Persia by Europeans. Both titles are now widely used.

Over the centuries, Persia was invaded by the Greeks, Arabs, Mongols and Turks. Yet the flavors of Persian cooking are distinct and identifiable primarily due to pleasant spices and fruits or vegetables found in most dishes.

The true beauty of Persian cuisine is its healthy, wholesome nature, its uncomplicated cooking method and simple presentation. These qualities make it ideal for those with special dietary needs, particularly when the restaurant cooks from scratch.

Major Persian ingredients include: Rice, dried fruits, nuts, beans, fresh fruits, tomato paste, *whey*, yogurt, olive oil, lamb, chicken and beef.

Spices include cinnamon, cardamom, nutmeg, curry powder, *sumac*, vanilla, saffron, ginger and turmeric. Vegetables are rarely served on the side since they are incorporated into many of the dishes.

Persian

Italicized words further explained in "A Mini Cooking Course" section beginning on page 47.

Naturally, this is all a generalization since there is a considerable amount of variation from one Iranian restaurant to another—as is true for all restaurants

Major Food Allergens or Intolerances:

Milk and casein found in yogurt, milk, butter, ghee. Ghee may be their oil of choice in some menu items. Nuts are included in some dishes or as a garnish.

Wheat, gluten, soy and perhaps other allergens/intolerances in commercially prepared items.

Dining Ideas at a Persian Restaurant:

After verifying all the ingredients meet your dietary needs.

For someone on a gluten-free diet, we found dining at a Persian Restaurant, like India Restaurants, to be a welcoming experience. We easily enjoyed a great number of the dishes.

Homous Dip (Hummus) is made of garbanzo beans, tahini sauce (sesame seed paste) olive oil, garlic and lemon juice. Verify they make it from scratch. During our research we were disappointed to find a jar of hummus with wheat as an ingredient. So you must always check—and while checking, verify the sesame seed paste is simply that, without any allergens. This dip is usually served with pita bread (wheat, gluten, eggs, etc.) either bring your own crackers or ask if they have any raw vegetables you may use for dipping.

Dolmeh is loosely interpreted as a stuffed vegetable. This could be an eggplant stuffed, or tomatoes, grape or cabbage leaves.

Stuffed Grape Leaves, called **Dolmeh-ye-bag-e-mo** are usually prepared with rice, onions, *broth*, dill weed, olive *oil*, sugar, vinegar, mint and spices. The grape leaves are usually *blanched*, rice is cooked in a *liquid*, the meat may be *browned* and a *broth* is poured over the leaves prior to baking. Pine nuts or raisins may also be used as a filling.

Yogurt and Cucumber Dip is usually yogurt, cucumbers, onions and vinegar. Sometimes the yogurt may be homemade. Chopped mint may be added. Use as a side or for dipping.

Tah Dig is rice that has been cooked in a *liquid* until it has a crispy and crunchy crust. When prepare correctly, this wonderful rice is an accompaniment to stews.

Kababs (Kabobs) means pieces of *marinated* lamb, chicken, beef and/or vegetables placed on a stick and *grilled*. The meat or vegetables may be *basted* while grilling.

If you order a Kabab, verify they do not use a piece of bread to remove the meat from the skewer if sensitive to wheat or gluten and the plate not be lined with bread upon serving.

Rice (long-grain is usually used) is usually made with water, and perhaps *oil*. Other rice dishes may have raisins, yogurt, spices, sugar, nuts, lentils, dates, oranges, vegetables or meat/fish/chicken added. Some rice dishes may include wheat noodles.

Stews are a favorite in Persian dining. They are usually served over Basmati rice cooked in a *liquid*. Vegetables are usually *sautéed* then added to the stew. The beef may be *browned* before adding to the stew. *Sauces* may be made from scratch or commercially prepared. These dishes are worth taking the time to ask questions.

Special Notes:

A **Marinade** in many Persian dishes may mean a combination of onion, garlic, red wine vinegar, olive oil, pepper, salt, or herbs; perhaps yogurt, butter, ghee or broth.

Basted in many Persian dishes may mean brushed intermittently with oil, butter, ghee, lime juice, salt, or pepper or special herb blend.

Bulgur, couscous or green wheat may be on the menu – none of which are wheat-gluten-free.

Gyros A Greek word for minced lamb that is molded around a spit and vertically roasted. The meat is sliced, enfolded in pita and topped with grilled onions, sweet peppers, and a cucumber-yogurt sauce. **Shawerma** is a Turkish or Persian word for the Gyros—or Gyros is the Greek word for the Persian Shawerma, depending on which countryman you talk to. This meat is delicious, however, unless the restaurant makes it themselves, it probably is commercially prepared from a manufacturer like Kronos and contains bread crumbs (wheat and eggs).

Please remember this is not an all-inclusive list of ingredients, foods or techniques. Do not rely upon this listing as your only source of information. Read labels, ask questions and add your own notes to this section to suit your special dietary need.

Thailand Cuisine

The food of Thailand, once known as Siam, has been influenced by the Burmese and Japanese who colonized Thailand at different times in history. While the French and neighboring countries of Laos, Cambodia, China and Vietnam also influenced the food, Thai cuisine is unique, supporting the definition of 'Thailand—Land of the Free.'

Thai cuisine is an international favorite due to its healthy preparation techniques and distinguishable blend of flavors and taste sensations. The balance of hot, sour, salty and sweet appears in almost every dish. While Thai cuisine is noted for the heat of its chilies, many Thai dishes are mildly spiced. Rice is a staple in Thai cuisine and Thailand is one of the largest exporters of rice.

Rice, noodles, fish, chicken, vegetables, fruit, *fish sauce*, shrimp paste, peanuts and curry sauces made with coconut milk, are integral to Thai cooking. Very little dairy is used in classic recipes. However, Thai restaurants in the United States may offer an 'Americanized' or 'euro-fused' Thai cuisine that is milder in spices, with different main ingredients and more meat on the menu.

Major Allergens or Intolerances:

Peanuts are frequently incorporated into a dish or served at the table. Soy is a common ingredient. Commercially prepared *sauces* and pastes may contain wheat or other allergen/intolerances. Always verify ingredients.

Italicized words further explained in "A Mini Cooking Course" section beginning on page 47.

Dining at a Thai Restaurant

Thai cuisine can be adapted for many people with food allergies or intolerances.

Some Thai restaurants will start their curry paste from scratch, thus eliminating the need for commercially prepared powders and pastes. Major flavorings include cilantro (coriander) turmeric, chilies, basil, lemongrass, lime, garlic, ginger, tamarind and mint.

Some of the items most likely to be wheat-gluten free or may be made free of some allergens include Pad Thai, Chicken in Coconut Milk Soup, Jasmine Rice, Sticky Rice, sweet and sour cucumber relish and more.

Pad Thai   One of the national rice noodle dishes of Thailand. Even though restaurants will create the dish a little different in order to attract patrons, many of the basics remain the same. Rice noodles, shrimp, chicken or tofu and egg are lightly fried in *oil*. *Fish sauce*, sugar, mung bean or soybean sprouts, garlic, chilies, onions, peanuts, rice vinegar and lime are ordinarily added to the dish. Some restaurants may season with tamarind or add *oyster sauce*. Peanuts are usually served on the side.

Verify the Pad Thai sauce is made from scratch rather than a paste, seasoning packet, or starter from a jar, bottle, envelope or can. If any of these items is used, ask to see the label since it may contain a food allergen or gluten item. If you have made it clear in the beginning about your dietary restrictions, the restaurant should feel comfortable in fulfilling your request.

Ask to see the label from the rice noodles to verify no wheat is included in the ingredients. The restaurant may insist there is no wheat, but during our research, we saw rice noodles, albeit extremely few, that had wheat flour listed on the package as well as rice flour.

Many of the allergens may be omitted in the preparation of the dish, if the dish is freshly made. Some restaurants may insist the dish will not be the same as the original. The restaurant may be concerned about their reputation; that you will not enjoy the meal, or their staff will not be able to understand the exclusion of the item. Take your time to make it clear the change is okay and you will return again if they can adjust the food so you can eat comfortably.

Chicken and Coconut Milk Soup

A classic Thai dish. Other names may be Chicken Soup and Lemongrass, Chicken and Galangal (Thai ginger) or Tom Kha Gai

The major ingredients are chicken (usually not marinated, but ask), water or *stock*, coconut milk (usually a non-dairy item), galangal, chilies, mushrooms, ginger, *fish sauce*, and lime. (Do not eat the galangal or lime leaves —they can be tough.) Curry paste, shrimp paste or curry powder may also be used, depending on the chef. Some restaurants may allow fish as a substitute for the chicken.

The soup is excellent alone, as an appetizer or combined with a side order of Jasmine Rice.

Curry Dishes May be beef, chicken, tofu, vegetable or shrimp included in a curry paste. A curry paste is made either from scratch or from a commercial package bottle and combined with a wide assortment of ingredients such as chilies, ginger, lemon grass, garlic, rice vinegar, sugar, onions, curry leaves, water, *stock*, *oil*, cream of coconut, or coconut milk. Curry pastes may contain shrimp paste (kapi), peanuts, peanut butter, anchovies, *fish sauce* or other allergen/ intolerances.

Rice A staple in Thai restaurants. Jasmine is long grain rice. Thai Basmati Rice is another long grain favorite. Sticky Rice is short grain rice called glutinous rice because it sticks together after steaming. It does not contain wheat gluten. All rice is usually simmered or steamed in water that may or may not be seasoned. A *stock* may also be used instead of water.

Papaya Salad A refreshing signature salad of northeast Thailand. Its simple ingredients of papaya, garlic, lime juice, *fish sauce*, sugar, shallots and green beans demonstrate Thai's appreciation for color and texture. Other ingredients may include shrimp, tomatoes, and carrots. A sweet *sauce* either made fresh or commercially bottled may be added to the mixture.

Noodles Rice noodles or mung bean noodles are served at many Thai restaurants. Ask if they can be used in lieu of wheat or egg noodles, if intolerant to wheat or gluten.

More Ingredients Used in Thai Cuisine

Bean curd Tofu made from soybeans that may be used in soups or salads

Coconut cream Grated flesh of brown coconuts. It is unsweetened.

Coconut milk Coconut cream mixed with water. It adds a smooth flavor. Verify milk is not used instead of water for a richer flavor. The book *Dancing Shrimp: Favorite Thai Recipes for Seafood* suggests some light coconut milk may contain flour as a thickener. In our research we did not see any canned ingredients stating flour was included, but it doesn't hurt to verify, if wheat or gluten is an issue.

Cream of Coconut	Used mainly for desserts and beverages, is a sweetened commercially produced version of coconut cream.
Curry pastes	Either made from scratch or commercially prepared. Red and green curry pastes are made from red and green chilies. A golden color curry is the red curry paste enhanced with the spice turmeric and 'mussamun' is the name of a red curry paste enhanced with cinnamon, cloves and other spices. As stated above, curry pastes may contain a wide number of allergens/intolerances. Verify the paste is one you are able to enjoy.
Dried shrimp	Used in Thai cooking almost exclusively, not for the flavor of shrimp but for the saltiness. If shellfish is an issue, be aware of this seasoning.
Oyster mushrooms	Not oysters at all, but mushrooms shaped like oysters.
Rice Noodles and Rice Paper	Both used in Thai cooking. Verify 100% rice or tapioca flour or starch if gluten intolerant.
Tamarind	A fruit from the tamarind tree that has a sour taste. The fruit pulp is usually made into a paste used for cooking.

Please remember this is not an all-inclusive list of ingredients, components, processes, foods or techniques. Do not rely upon this listing as your only source of information. Read other sections of this book for more information. Read labels, ask questions and add your own notes to this section to suit your special dietary needs.

Vietnamese Cuisine

Vietnamese cuisine has been influenced by neighboring countries, political events and paths of trade throughout the centuries. Stir fries and chopsticks from China, curries and spices from India, wine and baguettes from the French and soups from Thailand incorporate into a truly 'fused' and distinctive cuisine that is characteristically fresh and healthy with mild, unique flavor combinations.

Noodles, sauces, soups, salads, salad rolls, rice and seafood are mainstays of a traditional menu. Vegetarian dishes are usually available due to the Buddhist philosophy and influence in Vietnamese culture.

Main Food Allergens or Intolerances:

Fish, shellfish—mostly shrimp, peanuts and soy are common ingredients. Peanuts are frequently in a dish, as a garnish or served on the side. Fish sauce is a basic component of many meals. Commercially packaged items may contain food allergens or intolerances such as wheat. Always verify ingredients.

Dining at a Vietnamese Restaurant:

Vietnamese cuisine is one of the easier Asian foods to enjoy. The more traditional restaurants may use the finest of ingredients for freshly made *broths (stocks), sauces,* dips

Italicized words further explained in "A Mini Cooking Course" section beginning on page 47.

and dishes. Items are frequently assembled together or cooked upon ordering. The more Americanized-restaurants may use commercially bottled sauces, pastes or starters. These bottled items may contain certain allergens or food intolerances, always ask for ingredients or check the label.

The most popular items that may be made free of allergens or intolerances include the Pho (rice noodle soup), rice paper spring rolls, salad and rice.

Pho	The famous Vietnamese soup usually made with a *broth* (*stock*), rice noodles, bean noodles, bean sprouts, herbs, chilies and perhaps scallions. Pho soup starts with a hot broth. The noodles are added and then topped with the meat or vegetables. Beef with rice noodles is the traditional soup but shellfish, fish, poultry or vegetarian may all be offered. *Fish sauce, hoisin sauce* and chili sauces are frequently offered on the side for your own seasoning. It is customary to slurp the noodles while enjoying the soup.
	Pho Soup is considered a meal in itself and is worth the effort to ask a few questions. When ordering a soup, be interested in the *Broth* (*Stock*). *Broths* may be beef, pork, vegetarian, chicken or seafood. Ask if your *broth* choice is made from scratch. If it is made from only the basics, the list of ingredients will be few Ask if the *fish sauce* has wheat or if a soup *base* or soup starter is used. Some restaurants believe if they use a

starter or base from a container, the broth is still made from scratch. Ask about *seasonings*. A pork *stock* may be seasoned with a fish or shellfish. Cornstarch, wheat starch, *fish sauce*, shrimp paste or beer may be used, depending on the chef's creativity.

Chicken, seafood and fish may be *marinated* in cornstarch and water. Some restaurants may use wheat flour or egg for coating the chicken, but that is not the norm.

Question if the noodles are rice, bean or wheat/egg noodles. If items are made fresh, it will be easy to combine broth and noodles that you can enjoy for a delicious dining experience.

Rice Paper Spring Rolls

Rice paper soaked in water and then filled with a variety of ingredients. Make certain the spring roll wrappers are made from rice, not wheat, if you are wheat/gluten-free. If they offer the spring rolls deep fried, ask if they can omit the deep frying process if cross contamination is an issue. Ask for specifics on the inside ingredients (filling) which may include mung bean noodles, also called cellophane noodles, garlic, sugar, pork (ask for the ingredients and if it was fried in a soy based oil), *fish sauce*, eggs, carrots, or your particular allergen or intolerance. Do they seal their spring rolls with a flour and water paste or with egg? Since these rolls are usually assembled as they are ordered, you have a good chance of being able to order a roll that fits your dietary needs.

Cucumber Salad and Table Salads

Easiest to order. The Cucumber Salad is extremely refreshing. Its ingredients are usually simply vinegar, lime juice and cucumbers, but each restaurant may have its own recipe. Sometimes a sweet and sour sauce is added to the cucumbers. Ask if the sweet and sour sauce is made fresh or is from a commercially prepared bottle. If you have been clear on your dietary needs, they will not find this question offensive.

Many Vietnamese salad dressings contain *fish sauce*.

Ask how the salad is plated and served to avoid any surprises of dried shrimp, fried onions or other accompaniments.

Rice

Rice on the menu will be a long grain rice like jasmine, sticky (glutinous) rice or fried rice. Ask if the **jasmine** rice is boiled or steamed in unseasoned water. If it has seasonings or is prepared in a *broth*, you will need to know the ingredients. True **sticky** rice, also known as sweet rice is short grain rice that literally sticks together when cooked. A person would think nothing could be easier than ordering rice, but some restaurants do not use true glutinous rice and cause a short grain rice to stick together by adding sugar, corn syrup or rice syrup that may contain malt, a non-gluten-free item. So make certain you ask. **Fried** rice may be fried in a soy based oil, seasoned with *fish sauce* or *soy sauce* or contain other allergens such as egg. There will usually be rice you can enjoy with your meal or topped with one of the delicious dipping sauces discussed below.

Primary Ingredients:

■ Fresh garlic, lime, chilies, cilantro, mint, shallots, Thai basil and ginger are major contributors to the fresh flavor combinations of the food.

■ **Fish Sauce** (nuoc mam) a bottled sauce usually made from fermented anchovies is a primary ingredient in almost every dish. Most brands of fish sauce do not usually contain wheat. However, brands such as Viet Huong and Phu Quoc all contain wheat, clearly shown on the label. Fish Sauce may be made from other sources of fish, but not usually shellfish. Ask them if you returned with a wheat-free fish sauce, if they would use it for your meal.

■ **Peanut Oil** may be used for deep frying or in a dipping sauce.

■ **Dried Shrimp** is used as a seasoning or as an ingredient in some dishes.

- **Shrimp Paste** is used as a seasoning or as an ingredient in many dishes. It is a mixture of shrimp and water. During our research, we searched for a bottle, jar or package of shrimp paste that showed any other ingredients, but did not find one. Yet that does not mean one does not exist.

- **Soy Sauce** is used in some dishes, but not to the extent it is used in Chinese cooking. Most restaurants use *Soy Sauce* made from soybeans fermented with wheat flour. See 'Mini Cooking Course' section beginning on page 47.

- **Oyster Sauce** is not usually used in Vietnamese restaurants, but is mentioned here since it contains food allergens. A vegetarian *oyster sauce* is available, but upon reading the ingredients and talking with an importer, they were unwilling to confirm the terms 'oyster flavoring' did not contain any traces of oysters or wheat.

- **Hoisin Sauce** may be used as a flavoring in a dish or served on the side. The primary ingredients are soybeans. Many restaurants use a bottled hoisin sauce that contains soybean paste and wheat as a thickener. There are hoisin sauces that do not contain wheat-gluten on the market.

- The soybeans in **Soybean Paste and Soybean Sauce** are usually fermented with wheat, rice or barley. A traditional Korean soybean paste or sauce may be available that uses a natural fermentation process without the wheat, rice or barley concerns. Some restaurants may use the Japanese *Miso*.

- Edible **Rice Papers** are used as wrappings for the salad rolls. These round shaped wrappers are also called Rice Paper **Spring Roll Wrappers or Tapioca Sheets**. 99% of the rice papers we have seen in Asian markets or on the internet are made from rice, potato starch or tapioca starch, along with salt and water. On only rare packages have we seen wheat listed as an ingredient along with rice.

■ **Wheat Spring Roll Wrappers**. Some restaurants will use a Spring Roll Wrapper made with wheat because they stand up better to deep frying than the Rice Papers or Tapioca Sheets. You must ask specifically which spring roll wrapper they are using.

■ **Rice Noodles or Mung Bean Noodles** are in many dishes and may be used as a substitute for dishes made with egg/wheat noodles. Some dishes may contain deep fried rice noodle—a cross contamination or allergy issue if flour items are fried in the same oil or if the oil has a soy or peanut base. 99% of the rice and bean noodles we have seen in Asian markets or on the internet are made from rice flour, potato starch, tapioca starch, or mung bean along with salt and water. On only rare packages have we seen wheat listed as one of the ingredients.

There is a wide range of **sauces**.

■ **Chili Sauce** from a bottle of red chilies

■ **Spicy fish sauce or hot sauce**—either may include soy sauce

■ **Sweet and Sour Sauce**—may contain fish sauce, soy sauce, sugar, ginger and lime

■ **Nuoc mam chan** is a traditional sauce often made with *fish sauce*, lime juice, vinegar, water, garlic and red chilies

- **Peanut Sauce**—could contain *hoisin sauce*, soy sauce or even shrimp

- Bean Sauce—often made with *hoisin sauce* or soybeans

- **Shrimp Sauce**—made with shrimp

- **Sweet plum sauce**—may contain wheat or other allergens

- Many *pre-bottled sauces may contain msg, wheat, or other allergens*

Please remember this is not an all-inclusive list of ingredients, components, processes, foods or techniques. Do not rely upon this listing as your only source of information. Read other sections of this book for more information. Read labels, ask questions and add your own notes to this section to suit your special dietary needs.

Beyond Conventional Cuisine

✍ **Don Matesz, M.A., C. H., Dipl. Nutrition**
Co-author of *The Garden of Eating: A Produce-Dominated Diet and Cookbook*

Don Matesz is a nutritionist and herbalist based in Phoenix, Arizona. He heads the holistic nutrition program at the Southwest Institute of Healing Arts in Tempe, Arizona.

Beyond Conventional Cuisine

If you have the opportunity, you may more easily obtain a meal that fits your special needs by leaving the beaten path for an alternative restaurant. In major cities and college towns you can find restaurants run by and for people who eat what many may consider to be unconventional diets.

Vegetarian, vegan, macrobiotic, and raw food restaurants cater to people who have decided to eliminate some foods from their diets. All of these cuisines involve restriction of animal products in varying degrees. In the last part of the twentieth century the number of people eating semi-vegetarian or vegetarian diets increased due to concerns about the health effects of meat-based diets and problems such as mad cow disease.

Most of these alternative restaurants provide high quality food and have menus helpful to some degree to people restricting common allergens. Perhaps more importantly, in these establishments you often can more easily find a manager or chef who follows an alternative diet and clearly understands your need to avoid certain foods.

Vegetarian or Vegan

A vegetarian diet includes fruits, vegetables, grains, legumes, nuts, seeds, and might include eggs or milk, but excludes all meat (animal flesh or organs), including meat of poultry and fish. A vegetarian diet that includes eggs is called ovo-vegetarian, one that includes milk is called lacto-vegetarian, and one that includes both is called lacto-ovo-vegetarian. A vegan diet excludes all foods of animal origin.

You may find that vegetarian restaurants will go the extra mile to try to prepare something that meets your special dietary needs.

Many vegetarians understand the difficulties involved in following restricted diets. Many have felt offended when being offered a dish that has 'just a little fish' by a person who doesn't understand that a vegetarian eats no meat at all. So when you tell a vegetarian chef that you can't eat soy, he will know that you don't want any, not even 'just a little'.

A **vegetarian** restaurant will not serve fish or shellfish, but may or not provide menu selections for people allergic to wheat, milk, eggs, soy, nuts, or peanuts. Many vegetarian dishes are largely composed of items from the latter list.

However, menus of vegetarian restaurants often specify the vegan items that contain no milk or eggs, and offer plain brown rice, steamed vegetable platters, and various a la carte vegetables free of common allergens. Since vegetarian dishes often include soy sauce, miso (fermented soy-barley or soy-rice paste), tofu, nuts, or peanuts, you will have to give the wait person or manager a list of foods you must avoid and have him/her check with the chef to identify acceptable items. If you can eat soy but not wheat, ask if they have wheat-free tamari soy sauce.

A **vegan restaurant** will serve no animal products at all. Here you may find creamy soups, sauces, casseroles, and desserts free of dairy products that fit your special needs. Seventh Day Adventist Restaurant chefs are particularly skilled at making dairy-free treats. However, you will find many items incorporating wheat, soy (soy sauce, miso, tofu, tempeh, soy milk), nuts, or peanuts. Give the wait person or manager a written list of things you must avoid and have him/her check with the chef to identify acceptable items. As in a vegetarian restaurant you will probably have the option of ordering a la carte items such as brown rice and vegetables prepared without foods that cause you grief.

Macrobiotic Restaurants

People following macrobiotic diets regularly eat cooked whole grains (especially brown rice), vegetables, legumes, nuts, seeds, fruits, and may occasionally eat fish. They rarely if ever eat eggs or poultry, and generally do not eat any dairy products or red meat. Macrobiotic diets that regularly include modest servings of fish, eggs, or poultry probably have health benefits similar to vegetarian diets. People eating vegan macrobiotic diets for more than three years have been found to develop vitamin B-12 deficiency.

Like vegetarians and vegan chefs, macrobiotic chefs usually have experience dealing with dietary restrictions and tend to be open to modifying recipes or creating on the spot a special meal for someone with dietary restrictions.

Since many people eating macrobiotic diets avoid all animal products for varying periods of time, macrobiotic restaurants generally clearly mark the menu to identify the few dishes containing fish, shellfish, or eggs.

Among grains, macrobiotic chefs favor brown rice and millet so many of the menu items in a macrobiotic restaurant will be wheat-free. Macrobiotic chefs also use brown rice noodles in some recipes. Look also for items including mochi, a pounded sweet, sticky brown rice product that is gluten-free.

Some macrobiotic chefs like to use nuts or nut butters in desserts, as garnishes, or in sauces or dressings, but you usually will have no trouble finding nut-free items on a macrobiotic menu.

Macrobiotic chefs use soy sauce or miso (fermented soy-barley or soy-rice paste) as seasonings in most of the dishes they prepare. If you tolerate soy but not wheat, ask if they can use wheat-free tamari to replace soy sauce. Some macrobiotic dishes contain soy in the forms of tofu, tempeh, or soy milk, and usually this will be noted on the menu. If in doubt, ask.

Macrobiotic restaurants will generally offer a la carte brown rice and vegetables, and remember that a macrobiotic chef will generally enjoy whipping up something that meets your special dietary needs.

Raw Food Cuisine

Raw foodists refuse to eat anything that has been heated to a temperature greater than about 110 degrees. Raw foodists will eat sprouted grains and legumes, raw vegetables, fruits, nuts, and seeds. They also eat soy sauce, despite the fact that it is made of boiled soy beans and grains, some of which may contain gluten.

Generally raw food diets exclude all animal products, although some include raw (unpasteurized) dairy products. Most states prohibit restaurants from selling raw dairy products so raw food restaurants will not have these on the menu.

The meals at an all-raw vegetarian restaurant are usually presented with color and variety. Allergen-free and gluten-free sauces, main meals and desserts may all be found on the menu.

All-raw vegetarian meals tend to be very bulky and may cause gas and bloating. Raw food establishments may serve many foods heated to about 100 degrees, but no higher.

Many people find the creativity of all-raw vegetarian restaurants to be an enjoyable and worthwhile experience on a limited basis.

Friendly Restaurants, Cafes, and Delicatessens

🍴 Friendly Restaurants Defined

🍴 Neighborhood Restaurant Locations

🍴 Multi-state Restaurants Defined

🍴 Multi-state Restaurant Locations

Action: If you own a Friendly Restaurant, or if you have had an excellent experience in a Friendly Restaurant not included here, please complete and send us the Submittal Form on page 357so all may enjoy the benefits in the next edition.

Friendly Restaurants Defined

A 'Friendly Restaurant' welcomes your business and will take steps to provide a meal that meets your dietary restrictions.

For this book, a 'Friendly Neighborhood Restaurant'
Was identified by:

- recommendation by a patron or a support group
- responding to a questionnaire
- referral from other restaurants

A Friendly Neighborhood Restaurant answered "Yes" when asked:

- Do you have experience with serving gluten-free and/ or allergen-free diets?

- Are your employees in a position to do the best they can for special dietary needs?

- Do you welcome and can you accommodate more gluten-free and allergen-free business?

- Shall we include your restaurant in *Waiter, Is There Wheat in My Soup?*

You may ask if any of these 'Friendly Restaurants' or any other restaurant can guarantee a meal to be totally free of gluten or a particular food allergen?

Probably not. As you read the Disclaimer, and through the rest of this book, you will become aware of some of the challenges that surround food ingredients and their preparations.

- Restaurants rarely grow, breed, transport, package and label the many food items they prepare in a day.

- They rely on information from their sources as to food handling and ingredients.

- In a restaurant environment, as in some homes, food cross-contact or the slim chance of human error is a possibility.

With all this in mind, and the litigious nature of the American public, it makes sense that restaurants refrain from making such a guarantee.

Restaurant doors open both ways

If you have a dietary restriction, you must know what you can and cannot eat; be able to read a menu in order to ask specific questions; be alert; know your level of tolerance, and accept the responsibility for your choices. In order to help restaurants and the next person dining there with a dietary restriction, it is very important that you communicate your needs in a friendly, clear and patient manner.

Avoid restaurants where you feel they do not listen to you, take your special diet seriously or make a multitude of mistakes on a variety of different occasions. Simply take your dollars, family, friends, and business associates elsewhere.

If you are very ill, extremely sensitive or too shy to communicate your dietary needs in an effective manner, ask your physician for guidance on how often you should dine out.

Stay alert!

Restaurant management philosophy, personnel, menus, ingredients, procedures and food preparation are always subject to change. This is true even when there is a special diet menu at the restaurant.

Become a Repeat Customer to the Restaurants That are 'Friendly'

Bring your family, friends, and business associates to their door. If the restaurant is publicly held, purchase their stock. If they are privately held, help spread the word. Support 'friendly restaurants' in their efforts, and they will happily respond to your needs and the special dietary needs of others over and over again.

Example of a Friendly Restaurant

I have celiac disease and own an Italian restaurant that offers both a regular and gluten-free menu. It is easy to service the gluten-free customer due to our special menu and attention to details.

The gluten-free menu consists of a selection of appetizers, entrees and desserts. We also have a gluten-free beer called La Messagere.

My cooks are well aware of the cross-contamination issue. We have been using the gluten-free menu for 5 years and we have more and more customers driving great distances in order to enjoy a delicious and safe meal.

We have an established system for serving the gluten-free guest. When the guest advises the wait person of his dietary needs, the wait person uses a special key on the computer to alert the kitchen staff. This draws special attention to the order in a professional, reliable and consistent manner.

Our favorite gluten-free appetizers are: French fries with mayo, small spaghettis, artichoke bottoms, palm hearts and garlic snails au gratin.

Our salads are individually prepared for the gluten-free customer. Our salad dressings are certified gluten-free by their manufacturers.

We use separate pots and drainers for gluten-free pastas and delicious sauces that do not contain flour.

Our first quality meat sauces are made with 100% beef and are all easily made gluten-free.

Freshly shredded Parmesan cheese is offered at the table.

For the gluten-free customer, we offer dessert of a caramel flan or an apple, or Queen Elisabeth Cakes, both with a delicious caramel sauce, all made here with dedicated mixer and pans.

We treasure our gluten-free customers. They are an important aspect of our customer base. They bring with them a sincere appreciation for the efforts we make as well as family, friends, or business associates who dine off our regular menu.

Come and visit us,
Mireille Normand
Casa du Spaghetti
450.372.3848
604 Principale
Granby, Quebec Canada
www.casagranby.com

Mireille is a diagnosed celiac and restaurant owner. She is the previous owner of four restaurants, a ham and smoke meat plant where these meats were processed and had 300 employees. Mireille is a prominent supporter of the celiac community, both in Canada and USA. She is co-host of the Delphi Support Group, a free internet discussion group and a recipe writer. She provides many of her recipes through the Delphi Support Group. Visit her at the Casa du Spaghetti: www.casagranby.com or on line at: http://forums.delphiforums.com/celiac/start.

Neighborhood Restaurant Locations

Suggestions from various restaurants:

- Call ahead to confirm location and hours

- Verify special diet accommodations are available

- When dining with a large special diet group, verify restaurant is capable of handling the group effectively

Alabama

Old Heidelberg Cafe
256.922.0556
6125 University Dr NW
Suite E14
Huntsville, AL 35806

P.F. Chang's China Bistro
For location(s) see page 332
www.pfchangs.com
Gluten-free menu

Alaska

Marx Bros. Café, The
907.278.2133
627 West Third
Anchorage, AK 99501
www.marxcafe.com

Arizona

Alberto Italian Restaurant
480.488.5800
7171 E Cave Creek Road, Ste S
Carefree, AZ 85377
Gluten-free pasta available

Guiseppe's
602.381.1237
2824 E Indian School Rd
Phoenix, AZ 85016
Gluten-free pasta available

Havana Cafe
602.952.1991
4225 E Camelback Rd
Phoenix, AZ 85018
   Serving authentic Cuban, Spanish and Latin American Cuisine. We offer an extensive gluten-free menu and cater to many special diets.
   Open for lunch 11 am-4 pm, Mon-Sat. Open for Dinner 4 pm-9:30 pm Sun-Thur, and until 10 pm Fri & Sat.

Havana Patio Cafe
480.991.1496
6245 E Bell Rd
Scottsdale, AZ 85254
   Serving authentic Cuban, Spanish and Latin American Cuisine. We offer an extensive gluten-free menu and cater to many special diets when possible

Open for lunch 11 am-4 pm, Mon-Sat. Open for Dinner 4 pm-9:30 pm Sun-Thur and until 10 pm Fri-Sat.

Kingfisher Grill
520.323.7739
2564 E Grant Rd
Tucson, AZ 85716

La Stalla Cucina Rustica
480.855.9990
60 West Buffalo
Chandler, AZ 85225

All items made from scratch; Southern Italian cuisine; gluten-free pasta.

Los Sombreros Mexican Café & Cantina
480.994.1799
22534 N Scottsdale Rd
Scottsdale, AZ 85257
www.lossombreros.com

Los Sombreros Mexican Café and Cantina serves authentic Mexican cuisine in a charming 1926 building complete with a cozy patio. Our spectacular dinner menu is made with the freshest ingredients available. We support local farms like Young's Farm and One Windmill. Adjustments may be made to many of our items for special dietary needs.

P.F. Chang's China Bistro
For location(s) see page 332
www.pfchangs.com
Gluten-free menu

Pei Wei Asian Diner
For location(s) see page 339
www.peiwei.com
Gluten-free menu

Pugzie's
602.279.3577
4700 N 16th St
Phoenix, AZ 85016
www.pugzies.com

Pugzie's Restaurant and Catering Co. is open Mon-Fri. 10 am- 4 pm. We serve gluten-free rolls for sandwiches, as well as gluten-free muffins, cookies, dressings and soups. The owner is gluten-free and experienced in the diet.

Red Sky Café
520.326.5454
1661 N Swan Rd Ste 120
Tucson, AZ 85712

Please call ahead regarding special dietary needs.

Ruffinos Italian Cuisine
480.893.8544
4902 E Warner Rd
Phoenix, AZ 85044

Rice noodles available. With prior notice will make gluten-free meatballs

Saigon Healthy Cuisine
480.967.4199
820 S Mill Ave
Tempe, AZ 85281

Thaifoon – Taste of Asia
480.998.0011
8777 N Scottsdale Rd
Scottsdale, AZ 85253
www.thaifoon.com
Gluten-free menu

Z'Tejas
480.893.7550
7221 W Ray Rd
Chandler, AZ 85226
www.ztejas.com
Gluten-free menu

Z'Tejas
480.948.9010
10625 N Tatum Blvd
Phoenix, AZ 85028
www.ztejas.com
Gluten-free menu

Z'Tejas
480.946.4171
7014 E Camelback Rd
Scottsdale, AZ 85251
www.ztejas.com
Gluten-free menu

Z'Tejas
480.377.1170
20 W 6th Street
Tempe, AZ 85281
www.ztejas.com
Gluten-free menu

California

Bistro of Santa Monica
310.453.5442
2301 Santa Monica Blvd
Santa Monica, CA 90404
www.bistroofsantamonica.com

Cafe Carolina
818.881.8600
17934 Ventura Blvd
Encino, CA 91316
   Gluten-free pasta, marinara, pesto and salad dressing. Many vegetarian dishes.

Cilantro Live
619.827.7401
315 Third Ave
Chula Vista, CA 91910
www.cilantrolive.com

Freshies
530.542.3630
3330 Lake Tahoe Blvd #3
Lake Tahoe, CA 96150

Maurizio's Italian Kitchen and Bar
818.247.5600
135 N Maryland Ave
Glendale, CA 91206

Natural Food Works
530.756.1862
624 Fourth Street
Davis, CA 95616
www.naturalfoodworks.com
A gluten-free restaurant

P.F. Chang's China Bistro
For location(s) see page 332
www.pfchangs.com
Gluten-free menu

Pei Wei Asian Diner
For location(s) see page 339
www.peiwei.com
Gluten-free menu

Ravens' at the Stanford Inn, The
by the Sea and Spa
707.937.5615
44850 Comptche Ukiah Rd
Mendocino, CA 95460
www.stanfordinn.com

Sojourner Cafe
805.965.7922
134 E Canon Perdido
Santa Barbara, CA 93101
www.sojournercafe.com

Staff of Life
831.423.8041
305 Water St
Santa Cruz, CA 95062

Thaifoon – Taste of Asia
949.585.0022
85 Fortune Dr
Irvine, CA 92618
www.thaifoon.com
Gluten-free menu

Thaifoon – Taste of Asia
949.644.0133
857 Newport Center Dr
Newport Beach, CA 92660
www.thaifoon.com
Gluten-free menu
Vintage Tea Leaf
562.435.5589
969 E. Broadway
Long Beach, CA 90802
www.vintagetealeaf.com
Call ahead for gluten-free baked goods.

Z'Tejas
714.979.7469
3333 Bristol Street Ste 1876
Costa Mesa, CA 92626
www.ztejas.com
Gluten-free menu

Colorado

Abrusci's Italiano Ristorante
303.232.2424
3244 Youngfield St Unit G
Wheat Ridge, CO 80033
www.abruscis.com
Gluten-free menu

Biaggi's Ristorante Italiano
For location see page 329
www.biaggis.com
Gluten-free pasta

Gertrude's Restaurant
719.471.0887
2625 W Colorado Ave
Colorado Springs, CO 80904

Hilltop Cafe
970.842.5312
29870 US Highway 6
Brush, CO 80723

HuHot Mongolian Grill
970.416.0555
259 S College Ave
Fort Collins, CO 80524
List at buffet indicates allergens and gluten-free items.

Jax Fish House
303.444.1811
928 Pearl St
Boulder, CO 80302
Gluten-free menu

John Holly's Asian Bistro
303.768.9088
9232 Park Meadows Dr
Lone Tree, CO 80124
www.ufeedme.com
Gluten-free soy sauce available.

Lola
720.570.8686
1469 S Pearl St
Denver, CO 80210
Gluten-free menu

Luke's —A Steak Place
303.422.3300
4990 Kipling St Ste 13
Wheat Ridge, CO 80033

Orchid Pavilion Chinese Restaurant & Lounge
303.449.4353
1050 Walnut St Ste 125
Boulder, CO 80302
www.orchidpavilion.com

P.F. Chang's China Bistro
For location(s) see page 332
www.pfchangs.com
Gluten-free menu

Pei Wei Asian Diner
For location(s) see page 339
www.peiwei.com
Gluten-free menu

Rhumba Café Caribbean
303.442.7771
950 Pearl St
Boulder, CO 80302
Gluten-free menu

Vesta Dipping Grill
303.296.1970
1822 Blake St
Denver, CO 80202
www.vetagrill.com
Gluten-free and allergen-free menus.

Wolfe's Barbecue
303.831.1500
333 E Colfax Ave
Denver, CO 80302

Zolo Grill
303.449.0444
2525 Arapahoe Ave
Boulder, CO 80302
www.zsologrill.com
gluten-free menu
Sensitive to food allergies.

Connecticut

Elizabeth's Restaurant
860.257.3511
825 I J Cromwell Avenue
Rocky Hill, CT 06067

Frascati Restaurant
203.353.8900
581 Newfield Ave
Stamford, CT 06905
www.frascatiofstamford.com
Frascati offers family-friendly dining and a very caring staff. A gluten-free menu includes soup,

bruschetta, pasta and dessert. Other dietary restrictions are catered to on an individual basis.

District of Columbia

Asia Nora
202.797.4860
2213 M Street NW
Washington, D.C. 20037
www.noras.com

Foggy Bottom Café
202.338.8707
924 25th St NW
Washington, D.C. 20037

Food for Thought Café
202.797.1095
1811 – 14th NW
Washington, DC 20009

Restaurant Nora
202.462.5143
2132 Florida Ave, NW
Washington, DC 20008
www.noras.com

Florida

Bee Line Diner
407.345.4460
In Peabody Hotel
9801 International Dr
Orlando, Fl 32819

Crabby Bill's
727.595.4825
412 1st St
Indian Rocks Beach, FL 33785
www.crabbybills.com

Good Food Conspiracy
Natural Market & Cafe
305.872.3945
US1 Mile Market 30.2
Big Pine Key, FL 33043

Govinda's Restaurant
386.462.4500
14603 Main St
Alachua, FL 32615

Nature's Food Patch
Bunny Hop Cafe
727.443.6703
1225 Cleveland St
Clearwater, FL 33755
Gluten-free meals and desserts.

Ophelia's On the Bay
941.349.2212
9105 Midnight Pass Rd
Sarasota, FL 34242

P.F. Chang's China Bistro
For location(s) see page 332
www.pfchangs.com
Gluten-free menu

Ragin' Ribs
813.410.0606
3636 Henderson Blvd
Tampa, FL 33609
www.raginribs.com
 No wheat gluten in BBQ sauce per Jim Cheatham, founder.

Ragin Ribs
813.985.3449
7511 North 56th St
Tampa, FL 33609
www.raginribs.com
   No wheat gluten in BBQ sauce
per Jim Cheatham, founder.

Saffron's Caribbean Cuisine
727.345.6600
1700 Park St North
St. Petersburg, FL 33710
www.saffronscuisine.com
   We are very experienced in preparing food for people on a gluten-free diet

Georgia

Life Grocery and Cafe
770.977.9583
1453 Roswell Rd
Marietta, GA 30062
   Our organic vegan cafe offers a huge selection of gluten-free foods. Sandwiches can even be prepared with gluten-free breads if requested.

P.F. Chang's China Bistro
For location(s) see page 332
www.pfchangs.com
Gluten-free menu.

R. Thomas Deluxe Grill
404.872.2942
1812 Peachtree St
Atlanta, GA 30309

Idaho

Louie's Italian Restaurant
208.344.5200
620 West Idaho
Boise, ID 83702
Gluten-free pasta

Illinois

Ben Pao
312.22.1888
52 West Illinois
Chicago IL 60610
www.leye.com
Accommodates special diets.

Biaggi's Ristorante Italiano
For locations see page 329
www.biaggis.com
Gluten-free pasta

Big Bowl
847.808.8880
215 Parkway Dr
Lincolnshire IL 60069
www.bigbowl.com

Bistro 110
312.266.3110
110 E Pearson
by Water Tower
Chicago, IL 60611
Gluten-free pasta available

Cafe Baba
773.935.5000
2024 N Halsted St
Chicago, IL 60614
www.cafebabareeba.com
Gluten-free menu

Cafe Luciano
312.266.1414
871 N Rush St
Chicago, IL 60611
www.cafeluciano.com
Gluten-free pasta available

Cafe Salsa & Catering
847.516.4441
412 NW Highway
Fox River Grove, IL 60021

Charlie Trotter's
773.248.6228
816 W Armitage
Chicago, IL 60614
www.charlietrotters.com

Chicago Diner
773.935.6696
311 N Halsted St
Chicago, IL 60657
www.veggiediner.com
Gluten-free menu

Cucina Roma
630.654.9600
Route 83 and Ogden Ave
800 E Ogden Ave
Westmont, IL 60559
Gluten-free pasta available

Enzo and Lucia's Ristorante
847.478.8825
343 Old McHenry Rd
Long Grove, IL 60047

Feats Restaurant and Bar
773.772.7100
1616 North Damen Ave
Chicago, IL 60647
Owner knows about special diets. Most of menu is gluten-free, except for obvious items. Soups thickened with potatoes.

Fireside Restaurant and Lounge
773.878.5942
5739 N Ravenswood
Chicago, IL 60660

Flat Top Grill
312.787.7676
319 W North Ave
Chicago, IL 60610
www.fronteracooking.com

Graziano's
847.647.4096
5960 W Touhy
Niles, IL 60714
www.grazianos.net

Guardi's Pizza
708.429.1166
16711 S 80th Ave
Tinley Park IL 60477
Take out gluten-free pasta and pizza.

Heartland Cafe
773.465.8005
7000 N Glenwood Ave
Chicago, IL 60626
www.heartlandcafe.com

Hubbard Street Grill
312.222.0770
351 W Hubbard St
Chicago, IL 60610
www.rumba351.com

Jedi's Garden
708.499.4545
9266 S Cicero Ave
Oak Lawn, IL 60453

Joe's Seafood, Prime Steak and Stone Crab
312.379.5637
60 E Grand Ave
Chicago, IL 60611

Julio's Cocina Latino
847.438.3484
99 S Rand Rd
Lake Zurich, IL 60047
www.julioslatincafe.com

La Piazza
708.366.4010
410 Circle Ave
Forest Park, IL 60130
Gluten-free pasta

Lucianos on Rush
312.266.1414
871 N Rush St
Chicago, IL 60611
www.lucianosonrush.com
Gluten-free pasta

Mai Thai Restaurant
630.455.4298
697 N Cass Ave
Westmont, IL 60559

Myron & Phil's Steakhouse
847.677.6663
3900 W Devon Ave
Lincolnwood, IL 60712
www.myronandphils.com

Pacini
708.403.5585
9549 W 151st Street
Orland Park, IL 60462

P.F. Chang's China Bistro
For location(s) see page 332
www.pfchangs.com
Gluten-free menu

Royal Thai Restaurant
773.509.0007
2209 W Montrose
Chicago, IL 60618

South Gate Cafe
847.234.8800
655 Forest Ave
Lake Forest, IL 60045

Stashu's Deli & Pizza
309.797.9449
4200 44th Ave
Moline, IL 61265

Va Pensiero
847.475.7779
1566 Oak Ave
Evanston, IL 60201
www.va-p.com

Vinci Restaurant
312.266.1199
1732 N Halsted St
Chicago, IL 60614
Gluten-free menu and pasta

Weber Grill
312.467.9696
539 N State
Chicago, IL 60611

Indiana

Biaggi's Ristorante Italiano
For locations see page 329
www.biaggis.com
Gluten-free pasta

Bloomingfoods Market & Deli
812.336.5400
3220 E 3rd St
Bloomington, IN 47401
www.bloomingfoods.coop

Cafe Elise
219.836.2233
435 Ridge Rd
Munster IN 46321

Encore Café
812.333.7312
316 W 6th St
Bloomington, IN 47404

P.F. Chang's China Bistro
For location(s) see page 332
www.pfchangs.com
Gluten-free menu

Iowa

Atlas World Grill
319.341.7700
127 Iowa Ave
Iowa City, IA 52240
Call ahead for special dietary needs.

Aunt Maude's
515.233.4136
547 Main St
Ames, IA 50010

Biaggi's Ristorante Italiano
For location see page 329
www.biaggis.com
Gluten-free pasta

Club Car, The
515.226.1729
13435 University Ave
Clive, IA 50325
Experienced in gluten-free food preparation.

Givannis
Italian Restaurant
319.338.5967
109 E College St
Iowa City, IA 52240
Call ahead with special dietary needs.

Godfather's Pizza
641.424.5133
1703 Highway 122 E
Mason City, IA 50401
Order gluten-free pizza crust in advance.

Godfather's Pizza
563.359.4418
3340 E Kimberly Rd
Davenport, IA 52807
   Call regarding gluten-free pizza
availability.

Martin's Brandenberg
319.352.9170
215 E Bremer Ave
Waverly, IA 50677
   Flexible when it comes to food
allergies.

Mondo's of West Des Moines
515.327.9000
4001 Westown Pkwy
Des Moines, IA 50265

**New Pioneer Co-op and
Bakehouse**
319.358.5513
1101 2nd St
Coralville, IA 42241
www.newpi.com
   Deli offers gluten-free items
and a seated area.

**Noah's Ark Restaurant & Fire-
side Lounge**
515.288.2246
2400 Ingersoll Ave
Des Moines, IA 50312

P.F. Chang's China Bistro
For location(s) see page 332
www.pfchangs.com
Gluten-free menu

Kansas

P.F. Chang's China Bistro
For location(s) see page 332
www.pfchangs.com
Gluten-free menu

Kentucky

Cafe Fraiche
502.894.8929
3642 Brownsboro Rd
Louisville, KY 40207
Gluten-free bread and dessert

Louisiana

Emeril's Delmonico
504.5225.4937
1300 St Charles Ave
New Orleans, LA 70130
www.emerils.com

P.F. Chang's China Bistro
For location(s) see page332
www.pfchangs.com
Gluten-free menu

Maine

Five Islands Lobster
207.371.2990
1447 Five Islands Rd
Georgetown, ME 04548
www.fiveislandslobster.com

Romeo's Pizza
207.883.8883
201 US Route 1
Scarborough, ME 04074

Maryland

Natural Health Food Store
410.560.3133
2149 York Rd
Timonium, MD 21093
   Freshly   made   gluten-free
sandwiches.

P.F. Chang's China Bistro
For location(s) see page 332
www.pfchangs.com
Gluten-free menu

Savory Café
301.270.2233
7071 Carroll Ave
Tacoma Park, MD 20912
Corn based wraps and salads

Massachusetts

Elephant Walk
617.247.1500
900 Beacon St
Boston, MA 02215
www.elephantwalk.com
Gluten-free and vegan menus

Elephant Walk
617.492.6900
2067 Massachusetts Ave
Cambridge, MA 02140
www.elephantwalk.com
Gluten-free and vegan menus

P.F. Chang's China Bistro
For location(s) see page 332
www.pfchangs.com
Gluten-free menu

Waterstreet Cafe
508.672.8748
36 Water St
Fall River, MA 02721
Gluten-free pasta available

Woodman's Restaurant
& Clambake Catering
978.768.6451
121 Main St
Essex, MA 01929

Michigan

Amical
231.941.8888
229 East Front St
Traverse City, MI 49684
www.amical.com

Apache Trout Grill
231.947.7079
13671 S W Bay Shore Dr
Traverse City, MI 49684

Blue Pelican, The
231.544.2583
10555 W Old State Rd
Central Lake, MI 49622
www.thebluepelican.com

Boathouse Restaurant
231.223.4030
14039 Peninsula Dr
Traverse City, MI 49686

Grand Hotel
906.847.3331
Mackinac Island, MI 49757
www.grandhotel.com
Main dining room

Hatties
231.271.6222
111 Saint Josephs St
Suttons Bay, MI 49682
www.hatties.com

Hunan's Chinese Restaurant
231.947.1388
1425 S Airport Rd W
Traverse City, MI 49686

Inn at Beulah Beach, The
231.882.5523
173 Lake St
Beulah, MI 49617

Kewadin Sault Casino
800.kewadin (539.2346)
906.632.0530
2186 Shunk Rd
Sault Ste Marie, MI 49783
    Will accommodate special dietary needs. Best if tell them what you can eat, rather than what you cannot eat.

Lulu's
231.533.5252
213 N Bridge Ln
Bellaire, MI 49615

Pearl's New Orleans Kitchen
231.264.0530
617 Ames St
Elk Rapids, MI 49629
www.magnumhospitality.com

P.F. Chang's China Bistro
For location(s) see page 332
www.pfchangs.com
Gluten-free menu

Red Mesa Grill
231.582.0049
117 Water St
Boyne City, MI 49712
www.magnumhospitality.com

The Fish
231.526.3969
2983 S State Rd
Harbor Springs, MI 49740
www.magnumhospitality.com

The House
231.929.4917
826 W Front St
Traverse City, MI 49684

Windows
231.941.0100
7677 S W Bay Shore Dr
Traverse City, MI 49684

Wood-Ruff's Supper Club
248.586.1519
212 West Sixth
Royal Oak, MI 48067
www.wood-ruffs.com

Minnesota

Basil's Restaurant
612.376.7404
7th & Marquette
Minneapolis, MN 55401

Biaggi's Ristorante Italiano
For location see page 329
www.biaggis.com
Gluten-free pasta available

Birchwood Café
612.722.4474
3311 East 25th St
Minneapolis, MN 55406
www.birchwoodcafe.com
   Many salads and specials are gluten-free.

City Café
507.289.1949
216 – 1st Ave SW
Rochester, MN 55902
Gluten-free menu

Ecopolitan
612.874.7336
2409 Lyndale Ave S, Suite 2
Minneapolis, MN 55405
www.ecopolitan.com
   Wheat, corn, soy-free and 95% gluten-free.

Fiesta Café
507.288.1116
1645 N Broadway
Rochester, MN 55906
Gluten-free menu

Fresh and Natural Foods
651.203.3663
1075 West Highway 96
Shoreview, MN 55126
www.freshandnaturalfoods.com
   Gluten-free sandwiches, some deli items and fresh baked goods.

Good Earth
952.925.1001
3460 West 70th (Galleria)
Edina, MN 55435
www.goodearthmn.com
Gluten-free menu.

Good Earth
651.636.0956
1901 West Highway 36
Roseville, MN 55113
www.goodearthmn.com
Gluten-free menu

Jensen's Supper Club
651.688.7969
3840 Sibley Memorial Hwy
Eagan, MN 55122

Manny's
612.339.9900
1300 Nicollet Ave
Minneapolis, MN 55403
www.mannyssteakhouse.com

P.F. Chang's China Bistro
For location(s) see page 332
www.pfchangs.com
Gluten-free menu

Sidney's Restaurants
7 locations in Minnesota
Ask for rice pasta cooked in fresh pot of water

Zorbas Bar
507.281.1540
924 – 7th St NW
Rochester, MN 55901
Gluten-free menu

Missouri

P.F. Chang's China Bistro
For location(s) see page 332
www.pfchangs.com
Gluten-free menu

Montana

Bullwackers (Holiday Inn)
406.443.2200
22 N Last Chance Gulch
Helena, MT 59601

John Bozeman's Bistro
406.587.4100
125 West Main
Bozeman, MT 59715

Fast Looie's
406.522.0800
815 West College
Bozeman, MT 59715

Jade Garden Restaurant
406.443.8899
3128 N Montana Ave
Helena, MT 59602

Montana City Grill & Saloon
406.449.8890
5 miles south of Helena on I-15
Montana City, MT 59634
www.montanacitygrill.com

Oak Street Natural Food Market, Deli and Bakery
406.582.5400
1735 West Oak St
Bozeman, MT 59715

Red Fox Supper Club
406.227.0099
4030 Fox Ridge Dr
Helena, MT 59602

Savory Olive
406.586.8320
105 West Main
Bozeman, MT 59715

The Depot
406.728.7007
201 West Railroad
Missoula, MT 59802

Three Forks Café
406.285.4843
24 Main St
Bozeman, MT 59715

Nebraska

Biaggi's Ristorante Italiano
For location see page 329
www.biaggis.com
Gluten-free pasta available

Happy Hollow Country Club
402.391.2341
1701 S 105th St
Omaha, NE 68124
Gluten-free pasta available

Nevada

P.F. Chang's China Bistro
For location(s) see page 332
www.pfchangs.com
Gluten-free menu

Pei Wei Asian Diner
For location(s) see page 339
www.peiwei.com
Gluten-free menu

Z'Tejas
702.732.1660
3824 S Paradise Rd
Las Vegas, NV 89109
www.ztejas.com
Gluten-free menu

Z'Tejas
702.638.0610
9560 W Sahara Ave
Las Vegas, NV 89117
www.ztejas.com
Gluten-free menu

New Hampshire

The Yankee Smokehouse
603.539.7427
Junction of 15 & 25
West Ossipee, NH
Gluten-free menu

New Jersey

Café Capri
201.664.6422
343 Broadway
Hillsdale, NJ 07642

Court Street
201.795.4515
61 Sixth St
Hoboken, NJ 07030
www.courtstreet.com
Menu indicates items gluten-free

Janice — A Bistro
201.445.2666
201.445.6789 fax
23 Sheridan Avenue
Ho-Ho-Kus, NJ 07423
www.janiceabistro.com

A gluten-free annotated menu is available at our cozy bistro, ranked among the best restaurants in New Jersey by the *New York Times* 2004 and received a three star rating in the *Bergen Record*. Our items are cooked fresh with an International flair. We are open for breakfast, lunch and dinner.

P.F. Chang's China Bistro
For locations see page 332
www.pfchangs.com
Gluten-free menu

Park & Orchard
201.939.9292
240 Hackensack St
East Rutherford, NJ 07073
www.parkandorchard.com
Special dietary needs friendly

New Mexico

Blue Corn Café
505.438.1800
4056 Cerrillos Rd
Santa Fe, NM 87507
www.bluecorncafe.com
Must speak to manager before ordering.

Cafe Next Door, The
505.266.7321
4013 Silver Ave SE
Albuquerque, NM 87108

Inn of the Anasazi
800.688.8100
113 Washington Ave
Santa Fe, NM 87501
www.innoftheanasazi.com
  Explain dietary needs to Executive Chef. They can accommodate allergies and intolerances

Paisano's Italian restaurant
505.298.7541
1935 Eubank Blvd NE
Albuquerque, NM 87112
Gluten-free menu

P.F. Chang's China Bistro
For location(s) see page 332
www.pfchangs.com
Gluten-free menu

Pei Wei Asian Diner
For location(s) see page 339
www.peiwei.com
Gluten-free menu

New York

Anderson's Frozen Custard
716.663.2671
Throughout New York
www.andersonscustard.com

Biaggi's Ristorante Italiano
For location see page 329
www.biaggis.com
Gluten-free pasta available

Bistango
212.725.8484
415 3rd Ave
29th St & 3rd Ave
New York, NY 10016

Bloom's Delicatessen Café
212.922.3667
350 Lexington Ave
Corner of 40th St
New York, NY 10016

Caffé Baldo
516.785.4780
2349 Jerusalem Ave
Long Island
Wantagh, NY 11793

Candle 79
212.537.7179
154 E 79th St at Lexington Ave
New York, NY 10021
www.candlecafe.com
Gluten-free menu

Ciao!
914.779.4646
5-7 John Jo Albanese Place
Eastchester, NY 10709

Curly's Bar & Grill
716.825.0619
647 Ridge Road
Lackawanna, NY 14218

Gedney Grille
914.428.1264
68 Gedney Way
White Plains, NY 10605
www.gedneygrille.com

Hampton Chutney Co
212.226.9996
68 Prince St
Between Crosby and Lafayette Sts
New York, NY 10016

Hutch's
716.885.0074
1375 Delaware Ave
Buffalo, NY 14209

Hyde Park Brewing Company
845.229.8277
4076 Albany Post Rd
Hyde Park, NY 12538
www.hydeparkbrewing.com

Ilio Dipaolo's
716.825.3675
3785 South Park Ave
Blaisdell, NY 14219
www.iliodipaolos.com
Gluten-free menu

Luna
914.242.5151
251 Main St
Mount Kisco, NY 10549

Mama's Italian and Seafood Restaurant
631.567.0909
1352 Montauk Hwy
Oakdale, NY 11769

Maud's Tavern
914.478.2326
149 Southside Ave
Hastings on Hudson, NY 10706

Owen Murphy Inn
845.294.0182
1700 Route 17M
Goshen, NY 10924
www.owenmurphyinn.com

Oyster Bar & Restaurant
212.490.6650
Grand Central Station
New York, NY 10017
www.oysterbarny.com

P.F. Chang's China Bistro
For location(s) see page 332
www.pfchangs.com
Gluten-free menu

Pizza Plant
716.632.0800
8020 Transit Rd
Buffalo, NY 14221
   Gluten-free pizza and beer on Wednesday nights.

Pure Food and Wine
212.477.1010
54 Irving Place
NYC, NY 10014

Risotteria
212.924.6664
270 Bleeker St
New York, NY 10014
www.risotteria.com

Sacred Chow
212.337.0863
522 Hudson St
Between W 10th & Charles
New York, NY 10014
www.sacredchow.com

North Carolina

Biaggi's Ristorante Italiano
For location see page 329
www.biaggis.com
Gluten-free pasta

P.F. Chang's China Bistro
For location(s) see page 332
www.pfchangs.com
Gluten-free menu

Ohio

Biaggi's Ristorante Italiano
For location see page 329
www.biaggis.com
Gluten-free pasta

Molly Woo's Asian Bistro
614.985.9667
1500 Polaris Pkwy, Suite 220
Columbus, Ohio 43240
www.cameronmitchell.com
   Please let your server know of any food allergy concerns. A gluten-free menu is available upon request.

P.F. Chang's China Bistro
For location(s) see page 332
www.pfchangs.com
Gluten-free menu

Oklahoma

P.F. Changs China Bistro
For location(s) see page 332
www.pfchangs.com
Gluten-free menu

Pei Wei Asian Diner
For location(s) see page 339
www.peiwei.com
Gluten-free menu

Oregon

Bob's Red Mill Kitchen
503.607.6455
5000 SE International Way
Milwaukie, OR 97266
   Kitchen located in Bob's Red Mill Retail Store.
   Gluten-free pastries are available in refrigerated/freezer section.
   Gluten-free sandwiches may be prepared using purchased bread. Kitchen staff aware of gluten- free diet. Hours: M-F 6 am-3 pm, Sat. 7 am-3 pm.

Corbett Fish House
503.246.4434
5901 SW Corbett Ave
Portland, OR 97239
www.corbettfishhouse.com

Cozmic Pizza
In Strand Building
541.338.9333
199 West 8th Ave
Eugene, OR 97401
   Call ahead for gluten-free crust and toppings.

Greenleaf Restaurant
541.482.2808
49 N Main St
Ashland, OR 97520
www.greenleafrestaurant.com

Old Wives' Tales
503.238.0470
1300 East Burnside
Portland, OR 97214

P.F. Chang's China Bistro
For location(s) see page 332
www.pfchangs.com
Gluten-free menu

Rico Bella Pizza
(Talarico's Oldstyle Pizza)
503.620.7723
14559 Westlake Dr
Lake Oswego, OR 97035
Gluten-free pizza

Pennsylvania

Nino's Restaurant
724.547.2900
Star Route 3
Mount Pleasant, PA 15666
    Reservations 48 hours in advance for gluten-free diet.

P.F. Chang's China Bistro
For location(s) see page 332
www.pfchangs.com
Gluten-free menu

Rhode Island

Sticky Fingers
401.272.7427
133 Douglas Ave
Providence, RI 02908
Gluten-free menu

South Carolina

La Place Bistro & More
843.342.7677
In Port Royal Plaza
95 Natural Drive
Hilton Head Island, SC 29926

South Dakota

Veggies and Abundant Health
605.348.5019
2050 West Main St #7
Rapid City, SD 57702

Tennessee

Hungry Bear Bistro
865.908.0321
1887 Bluff Mountain Rd
Sevierville, TN 37876

P.F. Chang's China Bistro
For location(s) see page 332
www.pfchangs.com
Gluten-free menu

St. John's Restaurant
423.266.4400
1278 Market St
Chattanooga, TN 37402

Texas

Biga on the Banks
210.225.0722
203 S Saint Mary's St., Suite 100
San Antonio, TX 78205
www.biga.com

Blue Mesa Grill
972.934.0165
5100 Belt Line Rd
Dallas, TX 75254

Caro's Mexican Restaurant
817.924.9977
3505 Bluebonnet Circle
Ft Worth, TX 76109
www.caros.biz

Classic Café
817.430.8185
504 N Oak St
Roanoke, TX 76262

Fresco's Cocina
817.498.6370
7432 Denton Hwy
Watauga, TX 76148
24 hour notice for special diets

P.F. Chang's China Bistro
For location(s) see page 332
www.pfchangs.com
Gluten-free menu

Pei Wei Asian Diner
For location(s) see page 339
www.peiwei.com
Gluten-free menu

Toys Café, Thai
214.528.7233
4422 Lemmon Ave
Dallas, TX 75219

Wildwood Art Café
512.327.9660
3663 Bee Caves Road #4A
Austin, TX 78746
www.wildwoodartcafe.com
  Wildwood, a wheat-free restaurant with gluten-free items offers foods that are so good everyone

likes them better than ordinary wheat-filled items.

York St
214.826.0968
6047 Lewis St
Dallas, TX 75206

Z'Tejas
512.346.3506
9400 A Arboretum Blvd
Austin, TX 78759
www.ztejas.com
Gluten-free menu

Z'Tejas
512.478.5355
1110 W 6th St
Austin, TX 78703
www.ztejas.com
Gluten-free menu

Utah

Biaggi's Ristorante Italiano
For location see page 329
www.biaggis.com
Gluten-free pasta

P.F. Chang's China Bistro
For location(s) see page 332
www.pfchangs.com
Gluten-free menu

Pei Wei Asian Diner
For location(s) see page 339
www.peiwei.com
Gluten-free menu

Thaifoon —A Taste of Asia
801.456.8424
7 North 400 West
Salt Lake City, UT 84103
www.thaifoon.com
Gluten-free menu

Z'Tejas
801.456.0450
191 South Rio Grande
Salt Lake City, UT 84101
www.ztejas.com
Gluten-free menu

Vermont

Hemingway's Restaurant
802.422.3886
4988 US Route 4
Killington, VT 05751
www.hemingwaysrestaurant.com
   Special dietary needs accommodated

Virginia

Casa Grande
804.378.8177
10921 Midlothian Turnpike
Richmond, VA 23235

P.F. Chang's China Bistro
For locations see page 332
www.pfchangs.com
Gluten-free menu

Washington

Café Flora Restaurant
206.325.9100
2901 E Madison St
Seattle, WA 98112
www.cafeflora.com

Kaili's Kitchen
206.542.1462
877.664.5883
9711 Firdale Ave
Edmonds, WA 98020
www.wheatlessinseattle.com
A gluten-free restaurant

LaFiamma Wood Fire Pizza
360.647.0060
200 East Chestnut
Bellingham, WA 98225
www.lafiamma.com
   Call ahead for gluten-free pizza.

Pearls on Pearl
509.962.8899
311 N Pearl St
Ellensburg, WA 98908
www.pearlsonpearl.com

P.F. Chang's China Bistro
For location(s) see page 332
www.pfchangs.com
Gluten-free menu

Z'Tejas
425.467.5911
535 Bellevue Square
Bellevue, WA 98004
www.ztejas.com
Gluten-free menu

Wisconsin

Biaggi's Ristorante Italiano
For locations see page 329
www.biaggis.com
Gluten-free pasta available

Monty's Blue Plate Diner
608.244.8505
2089 Atwood Ave
Madison, WI 53704
www.foodfightinc.com
   Gluten, dairy, and nut-free menus.

P.F. Chang's China Bistro
For location(s) see page 332
www.pfchangs.com
Gluten-free menu

Saz's State House Restaurant
414.256.8779
5539 W State St
Milwaukee, WI 53208
www.sazs.com
   Gluten-free barbecue sauces for pork, chicken, ribs or dipping sauce.

Tess Restaurant
414.964.8377
2499 N Bartlett Ave
Milwaukee, WI 53211

Wyoming

Tavern on the Creek
307.684.8800
4 S Main
Buffalo, WY 82834
Daily lunch and dinner specials. Open Tues-Sat 11 am-9 pm We cater to special diets.

Canada

Casa Pescara
514.253.2658
6752 Sherbrooke E
Montreal, Quebec

La Casa du Spaghetti
450.372.3848
Fax 450.372.9281
604 Principale
Granby, Quebec
www.casagranby.com
Gluten-free menu and beer

Magic Oven
416.466.0111
788 Broadview Ave
Toronto, Ontario
www.magicoven.com

Quejos Bakery, Café and Retail
604.420.0832
4129 Main St
Vancouver, British Columbia
www.quejos.com
   Delicious wheat, gluten and yeast free baked buns in three product lines: the cheese line with seven flavors, the soya line (also lactose and rennet free) with five flavors, and the dairy-free line with four flavors.

Swiss Chalet Rotisserie & Grill
866.450.2903
Throughout Canada, in New York and Florida
   Gluten-free menu on website
www.swisschalet.com

Multi-State Restaurant Defined

A 'Friendly Multi-State Restaurant' was identified by:

■ corporate personnel responding positively to telephone or e-mail inquiries

■ corporate personnel providing valuable ingredient, allergen and/or intolerance information or menus that are accessible via website or phone

Many restaurants shown have established policies on how to handle cross contact or cross contamination issues. Some restaurants may be more aware or experienced than others.

These restaurants are to be applauded for their efforts. They are the forefront runners of a movement to increase awareness in the Restaurant Industry. Give them your business and help them to understand your dietary needs. We will all benefit.

How to use this section:

■ **First column: Restaurant Name, general number of restaurants and locations.** Check which restaurants are in your area or the area of your destination. If you are uncertain, visit their website or call the corporate phone number listed.

■ **Second column: What is on their website and how else to get the information.** This tells you how to receive the most up to date information; through web, e-mail, phone or snail mail. Other comments may be included.

■ **Third column—the one on the right hand side of the page.** Blank space to record your favorite special diet meals from the restaurant on the left, information from their website or information you received by calling corporate.

This form provides you with the power to stay 'in the know', directly from corporate, rather than relying on others or outdated information that may not be in your best interests.

Dining Out is a personal choice.

Keep in mind that everything is subject to change.
Restaurants do not guarantee a 100% gluten-free or allergen-free meal. Cross contamination is always an issue and human error, always a possibility.

Restaurant Name Phone number Website Approximate number of locations and where to find them	Items on website at time of printing * gluten-free menu on website * Ingredient listing on website * Allergen information on site How to receive information if not on the Internet
Arby's 800.487.2729 www.Arbys.com 3256 locations nationwide	Info on Website: -no gluten-free -yes ingredients -yes allergens Call and ask for Food Safety Dept. The top 8 allergens available. No gluten-free information available at this time
Austin Grill 410.534.0606 www.Austingrill.com 7 locations: MD, DC, VA	Info on Website: -yes gluten-free -no ingredients -no allergens Call corporate or check at Grill
Baja Fresh 877.225.2373 www.bajafresh.com 300 locations nationwide	Info on Website: -no gluten-free -no ingredients -no allergens Call customer relations. They will provide a list or discuss individual items
Ben & Jerry's 802.846.1500 www.benjerry.com 450 locations nationwide	Info on Website: -no gluten-free -yes ingredients -no allergens All items list their ingredients on packaging
Biaggi's Ristorante Italiano 309.664.2148 www.biaggis.com 15 locations: IL, IA, IN, WI, NE, NC, CO, NY, UT - see back of book for addresses -	Info on Website: -no gluten-free -no ingredients -no allergens Gluten-free pasta from Enjoy Life is available upon request
Big Bowl Asian Kitchen www.bigbowl.com 14 locations: TX, MN, WI, IL, VA, NC	See **Brinker International** for more information

Obtain the most up to date information from the restaurant itself; write your favorite gluten-free and/or allergen-free food items here or on pages in the back of this book.

Establish a routine of calling the restaurant or checking their website to stay up to date. Take care of yourself. Do not rely on old information or rumors.

Arby's: Verified on: _____

Austin Grill: Verified on: _____

Baja Fresh: Verified on: _____

Ben & Jerry's: Verified on: _____

Biaggi's Ristorante Italiano: Verified on: _____

Big Bowl Asian Kitchen: Verified on: _____

Restaurant Name Phone number Website Approximate number of locations and where to find them	Items on website at time of printing * gluten-free menu on website * Ingredient listing on website * Allergen information on site How to receive information if not on the Internet
Bob Evans 550 locations: 800.272.7675 www.Bobevans.com Midwest, Mid-Atlantic, Southwest	Info on Website: -no gluten-free -no ingredients -no allergens Information is available by phone or e-mail. Or call 1 day ahead and review with manager what is available to you
Bonefish Grill 866.880.2226 www.Bonefishgrill.com 53 locations: North East, South East	Info on Website: -yes gluten-free -no ingredients -no allergens Gluten-free friendly menu available on website and in restaurant
Boston Market 800.365.7000 www.Bostonmarket.com 627 locations nationwide	Info on Website: -no gluten-free -no ingredients -no allergens Information is available by phone or e-mail
Brinker International 972.980.9917 www.brinker.com 1400 restaurants worldwide	"Brinker International values all customers and strives to meet their dining needs. Customers may request allergen information of all Brinker concepts at www.brinker.com or call our Guest Relations department at 800.983.4637"
Buca di Beppo 612.288.2382 www.bucadibeppo.com 95 locations nationwide	Info on Website: -no gluten-free -no ingredients -no allergens Information is available by e-mail or snail mail. An Allergy Awareness Guide listing top 8 allergens is available to manager at each location

Obtain the most up to date information from the restaurant itself; write your favorite gluten-free and/or allergen-free food items here or on pages in the back of this book.

Establish a routine of calling the restaurant or checking their website to stay up to date. Take care of yourself. Do not rely on old information or rumors.

Bob Evans: Verified on: _____

Bonefish Grill: Verified on: _____

Boston Market: Verified on: _____

Brinker Restaurant concepts include:
- Chili's Grill and Bar
- Romano's Macaroni Grill
- On the Border Mexican Grill and Cantina
- Maggiano's Little Italy
- Corner Bakery Café
- Big Bowl Asian Kitchen
- Rockfish Seafood Grill

Buca di Beppo: Verified on: _____

Restaurant Name Phone number Website Approximate number of locations and where to find them	Items on website at time of printing * gluten-free menu on website * Ingredient listing on website * Allergen information on site How to receive information if not on the Internet
Burger King 305.378.3000 www.Burgerking.com 11,335 locations worldwide	Info on Website: -no gluten-free -yes ingredients -yes allergens, top 8 Information on gluten-free not available at this time
Captain D's 615.391.5461 www.captainds.com 500 locations throughout US	Info on Website: -no gluten-free -no ingredients -no allergens Information available by phone
Carls Jr.,/ Green Burrito 877.799.7827 www.carlsjr.com 969 locations nationwide	Info on Website: -no gluten free -no ingredients -no allergens Call and ask Quality Assurance Dept to send ingredient and allergen listings
Carrabba's 813.288.8286 www.Carrabbas.com 161 locations: south and southwest	Info on Website: -yes gluten-free -no ingredients -no allergens Gluten-free menu on line and at restaurant
Carvel 800.322.4848 Ext 327 www.carvel.com 330 locations nationwide	Info on Website: -no gluten-free -no ingredients -no allergens Call for gluten-free and allergen listing
Charlie Brown's 800.518.1855 www.Charliebrowns.com 40 locations: NJ, NY, PA	Info on Website: -yes gluten-free -no ingredients -no allergens Gluten-free menu on website and may be at restaurant

Obtain the most up to date information from the restaurant itself; write your favorite gluten-free and/or allergen-free food items here or on pages in the back of this book.

Establish a routine of calling the restaurant or checking their website to stay up to date. Take care of yourself. Do not rely on old information or rumors.

Burger King: Verified on: _____

Captain D's: Verified on: _____

Carls Jr.,/ Green Burrito: Verified on: _____

Carrabba's: Verified on: _____

Carvel: Verified on: _____

Charlie Brown's: Verified on: _____

Restaurant Name Phone number Website Approximate number of locations and where to find them	Items on website at time of printing * gluten-free menu on website * Ingredient listing on website * Allergen information on site How to receive information if not on the Internet
Chart House, The 713.850.1010 www.Chart-house.com 27 locations nationwide	Info on Website: -no gluten-free -no ingredients -no allergens Ingredients available from server or call corporate
Cheeseburger in Paradise 813.282.1225 www.cheeseburgerinparadise.com 9 locations in NE, KS, WI, IL, IN, OH, SC, VA, NJ	Info on Website: -no gluten-free -no ingredients -no allergens Ingredients available from corporate office
Chevys 800.4-Chevys www.Chevys.com 108 locations nationwide	Info on Website: -no gluten-free -no ingredients -no allergens Information is available by calling or e mail
Chi-Chi 502.426.3900 120 locations: East, Midwest www.chi-chis.com	Info on Website: -yes gluten-free -no ingredients -yes allergens Gluten-free menu and vegetarian menu on web and may be in restaurants
Chick-Fil-A 866.232.2040 www.Chickfila.com 1,000 locations nationwide	Info on Website: -yes gluten-free -yes ingredients -yes allergen Gluten-free menu on web, may be in restaurants, or call
Chili's 1.800.983.4637 www.Chilis.com 887 locations nationwide	See **Brinker International** for more information

Obtain the most up to date information from the restaurant itself; write your favorite gluten-free and/or allergen-free food items here or on pages in the back of this book.

Establish a routine of calling the restaurant or checking their website to stay up to date. Take care of yourself. Do not rely on old information or rumors.

Chart House, The: Verified on: _____

Cheeseburger in Paradise: Verified on: _____

Chevy's: Verified on: _____

Chi-Chi: Verified on: _____

Chick-Fil-A: Verified on: _____

Chili's: Verified on: _____

Restaurant Name Phone number Website Approximate number of locations and where to find them	Items on website at time of printing * gluten-free menu on website * Ingredient listing on website * Allergen information on site How to receive information if not on the Internet
Chipotle 303.390.0660 www.chipotle.com 270 locations nationwide	Info on Website: -no gluten-free -no ingredients -no allergens Information is available by phone. Generally, 90% of items are gluten-free, except tortillas and taco shells
Chuck E. Cheese 972.258.8507 www.chuckecheese.com 490 locations nationwide	Info on Website: -no gluten-free -no ingredients -no allergens Case by case basis. Some restaurants will allow guests to bring in own pizza. Check with local restaurant
Cold Stone Creamery 480.348.1704 www.coldstonecreamery.com 1178 locations nationwide	Info on Website: -no gluten-free -yes ingredients -no allergens Information available by phone or mail. Most ice creams gluten-free
Cracker Barrel 800.333.9566 www.Crackerbarrel.com 473 locations nationwide	Info on Website: -no gluten-free -no ingredients -no allergens All information available by phone, mail or e-mail through guest relations representative
Culvers 608.643.7980 www.culvers.com 200 locations Midwest	Info on Website: -no gluten-free -no ingredients -yes allergens Information available by phone, mail or e-mail

Obtain the most up to date information from the restaurant itself; write your favorite gluten-free and/or allergen-free food items here or on pages in the back of this book.

Establish a routine of calling the restaurant or checking their website to stay up to date. Take care of yourself. Do not rely on old information or rumors.

Chipotle: Verified on: _____

Chuck E. Cheese: Verified on: _____

Cold Stone Creamery: Verified on: _____

Cracker Barrel: Verified on: _____

Culvers: Verified on: _____

Restaurant Name Phone number Website Approximate number of locations and where to find them	Items on website at time of printing * gluten-free menu on website * Ingredient listing on website * Allergen information on site How to receive information if not on the Internet
Dairy Queen 952.830.0200 www.dairyqueen.com 4000 locations nationwide	Info on Website: -yes gluten-free -no ingredients -no allergens All information available by phone, mail or e-mail
Dave & Buster's 214.357.9588 www.daveandbusters.com 48 locations nationwide	Info on Website: -no gluten-free -no ingredients -no allergens Call and dietitian will walk you through the menu
Del Taco 800.852.7204 www.deltaco.com 400 locations: west, MO, GA	Info on Website: -no gluten-free -no ingredients -no allergens Information available through corporate
Denny's 800.733.6697 www.dennys.com 1,700 locations nationwide	Info on Website: -no gluten-free -no ingredients -yes allergens All information available by phone, mail or e-mail or contact nutrition consultant at 864.597.7396
Don Pablo's 800.372.2567 www.donpablos.com 105 locations central, east	Info on Website: -yes gluten-free -no ingredients -no allergens Gluten-free and vegetarian menu on website and may be in restaurants
First Watch Restaurants 941.907.9800 www.firstwatch.com 52 locations: CA, FL, OH, KS, MD, AZ, OK, WV	Info on Website: -yes gluten-free -no ingredients -no allergens Menu available on website and may be in restaurants

Obtain the most up to date information from the restaurant itself; write your favorite gluten-free and/or allergen-free food items here or on pages in the back of this book.

Establish a routine of calling the restaurant or checking their website to stay up to date. Take care of yourself. Do not rely on old information or rumors.

Dairy Queen: Verified on: _____

Dave & Buster's: Verified on: _____

Del Taco: Verified on: _____

Denny's: Verified on: _____

Don Pablo's: Verified on: _____

First Watch Restaurants: Verified on: _____

Restaurant Name Phone number Website Approximate number of locations and where to find them	Items on website at time of printing * gluten-free menu on website * Ingredient listing on website * Allergen information on site How to receive information if not on the Internet
Flemings Steakhouse 949.222.2223 www.flemingssteakhouse.com 35 locations nationwide	Info on Website: -yes gluten-free -no ingredients -no allergens Call for menu
Fuddruckers/Koo Koo Roo 512.892.2162 www.Fuddruckers.com 202 in 34 states	Info on Website: -no gluten-free -no ingredients -no allergens Information available by phone or e-mail
Hardee's 877.799.7827 www.hardees.com 1000 locations: East	Info on Website: -yes gluten-free -yes ingredients -yes allergens Information available by phone or e-mail
Hard Times Cafe 703.683.8545 www.Hardtimes.com 15 locations: MD, VA, NC	Info on Website: -no gluten-free -no ingredients -no allergens Information available by phone or e-mail
Houston's 602.553.2111 www.Houstons.com 43 locations nationwide	Info on Website: -no gluten-free -no ingredients -no allergens Information available through corporate Research and Development office
IHOP 818.240.6055 www.IHOP.com 1,100 locations nationwide, Canada	Info on Website: -no gluten-free -no ingredients -no allergens Call for information. Omelets usually contain pancake mix

Obtain the most up to date information from the restaurant itself; write your favorite gluten-free and/or allergen-free food items here or on pages in the back of this book.

Establish a routine of calling the restaurant or checking their website to stay up to date. Take care of yourself. Do not rely on old information or rumors.

Flemings Steakhouse: Verified on: _____

Fuddruckers/Koo Koo Roo: Verified on: _____

Hardee's: Verified on: _____

Hard Times Cafe: Verified on: _____

Houston's: Verified on: _____

IHOP: Verified on: _____

Restaurant Name Phone number Website Approximate number of locations and where to find them	Items on website at time of printing * gluten-free menu on website * Ingredient listing on website * Allergen information on site How to receive information if not on the Internet
In-N-Out Burger 800.786.1000 www.ln-n-outburger.com 150 locations in southwest	Info on Website: -no gluten-free -no ingredients -no allergens Call, e-mail or write for information
Islands Restaurant 760.268.1800 www.islandsrestaurants.com 29 locations: AZ, CA	Info on Website: -no gluten-free -no ingredients -no allergens Call corporate to walk you through the menu
Jack in the Box 800.955.5225 www.jackinthebox.com 2000 locations nationwide	Info on Website: -no gluten-free -yes ingredients -yes allergens Manager may have a nutritional brochure and ingredient listing. Or call corporate for a copy
Jason's Deli 713.780.1295 800.444.3354 www.jasonsdeli.com 150 locations nationwide	Info on Website: -no gluten-free -no ingredients -no allergens Call corporate to walk you through the menu
Lone Star Steakhouse & Saloon 316.264.8899 www.lonestarsteakhouse.com 249 locations nationwide	Info on Website: -no gluten-free -no ingredients -no allergens call corporate for information
Maggiano's Little Italy 503.226.3440 www.Maggianos.com 24 locations nationwide	See **Brinker International** for more information

Obtain the most up to date information from the restaurant itself; write your favorite gluten-free and/or allergen-free food items here or on pages in the back of this book.

Establish a routine of calling the restaurant or checking their website to stay up to date. Take care of yourself. Do not rely on old information or rumors.

In-N-Out Burger: Verified on: _____

Islands Restaurant: Verified on: _____

Jack in the Box: Verified on: _____

Jason's Deli : Verified on: _____

Lone Star Steakhouse & Saloon: Verified on: _____

Maggiano's Little Italy: Verified on: _____

Restaurant Name Phone number Website Approximate number of locations and where to find them	Items on website at time of printing * gluten-free menu on website * Ingredient listing on website * Allergen information on site How to receive information if not on the Internet
McCormick & Schmick's 888.344.6861 www.mccormickandschmicks.com 41 locations nationwide	Info on Website: -no gluten-free -no ingredients -no allergens New menu printed daily speak with general manager
McDonald's Corp 800.244.6227 www.McDonalds.com 31,229 International locations	Info on Website: -yes gluten-free -yes Ingredients -yes Allergies Call for information
Melting Pot - A fondue restaurant 813.881.0055 www.meltingpot.com 75 locations nationwide	Info on Website: -no gluten-free -no ingredients -no allergens Information available by phone
Mimi's Cafe 714.544.4826 www.Mimiscafe.com 62 locations: West	Info on Website: -no gluten-free -no ingredients -no allergens Call for copy of gluten-free menu
Moe's Southwest Grill feedback@moes.com www.moes.com 17 locations in Alabama	Info on Website: -no gluten-free -no ingredients -no allergens Gluten-free menu available, e-mail for copy
Noodles & Co 303.554.1963 www.noodles.com 90 locations: TX, MN, IL, WI, CO, UT, MI, MD, VA, CA, NE	Info on Website: -no gluten-free -no ingredients -no allergens Food allergen and gluten list available at each location. Special cooking package available for seriously allergic guests

Obtain the most up to date information from the restaurant itself; write your favorite gluten-free and/or allergen-free food items here or on pages in the back of this book.

Establish a routine of calling the restaurant or checking their website to stay up to date. Take care of yourself. Do not rely on old information or rumors.

McCormick & Schmick's: Verified on: _____

McDonald's Corp :Verified on: _____

Melting Pot: Verified on: _____

Mimi's Cafe : Verified on: _____

Moe's Southwest Grill: Verified on: _____

Noodles & Co: Verified on: _____

Restaurant Name Phone number Website Approximate number of locations and where to find them	Items on website at time of printing * gluten-free menu on website * Ingredient listing on website * Allergen information on site How to receive information if not on the Internet
Outback Steakhouse 877.733.6774 www.Outbacksteakhouse.com 742 locations nationwide	Info on WebsIte: -yes gluten-free -no ingredients -yes allergens Gluten-free menu on website and in restaurants. Other information available by phone
P.F. Chang's China Bistro 602.957.8986 www.PFchangs.com 84 locations nationwide	Info on Website: -yes gluten-free -no ingredients -no allergens Gluten-free menu at each location and in back of this book. Sports training menu also available
Panera Bread 314.633.7100 www.panerabread.com 350 locations nationwide	Info on Website: -no gluten-free -no ingredients -no allergens Information available by phone or mail
Papadeaux Seafood Kitchen 713.869.0151 www.Pappadeaux.com 28 locations in Southwest, GA, IL	Info on Website: -no gluten-free -no ingredients -no allergens Corporate said to discuss meal with kitchen manager; a listing is not available
Pasta Pomodoro 415.431.2681 www.pastapomodoro.com 43 locations: CA, AZ	Info on Website: -no gluten-free -no ingredients -no allergens Non-wheat pasta may be available. Request clean pot with fresh water for cooking
Pei Wei Asian Diner 866.732.4264 www.peiwei.com 50 locations: AZ, CA, CO, NM, NV, OK, UT, TX	Info on Website: -no gluten-free -no ingredients -no allergens Gluten-free menu available at counter

Obtain the most up to date information from the restaurant itself; write your favorite gluten-free and/or allergen-free food items here or on pages in the back of this book.

Establish a routine of calling the restaurant or checking their website to stay up to date. Take care of yourself. Do not rely on old information or rumors.

Outback Steakhouse: Verified on: _____

P.F. Chang's China Bistro: Verified on: _____

Panera Bread: Verified on: _____

Papadeaux Seafood Kitchen: Verified on: _____

Pasta Pomodoro: Verified on: _____

Pei Wei Asian Diner: Verified on: _____

Restaurant Name Phone number Website Approximate number of locations and where to find them	Items on website at time of printing * gluten-free menu on website * Ingredient listing on website * Allergen information on site How to receive information if not on the Internet
Rock Fish Seafood 214.887.9400 www.rockfishseafood.com 25 locations: AZ, NM, NC, TX	See **Brinker International** for more information
Romano's Macaroni Grill 800.983.4637 www.Macaronigrill.com 187 locations nationwide	See **Brinker International** for more information
Ruth's Chris Steak House 800.544.0808 www.Ruthschris.com 90 locations nationwide	Info on Website: -no gluten-free -no ingredients -no allergens Information is available by calling corporate office
Ryan's Restaurant Group 864.879.1000 www.ryansinc.com *Fire Mountain, Hot off the Grill* 43 locations *Ryan's Grill, Buffet and Bakery* 299 locations All within 23 states located primarily in South and Mid-west. Visit website for locations: www.ryans.com	Ryan's Restaurant Group does not have an allergen list or ingredient list at this time, but has a gluten-free list based on information from vendors. Call and they will look up ingredients on an item by item basis
Sonic Drive-In 405.225.5004 866.657.6642 www.sonicdrivein.com 2500 locations nationwide	Info on Website: -no gluten-free -no ingredients -no allergens Call for gluten-free information presently available through corporate
Soup Plantation & Sweet Tomatoes 800.874.1600 www.soupplantation.com 94 locations nationwide	Info on Website: -no gluten-free -no ingredients -no allergens Ingredient books can be made available from the manager upon request during a non busy time and with advance notice

Obtain the most up to date information from the restaurant itself; write your favorite gluten-free and/or allergen-free food items here or on pages in the back of this book.

Establish a routine of calling the restaurant or checking their website to stay up to date. Take care of yourself. Do not rely on old information or rumors.

Rock Fish Seafood: Verified on: _____

Romano's Macaroni Grill: Verified on: _____

Ruth's Chris Steak House: Verified on: _____

Ryan's Restaurant Group: Verified on: _____

Sonic Drive: Verified on: _____

Soup Plantation & Sweet Tomatoes: Verified on: _____

Restaurant Name Phone number Website Approximate number of locations and where to find them	Items on website at time of printing * gluten-free menu on website * Ingredient listing on website * Allergen information on site How to receive information if not on the Internet
Steak'n Shake 317.633.4100 www.Steaknshake.com 416 locations: Central and Southeast	Info on Website: -no gluten-free -no ingredients -no allergens Information is available in the restaurants and by calling corporate
Subway www.Subway.com 22499 International locations	Info on Website: -yes gluten-free -yes Ingredients -yes allergens Ask local Subway owner or manager for information
Taco Bell 800.Taco Bell www.tacobell.com 6,500 locations nationwide	Info on Website: -no gluten-free -no ingredients -no allergens Information available by calling corporate
TCBY 212.645.6900 www.Tcby.com 650 locations nationwide	Info on Website: -no gluten-free -no ingredients -no allergens information available by calling corporate
Texas Roadhouse 800.839.7623 www.texasroadhouse.com 170 locations nationwide	Info on Website: -no gluten-free -no ingredients -no allergens Information available by calling corporate
Thaifoon – Taste of Asia 480.945.0088 www.thaifoon.com 4 locations: AZ, CA, UT	Info on Website: -no gluten-free -no ingredients -no allergens Gluten-free menu available at most locations or call corporate for a copy

Obtain the most up to date information from the restaurant itself; write your favorite gluten-free and/or allergen-free food items here or on pages in the back of this book.

Establish a routine of calling the restaurant or checking their website to stay up to date. Take care of yourself. Do not rely on old information or rumors.

Steak'n Shake: Verified on: _____

Subway: Verified on: _____

Taco Bell: Verified on: _____

TCBY: Verified on: _____

Texas Roadhouse: Verified on: _____

Thaifoon – Taste of Asia: Verified on: _____

Restaurant Name Phone number Website Approximate number of locations and where to find them	Items on website at time of printing * gluten-free menu on website * Ingredient listing on website * Allergen information on site How to receive information if not on the Internet
Timberlodge Steakhouse 952.929.9353 www.Timberlodgesteakhouse.com 24 locations: MN, WI, ND, SD, IL, NB, NY	Info on Website: -yes gluten-free -no ingredients -no allergens Information available by calling corporate
Wendy's 614.764.3100 www.Wendys.com 5500 locations nationwide	Info on Website: -yes gluten-free -yes ingredients -yes allergens Information available by calling corporate office. Call for most up to date information
Wildfire 888.lettuce www.wildfirerestaurant.com 5 locations: IL, MN	Info on Website: -yes gluten-free -no ingredients -no allergens Menu available in restaurant and by calling
Z'Tejas 480.612.6380 www.ztejas.com 10 locations: West	Info on Website: -no gluten-free -no ingredients -no allergens Gluten-free menu available at many restaurant or by calling corporate

Obtain the most up to date information from the restaurant itself; write your favorite gluten-free and/or allergen-free food items here or on pages in the back of this book.

Establish a routine of calling the restaurant or checking their website to stay up to date. Take care of yourself. Do not rely on old information or rumors.

Timberlodge Steakhouse: Verified on: _____

Wendy's: Verified on: _____

Wildfire: Verified on: _____

Z'Tejas: Verified on: _____

Friendly Restaurants, Cafes, and Delicatessens

The following Multi-State Restaurant Corporate Headquarters were contacted. Even though you, or someone you know, many may have dined at some of these restaurants successfully—or may even have seen a gluten-free menu created at a particular franchise unit, Corporate Headquarters did not respond to our inquiries for any of the following reasons: (1) they were working on the information but it would not be done in time for publication (2) they did not reply to numerous attempts to reach them or (3) they stated the information requested was not available.

We look forward to their joining us in the future.

Acapulco Mexican Restaurants	Landry's
Applebee's	Legal Seafood
Arthur Treacher's	Logan's Roadhouse
Bahama Breeze (a Darden restaurant)	Lone Star Steakhouse
Bakers Square	Longhorn Steakhouse
Benihana	Marie Callender Pie Shops
Bickford Grille	Max & Erma's
Bennigan's	Nathan's Famous
Country Kitchen	Miami Subs
Blimpies	Olive Garden (a Darden restaurant)
Boardwalk Fries	On the Border
Big Boy Restaurants	Original Pancake House
Bojangle's Bugaboo	Perkins
California Pizza Kitchen	Pick up Stix
California Tortilla	Ponderosa
Captain D's Seafood	Rainforest Café
Capital Grill	Red Lobster (a Darden restaurant)
Carrows	Red Robin
Church's Chicken	Roadhouse Grill
Coco's Bakery & Restaurant	Rubio's Fresh Mexican
Claim Jumper	Ruby Tuesday
Country Kitchen	Saladworks
Damon's	Shari's
Eat'n Park	Shoney's
El Torito	Smokey Bones (a Darden restaurant)
Famous Dave's	Sonny's BBQ
Fazoli's	T.G.I. Friday's
Fleming's	Taco Cabana
Hard Rock Café	Tony Romas
Houlihan's	UNO Chicago Grill
J. Alexander's	Village Inn
Johnny Carino's	Waffle House
Kenny Rogers	Whataburger

Dining Out Success Stories and Tips

⫻ Multiple dietary concerns

⫻ When the job includes food

⫻ Take the time to explain. It is worth it.

⫻ Problems do not deter me from dining out

⫻ Know cooking and menu terms

⫻ Send things back if necessary

⫻ Cultivate privately owned local restaurants

⫻ Be upbeat

⫻ Many restaurants make us feel welcome

⫻ Salad for dessert

⫻ A caring and creative chef

Dining out with multiple food intolerances

My family and I loved to eat out before we were diagnosed with celiac disease, and we still love it! In our family, we have always asked specific questions about the menu items, even before we were diagnosed with celiac.

Our allergies and intolerances include: wheat, rye, oats, barley, turkey, shellfish, fish, pineapple and nuts. (We are fortunate in that our oldest daughter has outgrown her milk and egg allergies!)

It became important to me (almost a 'mission') to be able to go to restaurants, and eat all those delicious foods, without the fear of becoming ill.

Most restaurants are very helpful, and willing to work with us and our dietary restrictions. We definitely attempt to go early, when they are not as busy. If possible, I download the menu from the Internet ahead of time so that we may look it over and choose a few possibilities. If there is time, I will call and ask to speak with the manager, and discuss our situation. Otherwise, I speak with the waiter or chef when we arrive.

My 'usual' questions delve into marinades, sauces, cooking methods, and garnishes or extras. I explain which foods we can not eat, and then ask specific questions about the choices we've made. If they seem unsure about an ingredient, I ask them to find out before we complete our order.

When I find a restaurant that was particularly helpful, I make a note of it, and what we ate successfully. Most often, we have a wonderful and delicious meal we feel confident eating.

I am happy to say that many of our more frequented restaurants know us by name, and know just what we would like to order—and bring it to us with a smile!

Suzie E., Arizona

Severely allergic to shellfish

I was ten-years-old when I discovered that I was deathly allergic to shellfish. It was during a long-awaited lobster dinner on our family vacation to Prince Edward Island in Canada. Within moments of my first taste, my lips started to swell, followed by an itchy throat, severe wheezing and hives. I'm not sure if it was my family's ignorance about allergic reactions, or the substantial investment in a restaurant meal for six, but my parents didn't seek medical care until we returned home from the trip. Fortunately, I recovered without medical intervention!

The doctor's appointment was frightening. I remember him saying that I was severely allergic to shellfish and needed to be extremely careful. "It could kill you if a chef stirred a shellfish dish with a spoon and then used the same spoon in your food," he warned me. I have always remembered his words and avoided shellfish exposure whenever possible. Our family does not eat at seafood restaurants, even on coastal vacations where we're surrounded by crab shacks!

Unfortunately, mistakes happen. At a company Christmas party, a shrimp appetizer accidentally touched my food. When eating at a hotel brunch, the chef didn't understand English and I was served a casserole containing lobster. And once we ordered the wrong item number in a Thai restaurant and received a dish that contained shrimp. These events were followed by a quick trip to the emergency room and a shot of life-saving epinephrine.

Two years ago—and more than thirty years after my initial exposure to shellfish—I was diagnosed with celiac disease. In the next nine months, my husband and two children were similarly diagnosed. Now we needed to be aware of a much more common ingredient—gluten.

My daughter is the most sensitive to gluten. It literally just takes a crumb for her to develop a severe stomach ache, as well as other symptoms. As a result, eating out has become a calculated risk for us. In my opinion, it is almost impossible for a restaurant to provide the strictly gluten-free environment that we need. For one thing, suppliers change. A previously gluten-free chicken now may be pre-packaged with soy sauce. Secondly, orders are subject to human mistakes such as mixing up plates or orders, or taking shortcuts such as removing croutons rather than making a fresh salad. Finally, kitchens are busy places. It is hard to understand how a chef has the time to focus on a single special dietary meal when the kitchen is working hard to fill so many orders. So, when dining out, we know that we do so at our own risk!

When we do dine out, we usually choose a restaurant with a gluten-free menu, or an extremely knowledgeable and unhurried staff.

When traveling, we reserve a room that has a fridge and microwave. I bring an electric frying pan and pack gluten-free foods and mixes. Our first stop at a destination is often grocery shopping for milk and meats.

For plane trips, I will pack a lunch if possible. If not, we make do with a pre-packed protein bar, gluten-free muffins from home, grocery store prepackaged fruits and vegetables and junk food from airport food locations.

For dinner, I carry a list of the most recent gluten-free items in selected restaurants, so that we have a choice from multi-location restaurants.

I've learned to be flexible when traveling. After all, food is only part of the experience. If we can avoid getting sick, and enjoy the trip, then it's a success. If that means traveling with back up food, eating potato chips for breakfast and ice cream for lunch, it's worth it!

—Sue C., Canada and Arizona

When the job includes food

It's not easy having celiac, as many of us know, and having the kind of job I have doesn't make having it any easier. I supervise people all over the State of Arizona, from Page to Douglas, Yuma to Springerville. My job requires that I attend many meetings, trainings and conferences at various locations around the state.

Meetings are generally held between 10 am and 2 pm to allow those who travel from various parts of Arizona to avoid rush hour traffic. To make things convenient we generally order lunch in and eat while finishing the meeting. I think you can guess which are the favorite foods to order, yes, pizza and submarine sandwiches.

Attending trainings and conferences has also had its challenges because breakfast, lunch and snacks are generally included in the registration fee. In this case, you don't always get what you pay for! There were many times that I had to drink black coffee and eat a bag of gluten-free candy or potato chips to sustain myself until I could go home and make dinner.

You don't have to have too many of these bad experiences before you start getting tough and become more proactive and assertive. I had a choice to make, either I quit the job that is perfect for me and that I love or, I start taking charge. Quitting was not my choice.

When at a meeting I would order a hamburger with lettuce, tomato and no bun, or have them make me a salad with the lettuce and tomato and order oil and fresh lemon to use for a dressing. I sometimes packed a lunch if I had some leftovers and the meeting place had a microwave oven. Once colleagues were familiar with my 'problem' they started making different restaurant choices without my having to bring it up.

At one meeting I was pleasantly surprised; one of the choices for lunch was a restaurant I was unfamiliar with at the time. While reading the menu, it suddenly occurred to me that it contained the words gluten-free over and over. I shouted out loud in delight. Lots of discussion ensued about celiac and the gluten-free diet. Apparently, while at the restaurant, the secretary saw the gluten-free menu and remembered that I had celiac. Since then, thanks to many, there have been a number of other restaurants in the area that offer gluten-free menu items.

The positives in all of my trials and tribulations, is many more people know about celiac and the gluten-free diet and I am more assertive and creative. I don't sweat the 'small stuff' anymore. After six years of traveling, attending meetings and conferences I have learned to relax about my meals. I used to be very anxious which made things worse. Now, I kick back and say "worse comes to worse I'll have to eat M&M's®"!

Linda, AZ

Take the time to explain. It is worth it.

I have been successful at eating gluten-free at many types of restaurants over the years. I carry a laminated restaurant card with me, which I made up myself. I have it in English, Spanish, German and several other languages.

I usually start by looking over the menu carefully and then discuss in detail the dishes I have chosen. I always order something that the chef/manager/server and I have discussed thoroughly and end with a reminder of no croutons, bread or gravies on or near my plate. Nine times out of ten, I eat successfully. Very seldom do I become ill from the meal.

Dining out can be risky. It takes time to explain things, but it is well worth a successful dining out experience.

Betty B., Texas

Problems do not deter me from dining out

It is most important to tell the wait staff that you have a problem with your diet and emphasize that you can get very sick if you eat food that contains gluten. If I have a chance, I call ahead when the restaurant is not busy and speak to the chef who answers all my questions. If I do not call ahead I usually ask several questions at the restaurant. On occasion, I have had a problem after the meal, but that does not deter me from eating out.

Mary F., NH

Send things back if necessary

I fall into the category of, "I won't have to go to the hospital if I get a bit of gluten", but I don't like the results if I get it. To help avoid a problem, I carry a restaurant card that I made that explains about the diet. I don't go out to eat when the places are so busy that they can't think straight. I tip really well and tend to go back to the same restaurants.

It is not uncommon for restaurants to add something to the plate that is not listed on the menu: chips, sauces, a garnish or something. You must be willing to ask questions when that happens – ideally before that happens by asking how they 'plate' or 'present' the meal

I encourage you to eat out as much as you want, depending on your health, just be willing to ask questions, explain things and send things back if necessary.

Deborah M., OKC

Cultivate privately owned local restaurants

I have found that one of the best ways to eat out successfully is to 'cultivate' small privately owned local restaurants. I'll pick one that has a promising menu—a good choice of meals that are either gluten-free by nature or can easily be made gluten-free (or free of other allergen). Then I'll make an appointment to talk to the chef or owner (who is often one and the same.) I'll explain the details of the diet and the issue with cross contact. I'll go over the selected menu items to see if she thinks it is doable.

When I return to eat, I arrive early, before it is so busy that mistakes are apt to be made. I bring my own pasta, salad dressing and gluten-free bread or crackers. I politely re-review some of the items I had discussed earlier, place my order—and then I relax and enjoy the meal and the company.

I always leave a generous tip and a thank you note for the server and chef.

—Barbara C., CT

Know cooking and menu terms

I think that if a person has a basic understanding of cooking and what menu items mean, they can safely order in any restaurant with very few questions. When looking at a menu, I take into consideration how I would cook the item. I have decided that I am not going to let the 'small stuff' worry me. Life is too short to give up the few times that I get to eat out!

Leah

Be Upbeat

My daughter and I both have celiac and like to dine out. I recently revised my restaurant card to be more positive and I have gotten great results. Here are some of my tips:

- Find a restaurant you like and keep going back.

- Get to know the servers and chef if possible. Tip the servers well.

- Make certain the restaurant card you use isn't intimidating. I had the head chef of one of Anchorage's best restaurants come out saying he was mortified and didn't really know what to do—that prompted me to update the card into something more positive.

- Read through the menu and have several selections ready to ask the chef if he could adapt them to gluten-free (or free of a particular allergen).

- Thank the chef after a successful meal—even if it is just with a nod.

- Know the food types at particular restaurants—don't go to the Hofbrau Haus and expect to leave satisfied. Many cuisines are less wheat based than typical American.

- And mostly, be upbeat. There are many possibilities for wonderful dinner results with gluten-free foods.

Alison, AK

Many restaurants are happy to make us feel welcome

I am not intimidated to dine out. We travel a lot and I always manage to find a place to eat safely. I do travel with a good selection of gluten-free foods for emergencies (such as peanut butter...a staple in my diet!) No celiac should be afraid to venture out. Most restaurants are more than happy to make us feel welcome in their establishments.

Our Dallas Fort Worth support group has a dining out group that contacts restaurants ahead of time to review their menu from top to bottom. They make arrangements with the chef for our group dinner and review every ingredient label. We have had a lot of success in dining out at very friendly restaurants that have gone out of their way for us.

Nothing is more fulfilling for someone with a restricted diet, then to be able to dine out without fear.

Betty Barfield, TX

An alternative to the steak house

My husband has been gluten-free for over a year. We decided to take a chance on a small local Vietnamese restaurant that we had enjoyed pre-diagnosis. Much to our amazement, the waitress, who was in college replied to our questions, "Oh, you can't eat gluten!" Seems one of her professors had celiac and the waitress went through all the condiments and cooking preparation techniques in the restaurant so he could dine there. She made an 'approved list' for him that included my husband's favorite dish, a light, savory rice-flour 'Happy Pancake' laden with meat and vegetables. It was a great alternative to yet another trip to the local steakhouse.

Salad for dessert

I followed a strict, no-cheating-ever gluten-free diet for almost two years before I tried eating out again. Because I have multiple food sensitivities, in addition to celiac, it can be difficult to find anything on a restaurant menu that is safe for me to consume. The fresher, healthier, and less fussy the food, the better.

This makes for a funny sort of paradox when it comes to choosing restaurants, as upscale, expensive restaurants tend to have the highest quality food, but also, what I'd call hyphenated ingredients—original combinations of spices and sauces and garnishes in complex and complicated combinations that chefs are often reluctant to alter or eliminate.

Recently, I had a wonderful experience, in a lovely bistro in St. Paul, Minnesota. For lunch I had a marvelous plate of fresh greens and tender haricot beans, topped with a small, plain roasted fillet of trout. The server successfully conveyed my wishes to the kitchen, so the chef omitted the fancy seasonings and sauce and the vegetables and spices I cannot tolerate. She took my order graciously and, on hearing my restrictions and requests, even remembered to ask if I wanted the salad dressing, which I had forgotten to say I did not want.

But that's not really what made the lunch so successful. It's what I had for dessert. Another plate of the salad and fish! With no appetizers or bread to help fill me up and no dessert in my future (fresh fruit is the only dessert I can eat), I was still a little hungry. So, while my companion enjoyed a luscious-looking slice of tiramisu, I had a second helping of lunch. The server didn't flinch when I ordered it, the second order was prepared perfectly to my specifications, just like the first, and the kitchen and wait staff timed it perfectly so that my 'dessert' arrived at the same time as the tiramisu and cappuccino. It was the most satisfying restaurant experience I've had since I started my never-break-the-rules-for-any-reason gluten-free multiple food sensitivities diet. It was the first time I ordered two lunches, but it won't be the last!

Sima, MN

A caring and creative chef

One of my best dining out experiences was at a neighborhood Italian and Mediterranean foods restaurant. I spoke with the chef and let him know of my special dietary concerns. He created a fabulous meal just for me that was not on the menu! Now, when I return to the restaurant, I no longer bother looking at the menu, I just ask him to make me something wonderful that fits my dietary needs—and he does.

Angela, CA

Shopping

'Fresh Baked' Gluten-Free Products

Includes walk in facilities, special order and baked-to-order companies.

Arizona

Gluten-Free Creations   *All Gluten-Free Environment*
602.485.5312
Scottsdale, AZ
www.glutenfreecreations.com

All items made to order with the finest of ingredients in a gluten-free environment. We offer delicious basic and artisan breads, pizza crusts, wraps, pretzels, éclairs, gourmet desserts, crackers, cookies, cakes and more. A variety of items dairy-, sugar-, soy-, or nut-free baked goods provided weekly to select store locations. A selection of our Artisan Breads and flavorful cookies and crackers are available for shipping. Visit website or call for more information.

California

Confections by Carol   *All Gluten-Free Environment*
818.845.8054
Carol Tipton
Burbank CA
Catipton@sbcglobal.net

Special order items include cakes, cookies, muffins, yeast and quick breads, recipe conversions, Holiday meals including GF bread stuffing, and more. All from a gluten-free kitchen. Pick up or delivery available. Place orders at least 7 days in advance. E-mail or call for a listing of available items.

Fresh Baked GF Products

Crave   *All Gluten-Free Environment*
415.826.7187
San Francisco, CA 94110
www.cravebakery.org

Crave is the first bakery in San Francisco committed to baking without wheat, gluten or dairy, using high quality, animal conscious and organic ingredients; we are devoted to the flavor and integrity of our creations. Crave supports free-range egg farmers, local and family owned operations. Our mission is for our products to be so scrumptious; you'll forget your cravings for traditional baked goods made with wheat! Products are available in San Francisco at Rainbow Coop, Whole Foods and Harvest Market; in Berkeley and special order.

Colorado

Outside the Breadbox   *All Gluten-Free Environment*
719.633.3434
1508 West Colorado Ave
Colorado Springs, CO 80904
www.outsidethebreadbox.com

We offer breads, croutons, pizza crusts, cakes, cupcakes, muffins, cookies, crackers, mini pies, dinner rolls, hamburger and hot dog buns. All products are nut free. Many are free of dairy, casein, corn and soy. Place your pick up order 48 hours in advance. Many of our products are available throughout Colorado and other states.

Connecticut

Gluten Free Pantry   *All Gluten-Free Environment*
860.633.3826
82 Oakwood Drive
Glatonsbury, CT 06033
www.glutenfreepantry.com

Illinois

Breadsmith
630.832.0992
174 North York
Elmhurst, IL 60126

Breadsmith
708.460.6061
9044 159th St
Orland Park, IL 60462

Breadsmith
630.584.2323
121 North 2nd St Ste E
St. Charles, IL 60174

Special Order Market and Bakery
630.264.7128   *All Gluten-Free Environment*
200 Butterfield Rd
North Aurora, Ill
www.specialordermarket.com

Looking for fresh baked bread, cakes, cookies or a decorated special occasion cake? You will be pleased with our selection of freshly baked items in a gluten-free environment. The majority of our items are dairy-free. Some are corn and soy-free. Located within the Special Order Gluten-Free Market, you will be able to easily shop for all your items. Open Mon-Fri 10-6 pm. Sat. 10-3 pm. Contact us for baking schedule.

Massachusetts

Gillians Foods, Inc *All Gluten-Free Environment*
781.586.0086
82 Sanderson Ave
Lynn, MA 01902
www.gilliansfoods.com
Breads, rolls, pizza crusts

Lo Carbaret Café
978.499.4443
45 Storey Ave
Newburyport, MA 01950
www.locarbaret.com

Pies by Maria, Gluten Free Bakery, Inc.
781.440.0875 *All Gluten-Free Environment*
48 Austin St
Norwood, MA 02062
www.glutenfreebakery.com
(just southwest of Boston, close to Foxboro Stadium)
    All items baked to order. Call 24 hours in advance for pick up. This is a full service gluten-free bakery specializing in gluten-free as well as other dietary needs. We bake breads, cakes, cookies, pies, and special occasion cakes. All products on our website are available for shipping across the country.

Michigan

Celiac Specialties *All Gluten-Free Environment*
586.598.8180
48411 Jefferson Avenue
Chesterfield Township, MI 48047
www.celiacspecialties.com
    Offering fresh baked gluten-free items daily in a 100% gluten-free facility. We specialize in casein-free and sugar-free items.

Hours: M-W 7:00am–2:30pm; Th. 7:00am–7:00pm
Fri 7:00am-2:30pm; Sat 8:00am–1:00pm

Sugar Kisses
248.542.5622
1025 S Washington
Royal Oak, MI 48067

Minnesota

Bittersweet Gluten-Free Bakery
651.686.0112   *All Gluten-Free Environment*
2105 Cliff Rd
Eagan, MN 55112
www.bittersweetgf.com
   Our unique bakery offers gluten-free and many dairy-free products made fresh daily.

Bread Art
651.351.1475
110 Third St. North
Bayport, MN 55003

Bread Baker Company
507-289-7052
16 - 17th Ave NW
Rochester, MN 55901
www.breadbakercompany.com

Missouri

Breadsmith
314.822.8200
10031 Manchester Rd
St. Louis, MO 63122

New Jersey

Foods by George   *All Gluten-Free Environment*
201.612.9700
3 King St
Mahwah, NJ 07430
www.foodsbygeorge.com

New Mexico

Great Harvest Bread Company
505-293-8277
El Dorado Square, Ste 4
11200 Montgomery NE
Albuquerque, NM 87111
www.greatharvest.com

Great Harvest Bread Company
505-922-8817
6301 Riverside Plaza Ln., NW, Ste 1
Albuquerque, NM 87120
www.greatharvest.com

New York

Joseph's Organic Gluten-Free Bakery
718.336.9494   *All Gluten-Free Environment*
1712 Avenue M
Brooklyn, NY 11230
www.joesephsorganic.com

North Dakota

Breadsmith
701.478.8000
1617 – 32nd Ave S
Fargo, ND 58103

Ohio

Kathy's Creations   *All Gluten-Free Environment*
330-821-8183
866-821-8183
460 E. Main St.
Alliance, OH 44601

Products are made from scratch and taste like homemade 'regular' baked goods, not like gluten-free ones. Coffee, tea and other refreshments are available to enjoy with your fresh baked items. Gluten-free pizza is served on Saturdays. Hours: T-F 8:00am-5:00pm; Sat. 9:00am-4:00pm

Oregon

Angeline's Bakery & Café
541.549.9122
121 West Main Ave
Sisters, OR 97759

Grassroots Baking Company
503.293.6025   *All Gluten-Free Environment*
Portland, OR
www.grassrootsbakingcompany.com

Special orders accepted for fresh baked items made in a totally gluten-free environment. Our products may be found in Portland at the Corbett Fish House, Bob's Redmill Kitchen and Market of Choice. Look for freshly baked cookies, mini pies, bars, breads and the best cheesecake to be found. Fresh baked gluten-free pizza using our crust is available at Talarico's Mercado. A complete listing of our special order items is available on our web or by calling us.

Sweet Life Desserts
541.683.5676
755 Monroe
Eugene, OR 97402
www.sweetlifedesserts.com

Pennsylvania

Mr. Ritts Gluten Free Bakery
877.677.4887   *All Gluten-Free Environment*
709 E Passyunk Ave
Philadelphia, PA 19147
www.mrritts.com

Grainless Baker, The   *All Gluten-Free Environment*
570.342.1876
Scranton, PA 18505
www.grainlessbaker.com

Texas

Cakes by Monica   *All Gluten-Free Environment*
281.998.2569
Pasadena, Texas 77505
E-mail: GFCakesbymonica@aol.com

Cakes by Monica specializes in the creation of gluten-free wedding cakes, birthday cakes, cheesecakes, cupcakes, pies and cookies. All confections taste and have the texture just like a product made with wheat flour. Some cakes and cheesecakes can be made lactose free, soy-free, in addition to gluten-free. We currently service the Houston metropolitan area. In order to insure freshness, orders should be placed 5-7 days ahead of time.

Francis Simun Bakery
214.741.4242
3106 Commerce St
Deepellum (Dallas) TX 75226
www.francissimunbakery.com

For 22 years specializing in baked goods made from the very best organic ingredients and without the use of dairy, eggs, or leavening agents. Ingredients include high energy water, filtered by reverse osmosis and activated carbon. We use the very finest high quality sea salt. We bake both gluten-free and non-gluten-free products.

Wild Wood Art Café & Bakery
512.327.9660
3663 Bee Caves Rd. #4 A
Austin, TX 78746
www.wildwoodartcafe.com

We make a surprisingly large selection of unique home-made gluten-free entrées and bakery goods. All are so tasty and wholesome, that your friends and family can enjoy a meal with you. Shipping of baked items is available.

Virginia

Baker's Palette, The
434.295.3009
126-B Garrett St
Charlottesville, VA 22902

The Hungarian Bakery *All Gluten-Free Environment*
434.973.8863
Earlysville, VA 22936
www.hungarianbakery.com

Washington

Kaili's Kitchen   *All Gluten-Free Environment*
877.664.5883
206.542.1462
9711 Firdale Ave
Edmonds, WA 98020
www.wheatlessinseattle.com
E-mail: kailiskitchen@aol.com

Wisconsin

Grandma Ferdon's   *All Gluten-Free Environment*
800.464.2415
16052 West U.S. Highway 63
Hayward, WI 54843
www.grandmaferdons.com

Special Note:

Whole Foods Market dedicated gluten-free bakery ships
fresh-baked flash-frozen baked goods to many of its locations along the east coast. www.wholefoods.com.

Fresh Baked Gluten-Free Products in Canada

Some in a non gluten-free environment

Choices Market Rice Bakery
604.736.0301
2595 West 16th Avenue
Vancouver, British Columbia, Canada V6K 3B9
www.choicesmarket.com

Earth's Oven
403.686.4810
2133B-33 Avenue SW
Calgary, Albany, Canada T2T 1Z7
www.earthsoven.com
E-mail: baker@earthsoven.com

Elpeto Products, Ltd.
519.650.4616
800.387.4064
65 Saltsman Drive
Cambridge, Ontario, Canada N3H 4R7
www.elpeto.com

Glutino
800.363.3438
3750 Francis Hughes
Laval, Quebec, Canada H7L 5A9
www.Glutino.com

Kinnikinnick Foods, Inc.
780.424.2900
10940-120nd St
Edmonton, Alberta, Canada T5H 3P7
www.kinnikinnick.com

Panne Rizo Bakery
604.736.0885
1939 Cornwall Ave
Vancouver, British Columbia, Canada V6J 1C8
www.pannerizo.com

Fresh baked breads, pastries, cookies, muffins. Open 10 am-4 pm Tues-Sat. We ship our 'baked from scratch' items to the U.S. every Wednesday via FedEx. Order ahead on our website. A gluten-free bakery.

Quejos Bakery and Café
604.420.0832
4129 Main St
Vancouver, British Columbia, Canada V5V 3P6
www.quejos.com

Delicious wheat, gluten and yeast free baked buns come in three product lines: the cheese line with seven flavors, the soya line (also lactose and rennet free) with five flavors, and the dairy-free line with 4 flavors. Thin 10" crusts used as pizza shells or wraps are available in cheese or dairy free. All products are available for shipping to destinations across North America. Please check our website or email us for further information.

Slice of Life Bakery
416.463.5974
285 Coxwell Avenue
Toronto, Canada

Sterks Bakery
905.562.3086
800.608.4501
3866 –23 St.
Vineland, Ontario, Canada L0R 1S0

Friendly Store Defined

A friendly Store, for the purpose of this book, is one that carries a significant and varied amount of gluten-free and allergen-free food items

All individually listed Stores were contacted and included in this book based on:

■ A referral from a happy customer or manufacturer.

■ The store's marketing program.

■ The store answering 'Yes' when asked: *Do you carry a significant amount of gluten-free and allergen-free foods? Do you carry both dry goods and frozen items? If a customer were to drive for an hour to reach you, do you think they would leave as a satisfied customer due to their special diet shopping experience?*

Of the large number of stores recommended, many contacted did not meet the above criteria. Some said they 'carried some' items; others did not return phone calls faxes or e-mails after three attempts to reach; or had gone out of business.

Some stores offer the following services:

■ web page ordering.

■ lists of gluten-free or allergen-free items found in their store.

■ support group meetings held in store location.

■ gluten-free lecture series.

■ special diet cooking classes or tastings.

■ catering to the customer by ordering items not stocked at present time.

Some of the stores listed are totally gluten-free, while others offer a significant percentage of their shelf space to gluten-free and allergen-free items.

Action: If you own or manage a store, or if you had an excellent shopping experience in a store that is not included here, please complete and send us the Submittal Form on page 357 so all may enjoy the benefits in the next edition.

Friendly Store Locations

Call to verify store location has not changed
and hours of business.

Alaska

Natural Pantry
907. 770.1444
1200 W Northern Lights Blvd
Anchorage, AK 99503

Arizona

AJ's Fine Foods
480.563.5070
23251 N Pima Rd
Scottsdale, AZ 85255

Gluten-Free For You
602.749.1392
3122 E Indian School Rd
Phoenix, AZ 85016
www.glutenfreeforyou.com
   Specializing exclusively in gluten-free products. Baked goods and other specialty items. Centrally located in Phoenix, AZ

Nature's Finest
480.837.4588
16838 E. Parkview Ave
Fountain Hills, AZ 85268

Nature's Finest
480.962.8288
1925 E. Brown Rd Ste 8
Mesa, AZ 85203

Aspire Markets
480.348.9124
6339 E Greenway Rd
Ste 102-190
Scottsdale, AZ 85254
www.aspiremarkets.com
   At Aspire Markets, we believe that it's not what you can't eat that counts, it's what you can. We carry freshly prepared gourmet meals and bakery items for all dietary needs, as well as an international selection of foods and ingredients to tempt the most discerning palate. Our philosophy of catering to you, whatever diet you are on, is seen in everything we do. At Aspire Markets diet means delicious.

New Life Health Centers
520.747.9413
5612 E Broadway
Tucson, AZ 85711
www.newlifehealth.com

Whole Foods Market
602.569.7600
10810 N Tatum Blvd
Phoenix, Arizona 85028
www.wholefoodsmarket.com
   Store hours: 8 am-10 pm, 7 days a week.

We carry a large selection of gluten-free and allergen-free products.

Whole Foods Market
480.456.1400
5120 S Rural
Tempe, AZ 85282
www.wholefoodsmarket.com
Store hours: 8 a.m. to 10 p.m. seven days a week
We carry a large selection of gluten-free and allergen-free products.

Arkansas

The Kitchen Store
501.327.2182
704 Locust St
Conway, AR 72034

California

Country Sun Natural Foods
650.324.9190
440 S California Ave
Palo Alto, CA 94306

Erewhon Natural Foods Market
213.937.0777
7660 Beverly Blvd
Los Angeles, CA 90036
www.erewhonmarket.com

Gelson's The Super Market
818.906.5700
From Santa Barbara to Dana Point California
www.gelsons.com

One Life Natural Foods
310.392.4501
3001 Main St
Santa Monica, CA 70405

Staff of Life Natural Foods Market
831.423.8041
1305 Water St
Santa Cruz, CA 95062

Colorado

Bamboo Market
970.879.9992
116 9th St
Steamboat Springs, CO 80487

Sundrop Grocery
970.243.1175
321 Rood Ave.
Grand Junction, CO 81501

Water To Go
303.688.9536
562 E Castle Pines Pkwy Unit C-10
Castle Rock, CO 80108
Robert@watertogo.com
www.watertogo.com
We offer over 400 gluten-free food products and G/F vitamins and supplements. Many of our food products are also free of other allergens. We have breads, bagels, pizza crusts, cakes, pies, cookies, donuts, waffles, cereals, pastas and much more. We are here for those with special diet needs and we respond to new product requests every week.

Connecticut

Foodworks
203.458.9778
1055 Boston Post Rd
Guilford, CT 06437

Fountain of Youth
203.259.9378
1789 Post Road East
Westport, CT 06880

Harvest Moon Marketplace & Bistro
860.945.1003
465 Main St
Watertown, CT 06795

Healthfare
203.966.5400
2 Morse Court
New Canaan, CT 06840

Water To Go
203.268.6766
401 Monroe Turnpike, Rt 111
Monroe, CT 06468
www.watertogo.com

Delaware

Country Health Food Store
302.995.6620
2199 Kirkwood Hwy
Wilmington, DE 91805

Newark Natural Foods
302.368.5894
280 E Main St
Newark, DE 19711

District of Columbia

Yes Organic Market
202.363.1559
3425 Connecticut Av NW
Washington, DC 20008

Florida

A New Dawn
904.824.1337
110 Anastasia Blvd
St. Augustine, FL 32080

Abbey's Health & Nutrition
813.265.4951
14374 N. Dalemabry
Tampa, FL 33618

Chamberlin's Natural Foods Market
407.846.7454
1114 N John Young Pkwy
Kissimmee, FL 34741
www.chamberlins.com
Near Disney attractions!

Chamberlin's Natural Foods Market
407.647.6661
430 N Orlando Ave
Winter Park, FL 32789
www.chamberlins.com

The Health Food Store
850.671.1452
1989 Capital Circle NE
Tallahassee, FL 32308

Georgia

Life Grocery and Café
770.977.9583
1453 Roswell Rd.
Marietta, GA 30062
www.Lifegrocery.com

We carry a full line of gluten-free products and our organic vegan café' offers a huge selection of gluten-free foods. Sandwiches can even be prepared with gluten-free breads if requested. The café features a large living foods menu which is entirely gluten-free.

Sevananda Co-op
404.681.2831
467 Abernathy Blvd SW
Atlanta, GA 30307

Water To Go
678.205.5314
8725 Roswell Rd, Ste 14
Atlanta, GA 30350
www.watertogo.com

Water To Go
678.422.7266
1510 S Lake Parkway, Ste 1-G
Morrow, GA 30260
www.watertogo.com

Idaho

Pilgrim's Natural Market
208.676.9730
1316 N 4th St
Coeur de Alene, ID 83814

Illinois

A Way of Life
847.966.5565
9359 Milwaukee Av
Niles, IL 60714

Special Order (Gluten-Free) Market And Bakery
630.264.7128
200 Butterfield Rd
North Aurora, IL 60542
www.specialordermarket.com

We specialize in gluten-free wheat-free items. Our wide selection makes your life easier by omitting most label reading and searching among brands for items that suit your gluten-free needs. We are family owned and operated and offer freshly-baked gluten-free items made within a gluten-free environment. We are also sensitive to those with other food concerns such as dairy and casein-free. Let us become your major shopping market.

Gluten-free Market
847.419.9610
174 McHenry Rd
Buffalo Grove, IL 60089
www.glutenfreemarket.com

Sunrise Health Foods
708.365.5400
3203 Vollmer Rd
Flossmoor, IL 60422
Also in Lansing and Tinley Park
www.sunrise2you.com

Sunset Foods
847.272.7700
1127 Church St
Northbrook, IL 60062
Also in Highland Park, Lake
Forest and Libertyville
www.sunsetfoods.com

Indiana

Wise Way
219.464.3571
2800 N Calumet Ave
Valparaiso, IN 46383

Iowa

Health Country
641.423.6723
1631- 4th St SW
Mason City, IA 50401
    We specialize in gluten-free
foods. Open Mon-Fri. 10:00 am
-5:30 pm. Closed Saturday, open
Sunday 1:00-4:00 pm.

**New Pioneer Co-op and
Bakehouse**
319.358.5513
1101- 2nd Street
Coralville, IA 42241
www.newpi.com
    We carry a large selection of
gluten-free items

New Pioneer Co-op Deli
319.338.9441
22 S Van Buren St
Iowa City, IA 52245
www.newpi.com
    We carry a large selection of
gluten free items

Water To Go
515.225.8100
8812 Swanson Blvd #B
Clive, IA (Des Moines) 50325
www.watertogo.com

Kansas

Akin's Natural Foods Market
785.228.9131
2913 SW 29th St
Topeka, KS 66614
www.akins.com

Kentucky

**Amazing Grace Whole Foods
& Nutrition**
502.485.1122
1133 Bardstown Road
Louisville, KY 40204
www.amazinggracewholefoods.com

Louisiana

Conrad Rice Mill, Inc.
800.551.3245
307 Ann Street
New Iberia, LA 70560
www.holgrain.com

KONRIKO Company Store
337.364.7242
537 St. Ann Street
New Orleans, LA 70116
www.holgrain.com
    Hol-Grain gluten-free rice
crackers, baking mixes, rice bread
crumbs, rice and rice flour. Recipes, mail order catalogue and
complete gluten/wheat-free list
available.

Nature Lovers Health Foods
504.887.4929
3014 Cleary Ave
Metairie, LA 70002

Maine

Fresh off the Farm
207.236.3260
495 Commercial Street
Rockport, ME 04856

Lois' Natural Marketplace
207.885.0602
152 US Route One
Scarborough, ME 04074

Natural Living Center
207.990.2646
209 Longview Dr
Bangor, ME 04401

Maryland

Laurel Health Food
301.498.7191
131 Bowie Rd
Laurel, MD

Natural Health Food Store
410.560.3133
2149 York Rd
Timonlum, MD 21093

Water To Go
301.340.0004
Talbot Center
1085 Rockville Pike
Rockville, MD 20852
www.watertogo.com

Water To Go
301.424.1322
2232 Veirs Mill Rd
Rockville, MD 20851
www.watertogo.com

Massachusetts

Cape Cod Natural Foods
508.771.8394
1600 Falmouth Rd, Ste 27
Centerville, MA 02632

Green St. Natural Foods
781.662.7741
164 Green St.
Melrose, MA 02176

Harvest Co-op
617.661.1580
581 Massachusetts Ave.
Cambridge, MA 02139

Simple Enough Natural Foods
508.366.7037
18 Lyman St
Westborough, MA 01581

Michigan

Celiac Specialties
586.598.8180
48411 Jefferson
Chesterfield Township, MI 48047
www.celiacspecialties.com
  We offer a 100% gluten-free facility for all your shopping and freshly baked goods. Try our new Take & Bake Pizza as well as casein-free and sugar-free items. Hours Mon-Wed 7 am-2:30 pm, Thurs 7 am-7 pm, Fridays 7 am-2:30 pm Saturdays 8am-1pm.

Foods for Living
517.324.9010
2655 E. Grand River Ave
East Lansing, MI 48823

People's Food Co-op
734.994.9174
216 N Fourth Avenue
Ann Arbor, MI 48104

Minnesota

Fresh & Natural Foods
651.203.3663
1075 West Highway 96
Shoreview, MN 55126
www.freshandnaturalfoods.com
  Gluten-free Swedish meatballs, meatloaf, cakes, sandwiches and frozen foods. Fresh baked goods by Bittersweet Bakery. Large assortment of allergy-free and gluten-free items. Hours: Mon- Sat 9-9 pm Sunday 9-7 pm.

Gluten Free Cupboard
507.529.1132
1833 3rd Ave S.E.
Rochester, MN 55904
www.glutenfreecupboard.com

Good Food Store
507.289.9061
1001 6th Street NW
Rochester, MN 55901
www.rochestergoodfood.com

Mississippi Market
Natural Foods Co-op
651.310.9499
622 Selby Avenue
St. Paul, MN 55104
www.msmarket.org

River Market Community Co-op
651.439.0366
221 N Main St
Stillwater, MN 55082
www.mwnaturalfoods.coop

Sassafras Health Foods
651.426.0101
2186 Third St
Ste 110
White Bear Lake, MN 55110

Wedge Community Coop
612.871.3993
2105 Lyndale Ave So
Minneapolis, MN 55405
www.wedge.coop

Missouri

Country Mart
417.334.2101
1447 State Hwy 248
Branson, MO 65616

Nature's Sunshine
417.335.4372
1129 W Hwy 76
Branson, MO 65616

Montana

Oak Street Natural Market
406.582.5400
1735 West Oak Street, Ste F
Bozeman, MT 59715

Food Works Natural Market
406.222.8223
412 East Park St
Livingston, MT 59047

Nebraska

Akin's Natural Foods Market
402.466.5713
6900 "O" St, Ste 100
Lincoln, NE 68510
www.akins.com

Nevada

Water To Go
702.242.0777
1930 Village Center Circle #4
Las Vegas, NV 89134
www.watertogo.com

New Jersey

Harmony Natural Foods
732.671.7939
1077 State Hwy 34
Aberdeen Township, NJ 07748

Health Shoppe, The
973.538.9131
66 Morris St
Morristown, NJ 07960

Nature's Way Nutrition Center
973.667.6453
231 Franklin Ave
Nutly, NJ 07110

Sussex County Food Co-op, Inc.
973.579.1882
30 Moran Street
Newton, NJ 07860
www.sussexcountyfoods.org

Water To Go
732.452.0440
1199 Amboy Ave-Tano Mall
Edison, NJ 08837
www.watertogo.com

Water To Go
856.608.0777
3131 State Highway 38
Mt. Laurel, NJ 08054
www.watertogo.com

Water To Go
856.910.8881
3501 Haddonfield Rd
Pennsauken, NJ 08109
www.watertogo.com

New Mexico

Water To Go
505.792.9778
8201 Golf Course Rd NW, #A-4
Albuquerque, NM 87120
www.watertogo.com

New York

Capitol Health & Nutrition Mart
631.271.5577
357 New York Ave
Huntington, NY 11743

Green Star Cooperative Market
607.273.9392
701 W Buffalo St
Ithaca, NY 14850
www.greenstarcoop.com

Pitcher of Health
585.388.3802
114 N Main St
Fairport, NY 14450
www.pitcherofhealth.com

Sunrise Health Food Store
516.379.3111
129 W Sunrise Hwy
Freeport, NY 11520

Westerly Natural Market
212.586.5262
911 8th Ave
New York, NY 10019
www.westerlynaturalmarket.com

North Carolina

Talley's Green Grocery
704.334.9200
1408-C East Blvd
Charlotte, NC 28203
www.talleys.com

Ohio

Water To Go
330.864.5880
2281 W Market St
Akron, OH 44313
www.watertogo.com

Oklahoma

Akin's Natural Foods Market
800.800.3133
7807 E 51st
Tulsa, OK 74143
www.akins.com

Akin's Natural Foods Market
405.843.3033
2924 NW 63rd St
Oklahoma City, OK 73116
www.akins.com

Oregon

Bob's Red Mill Natural Foods
800.349.2173
5209 SE International Way
Milwaukie, OR 97222
www.bobsredmill.com

New Seasons Market
503.445.2888
1954 SE Division St
Portland, OR 97202
www.newseasonsmarket.com

Pennsylvania

Essentials
800.834.1056
125 W. Main St
Ligonier, PA 15658
www.essentialshealthfood.com
    We specialize in helping those with special dietary needs such as diabetes, food allergies or gluten intolerance. Gift baskets are available, and we ship. Located just 60 miles east of Pittsburgh,

Garden Gate Natural Foods
610.433.8891
17 S 9th St
Allentown, PA 18102

Martindale's Natural Foods
610.543.6811
1172 Baltimore Pike
Springfield, PA 19064

Rose Garden Natural Foods
717.338.0835
39 West Street
Gettysburg, PA 17325

Water To Go
610.438.2865
1315 Tatamy Rd
Easton, PA 18045
www.watertogo.com

Water To Go
717.545.1333
Plaza 5000
Linglestown Rd. Ste 9&10
Harrisburg, PA 17112
www.watertogo.com

Rhode Island

Water To Go
401.615.0665
1094 Bald Hill Rd
Warwick, RI 02868
www.watertogo.com

South Carolina

Natural Choice
803.547.1142
1741 Gold Hill Rd Ste 106
Fort Mill, SC 29708

Nature's Cupboard
864.225.7199
1630 N Main St
Anderson, SC 29621

Water To Go
803.325.8080
2738 Celanese Rd
Rock Hill, SC 29732
www.watertogo.com

South Dakota

Staple & Spice Market
605. 343.3900
601 Mt. Rushmore Rd
Rapid City, SD 57701

Tennessee

The Olive Branch II
731.660.7128
603 Vann Drive #E
Jackson, TN 38305

The Turnip Truck Natural Market
615.650.3600
970 Woodland
Nashville, TN 37206

Texas

FM Specialty Foods
972.724.3388
1001 Cross Timbers Rd
Ste 1060
Flower Mound, TX 75028

Healthy Approach Market
817.399.9100
5100 Hwy 121
Colleyville, TX 76034

Ranch Creek Natural Food Market
713.467.8900
13211 Memorial Drive
Houston, TX 77079

Roy's Natural Market
214.987.0213
130 Preston Royal Village
Dallas, TX 75230

Sunflower Shoppe
817.738.9051
5817 Curzon at
Camp Bowie Blvd
Fort Worth, TX 76087

Utah

Sunshine Nutrition
435.586.4889
111 W 535 S
Cedar City, UT 84720

Water To Go
801.474.1021
2921 E 3300 South
Salt Lake City, UT 84109
www.watertogo.com

Water To Go
435.627.8791
740 W Telegraph Rd, Ste #2
Washington, UT 84780
www.watertogo.com

Vermont

Newport Natural Foods
802.334.2626
194 Main St
Newport, VT 05855

Virginia

Kennedy's Natural Food
703.533.8484
1051 W Broad St
Falls Church, VA 1053

My Organic Market
703.535.5980
3831 Mt Vernon Ave
Alexandria, VA 22305

Rebecca's Natural Food
434.977.1965
1141 Emmet St N
Charlottesville, VA 22903

Heritage Store
757.428.0500
314 Laskin Rd
Virginia Beach, VA 23451

Water To Go
703.493.9349
8921 Ox Rd, Ste 40
Lorton, VA 22079
www.watertogo.com

Washington

Manna Mills
425.775.3479
21705 66th Ave W
Mountlake Terrace
Seattle, WA

Morning Harvest Natural Foods
360.876.6688
1037 Bethel Rd
Port Orchard, WA 98366

Nature's Pantry
425.454.0170
10201 NE 10th St
Bellevue, WA 98004

**Okanogan River Natural
Foods Co-op**
509.486.4188
21 West 4th St
Tonasket, WA 98855

Pilgrims Natural Foods
509.535.2264
2927 E 29th Ave #A
Spokane, WA 99223

Water To Go
253.752.1700
5401 6th Ave #K-807
Tacoma, WA 98406
www.watertogo.com

West Virginia

Earth Zone Nutrition Center
304.726.7316
RT 956 & RT 28
Ridgeley, WVA

Healthy Life Market
304.204.2091
909 Cross Lanes
Cross Lanes, WVA 25313

Wisconsin

**Gluten Free Family Country
Store**
920.693.2833
15007 County Rd XX
Keil, WI 53042

Gluten-Free Trading Co., LLC
888.993.9933
604A West Lincoln Ave.
Milwaukee, WI 53215
www.gluten-free.net

Outpost Natural Foods
414.961.1676
100 E Capitol Dr
Milwaukee, WI 53212
www.outpostcoop.com

Outpost Natural Foods
414.778.2012
7000 W State St
Wauwatosa, WI 53213

Wyoming

Bino's Grocery
307.674.8262
801 Main
Sheridan, WY 82834

Buffalo Health Mart
307.684.9062
201 Aspen Dr
Buffalo, WY 82834

Shirlyn's Natural Foods
307.754.9266
139 North Bent
Powell, WY 82435

Multiple Location Stores

Many main stream grocery stores are now carrying special dietary groceries in their Natural Food or Healthy Living Sections. For instance, Basha's has 42 stores with Natural Choice Departments throughout Arizona www.bashas.com.

Akin's Natural Food Markets
800.800.3133
14 locations in FL, OK, MO, NE, KS
www.akins.com

Basha's
42 stores with Natural Choice departments in Arizona
www.bashas.com

Trader Joe's Company
800.746.7857
P.O. Box 3270
South Pasadena, CA 91031
In 17 states
www.traderjoes.com

Vitamin Cottage Natural Grocers
800.817.9415
19 locations in NM, CO
www.vitamincottage.com

Wegman's Food Markets
800.934.6267
NY, PA, MD, NJ, DE, VA
Gluten-free, vegan, low fat and allergens listed on products
www.wegmans.com

Whole Foods Market
512.477.4455
601 N Lamar, Ste 300
Austin, TX 78703
www.wholefoodsmarket.com
    Also operates as: Fresh Fields, Bread & Circus and Wellspring Grocery

Wild Oats Markets, Inc.
800.494.9453
3375 Mitchell Lane
Boulder, CO 80301
www.wildoats.com
Also operates as Alfalfa's Markets, Capers Markets, Henry's Marketplace, Sun Harvest, Up- town Whole Foods and under other names.

Travel in the USA and Beyond

- 🍴 Take Along Ideas

- 🍴 Air Travel

- 🍴 Bed & Breakfasts

- 🍴 Camps

- 🍴 Cruises

- 🍴 Hospitals

- 🍴 National Parks

- 🍴 Theme Parks

- 🍴 Trains

- 🍴 Vacations

- 🍴 International Travel Stories

Take Along Ideas

Whether visiting a neighbor, traveling great distances, or staying at home, you will enjoy these creative take-along ideas from some of our sponsors.

Traveling with Amy's convenience food is easy. Place Amy's easy to prepare meals in a cooler with blue ice. Stop at a restaurant along the way and ask them to microwave your meal or use the microwave in a quick stop. On a long airplane flight, ask the flight attendants if they will warm up your Amy's meal in the microwave before or after all the passengers have been served. By bringing along your own Gluten Free Amy's meals, you can enjoy a stress free trip without wondering if there is gluten in your soup.

Amy's Kitchen, Inc.
707.578.7188
www.amys.com

We offer prepared meals so delicious they even tempt people who aren't on a diet. From a snack to an entire meal, and, of course, everything for the do it yourself chef, we cater to your needs for dining at home or on the road.

Aspire Markets, Inc.
480.348.9124
ww.aspiremarkets.com

All of our eight different flavored nutritious and convenient bars travel well.

Bumble Bars
888.453.3369
www.bumblebar.com

Are you planning a trip? Is your child going off to school or camp? How do you know which restaurants or cafeterias accommodate a gluten-free diet? Let Dietary Specialties help! We have a wide selection of foods including pastas, frozen entrees, and desserts. Just ask us and we'll ship your order to your vacation destination or your child's school. We at Dietary Specialties want to make mealtimes for you and your family an enjoyable experience.

Dietary Specialties
888.640.2800
www.dietspec.com

Our pocket sized Throat Soothers, Sweets, Tarts and Pastilles are perfect for on the road. Use them as a remedy for sore, scratchy throat, an upset stomach, a breath freshener or a simple treat.

EcoNatural Solutions, Inc.
877.684.5195
www.econaturalsolutions.com

Our extensive line of gluten-free and allergen free foods makes it easy for you to take along healthy smoothies, sandwiches, cookies and crackers.

Fresh & Natural Foods
651.203.3663
www.freshandnaturalfoods.com

When traveling, I always bring with me a small cooler to keep safe foods. In this cooler, I pack a zip-lock bag full of gluten-free snack mix, bread, peanut butter (the squeeze tubes of peanut butter are great for traveling.), fruit and a few cookies. In addition, I pack napkins, plastic forks and knives. Friends love traveling with me because I always have snacks! So remember to bring enough to share.

Gluten-Free Baking and More
518.279.3884
www.glutenfreebakingandmore.com

Gluten-Free Living contains a wealth of information on living the gluten-free life. You'll refer to it time and again.

Gluten-Free Living
914.741.5420
www.glutenfreeliving.com

Our Meals in a Cup provide the easiest take-along meal.

Gluten-Free Pantry
800.291.8386
www.glutenfreepantry.com

Our healthy dairy free and gluten-free shakes and rice nog travel well in a cooler. Combine with pre-baked Mochi squares for a nutritious snack.

Grainaissance, Inc.
800.472.4697
www.grainaissance.com

Before you venture out on your trip, call ahead and order a travel bag filled with freshly baked peanut butter cookies, Chocolate Brownies, Lemon Pound Cake and Sandwich/ Hamburger Buns complete with napkins and travel silverware.

Grassroots Baking Company
503.293.6025
www.grassrootsbakingcompany.com

Gourmet Tea Cakes are the perfect take along quick meal. Throw a two pack in your lunch bag, several in the picnic basket, in your purse or briefcase for that long plane trip. Take Tea Cakes to work, coffee and tea parties, or club and board meetings to treat your colleagues to something wonderful and gluten-free to replace those awful doughnuts and cookies that you can't eat anyway!

Madwoman Foods
612.728.2679
www.madwomanfoods.com

Make up a batch of our Hush Puppies the night before your trip. They are a great snack for the road with ketchup, mustard or mayonnaise; use as croutons for your salad or as breadsticks with marinara sauce on the side.

Marlene's Mixes
903.839.3892
www.marlenesmixes.com

Take along some of our delicious, nutritious easy-to-eat Whole Life Flax Krisps. We have seven Savory flavors. On a sweeter note, try our Fruity Flax Krisps or our crunchy Flax 'n' Fruit cereals with ground flax, nuts and dried fruits. All are wheat and gluten-free, organic, raw and delicious.

Matter of Flax
888.541.3529
www.matterofflax.com

Most of our products are 'suitcase friendly'. We will also ship to your point of destination, whether it is a family, friend or your vacation cruise liner.

Miss Roben's, Inc.
800.891.0083
www.allergygrocer.com

Our Brownies, Cookies and Muffins freeze perfectly and make excellent traveling treats! Add nuts, raisins, coconut, chocolate chips or any other combination that pleases your palate, freeze in individual plastic baggies and a scrumptious treat is ready to go when you are!

Namaste Foods
866.258.9493
www.namastefoods.com

We have wonderful products for traveling. Our Amaranth Mini-Ridges Snacks (Cheddar, Rosemary-Basil, Sun-dried Tomato Basil), and new Amaranth O's Cereals (Peach, Strawberry, Original) are great pack-and-go foods.

Nu-World Amaranth, Inc.
877.692.8899
www.nuworldfamily.com

Take our meals and snacks along on your trip or plan ahead and have your gluten-free meals delivered right to your door!

Pam's Celiac Kitchen
201.230.9292
www.celiackitchen.com

For a quick treat, remember to bring along a box or two of our cookies or biscotti.

Pamela's Products, Inc.
707.462.6605
www.pamelasproducts.com

Cold or hot, you will find Rizopia Pastas retain their shape and hold up to sauces. Take a couple of unopened boxes on the road with you the next time you travel.

Rizopia Food Products
866.749.6742
www.rizopia.com

If you have one mix to take along, just bring our Pancake & Waffle Mix. A recipe for making biscuits is included in this mix that also makes a great pie crust. This mix was the one mix to go with a crew rafting down a river in Alaska, because the entire crew enjoyed the flavor and versatility.

Sylvan Border Farm
707.459.1854
www.sylvanborderfarm.com

Our Buckwheat Porridge makes a hearty breakfast and hemp nuts makes a healthy snack. Bring a bag or two on the road with you for ease and safe snacking.

Trigone, Inc.
418.259.7414

Our wheat and gluten-free waffles are also free of dairy, egg and yeast. Toast up a box before your trip and use them for dips, as chips or spread them with jelly and peanut butter for a food that is fun to eat.

Van's International Foods
310.320.8611
www.vanswaffles.com

The next time you travel be sure to stock up on gluten-free items from Water To Go Diet & Nutrition Center™! We have an inviting store layout so you can easily find your favorite gluten-free items in a one-stop shop. Don't forget to pick up our pure and fresh purified drinking water and gluten-free vitamins in addition to gluten-free foods!

Water To Go Diet & Nutrition Center™
800-976-9283
www.watertogo.com

Airline Information

Air Canada

888.247.2262

www.aircanada.com

Gluten-free meals offered but certain restrictions may apply. Call ahead

Other special meals: Asian, vegetarian, bland/soft, child's, diabetic, fruit platter, gluten-free, Hindu, Kosher, low calorie, low cholesterol/low fat, low sodium, Muslim, oriental, vegetarian, lactose intolerant. All special meals must be ordered at least 18 hours prior to flight departure. Kosher at least 24 hours in advance.

American Airlines

800.433.7300

www.american.com

Gluten-free meals offered on International flights.

Other special meals: Vegetarian, diabetic, low-cal, lactose-free, Kosher, Hindu, Muslim, low-sodium, low-cholesterol, non-dairy and peanut-free. Call 'Special Assistance' after making reservations for special dietary requests. Reservations will provide number.

British Airways

800.247.9297

www.ba.com

Gluten-free meals offered on certain flights except for UK domestic routes and Euro Traveler flights to Paris, Luxembourg, Düsseldorf, Jersey, Cologne, Amsterdam and Brussels.

Other special meals: Ask when making reservations. Minimum of 24 hours advance notice for special meals.

Airlines

Continental

800.525.0280
www.continental.com

Gluten-free meals offered with a special 'Service Request' and in select markets on coast to coast and international flights.

Other special meals: lactose-free, low-fat, low-cholesterol, diabetic, low-sodium, Hindu, Muslim, Kosher.

Delta

800.221.1212
www.delta.com

Gluten-free meals offered on select flights.

Other special meals available in first class only. Baby, toddler and children's meals, bland, diabetic, fruit plate, gluten-free, Kosher, low calorie, low cholesterol, low fat. low sodium, Muslim, seafood, vegetarian, lactose free, Asian (Hindu).

Japan Airlines

800.525.3663
www.jal.co.jp/en

Ask if special meal is available when making reservations. If so, reserve at that time.

Northwest Airlines KLM

800.447.4747
www.nwa.com

No gluten-free meals offered on Northwest domestic flights at this time.

Gluten-free meals offered on KLM Int'l. flights

Other special meals of fruit and vegetarian plates may be available in first class domestic flights. Some meals may be purchased on flight.

Qantas

800.227.4500

www.qantas.com.au

Gluten-free meals available on the majority of its flights. Make request at time of booking flight.

Other special meals may be requested at time of booking.

Southwest Airlines

800.248.4377

www.southwest.com

No meals provided. No first class sections in their planes.

Swiss International Air

877.359.7947

www.swiss.com

Gluten-free meals offered

Other special meals available from Asian-vegetarian to no-spice. Call for the full list. Choice of all special meals must be made 72 hours before departure.

U.S. Airways

800.428.4322

www.usair.com

Gluten-free meals offered in First Class only for both domestic and international depending on length of flight. Business and coach may purchase meals provided by TGI Fridays. Or visit www.bobonline.com (buy on board online) or bring own food.

Other special meals: Vegetarian or lactose-free.

United Airlines

800.241.6522

www.united.com

No gluten-free meals available on domestic or international flights. Gluten-free meals may be reconsidered in 2005.

Other special meals include: Medical (diabetic, low-fat, low-cholesterol, low calorie, high fiber, low protein, and low-sodium), Vegetarian, Religious (Kosher, Muslim and Hindu), Children and babies, and fruit plates

---

Disclaimer: We (Airlines) do not guarantee any of our meals 100% free of food allergens or food intolerances.

Note: Many airlines do not offer peanuts on their flights; however, passengers may bring peanuts or peanut items on board.

All information subject to change without notice. It is the responsibility of the individual with the special diet, or his/her parent/guardian to obtain the most up to date information.

Friendly Bed & Breakfasts

A friendly Bed & Breakfast (B&B), for the purposes of this book, is one that welcomes people with specialized medical diets.

All Bed & Breakfasts were contacted and included in this book based on:

- A referral from a previous guest

- The Bed & Breakfast's marketing program

- Their answering "Yes" to the questions: *Do you have experience preparing foods for people on specialized diets? Do you have experience and are you comfortable serving gluten-free guests? Do you welcome more specialized diets and gluten-free guests into your Bed & Breakfast?*

Many of the B&Bs we spoke with have experience in the special diets category because either they, a family member or a friend is gluten-free or has other dietary restrictions.

Some B&Bs welcome guests to bring along or send ahead, their favorite gluten-free products. Others said they keep gluten-free products in their pantry; were familiar with gluten-free mail order, or that nearby stores carry items.

All B&Bs asked to be notified of the special dietary needs at the time of booking, and if possible, to remind them a couple of days prior to your arrival.

Each Bed & Breakfast Inn is unique. This uniqueness, their location, ambiance, food and owners are usually what attract guests. Ordinarily the guest has use of the bedroom as well as the house sitting rooms during their stay.

Bedrooms may be within the home, as an addition to the house, or even a stand alone building. Some B&Bs are in cottages while others are in ranches. Breakfasts are available in many different styles. They may be simple rolls and coffee in the morning; a full meal that is shared with most of the people in the Inn; or prepared to order.

If it is important to your trip make certain you inquire if the rooms have a separate bath, they allow children, pets, and smoking or if the staff is available to schedule any activities for you.

It is estimated there are over 2,500 bed & breakfasts in the United States and Canada. Our research quickly showed us that not all Bed & Breakfasts had the experience, nor wanted the experience of offering services to those on special diets.

Action: If you own a Bed & Breakfast, or if you have had an excellent experience in a Bed & Breakfast that is not included here, please complete and send us the Submittal Form on page 357, so all may enjoy the benefits in the next edition of this book.

Friendly Bed & Breakfast Locations

Alaska

Big Bear Bed & Breakfast
907.277.8189
3401 Richmond Ave
Anchorage, AK 99508
www.alaskabigbearbb.com

We enjoy providing our guests with a 'taste' of Alaska by sharing our food, surroundings and our 'Old Fashioned Alaskan Hospitality.' Special diets accommodated with advance notice.

Arizona

Inn at 410 Bed & Breakfast, The
800.774.2008
410 N Leroux St
Near the Grand Canyon
Flagstaff, AZ 86001
www.inn410.com

Natural Bed & Breakfast and Retreat
888.295.8500
3150 E Presidio Rd
Tucson, AZ 85716
www.tucsonnatural.com

California

Compassion Flower Inn
831.466.0420
216 Laurel St
Santa Cruz, CA 95060
www.compassionflowerinn.com

Yosemite Peregrine Inn
A unique Bed & Breakfast
209.372.8517
7509 Henness Circle
Yosemite National Park, CA 95389
www.yosemiteperegrine.com

Colorado

Two Sisters Inn
800.274.7466
Ten Otoe Place
Manitou Springs, CO 80829
www.twosisinn.com

Hawaii

Shipman House Bed & Breakfast Inn
800.627.8447
808.934.8002 phone/fax
131 Kaiulani Street
Hilo, Hawaii 96720
www.hilo-hawaii.com

Shipman House is located on the edge of Historic Downtown Hilo, yet great stands of palms, mango and bamboo hide the buildings, allowing one to look beyond to Hilo Bay and the Pacific Ocean. Waterfalls, snorkeling, hiking, and volcanoes are within an hour of the Shipman House Bed & Breakfast. Guests return again and again to this antique Victorian, and make a point of never missing our beautiful tropical breakfasts. We can even give you a short hula lesson!

Indiana

Old Bridge Inn, The
812.284.3580
866.284.3580
131 W Chestnut St
Jeffersonville, IN 47130
www.oldbridgeinn.com

Seconds to Louisville, Kentucky, this neoclassical was built by a prominent Jeffersonville family and dates to 1836. The entire house, is decorated with antiques and features five beautiful bedrooms, with private baths, and can accommodate up to 18-20 people. Among the many amenities you will enjoy are a full breakfast and complimentary beverages. The Old Bridge Inn is conveniently located in the heart of Jeffersonville's Historic District, seconds to the interstate (I-65), Louisville, KY and within walking distance of antique shops, restaurants and the Ohio River. The Falls of the Ohio State Park and the Howard Steamboat Museum are just five minutes from the Inn.

Iowa

Mandolin Inn, The
563.556.0069
199 Loras Blvd
Dubuque, IA 52001
www.mandolininn.com

Louisiana

Avenue Inn Bed & Breakfast
800.490.8542
4125 St. Charles Ave
New Orleans, LA 70115
www.avenueinnbb.com

Maine

EdgeWater Farm Bed & Breakfast
877.389.1322
71 Small Point Rd
Phippsburg, ME 04562
www.ewfbb.com

Rivendell House Bed & Breakfast
207.824.0508
16 Park St
Bethel ME 04217
www.rivendellhouse.com

Roaring Lion Bed & Breakfast, The
207.832.4038
995 Main St
Waldoboro, ME 04572
www.roaringlion.com

Enjoy a Maine vacation at our Waldoboro Bed & Breakfast, near Maine's best cross country skiing and the Farnsworth Art Museum. The Roaring Lion Bed & Breakfast is a country Victorian Inn located in a quiet New England village at the center of Maine's East Coast. Advise of special diets when making reservations.

West of Eden
207.244.9695
Route 102 and Kelleytown Rd
Seal Cove, ME 04674
www.acadia.net/westofeden

Maryland

Georgian House Bed & Breakfast
800.557.2068
170 Duke of Gloucester St
Annapolis, MD 21401
www.georgianhouse.com

Massachusetts

Windflower Inn
800-992-1993
684 S Egremont Rd
Great Barrington, MA 01230
www.windflowerinn.com

Michigan

Country Hermitage Bed & Breakfast
231.938.5930
Traverse City, MI
www.countryhermitage.com
info@countryhermitage.com

Minnesota

Wildwood Inn Bed & Breakfast
888.212.7031
3361 Cottonwood Rd NW
Wheeler's Point, Lake of the Woods
Baudette, MN 56623
www.wildwoodinnbb.com

Nebraska

Atwood House Bed & Breakfast
402.438.4567
740 S 17th St
Lincoln, NE 68508

New Hampshire

Inn of the Tartan Fox
877.836.4319
350 Old Homestead Hwy
Swanzey, NH 03446
www.tartanfox.com

New Jersey

Pillars of Plainfield Bed & Breakfast, The
888.745.5277
922 Central Ave
Plainfield, NJ 07060
www.pillars2.com

Serendipity Bed & Breakfast
800.842.8544
609.399.1554
712 Ninth St
Ocean City, NJ 08226
www.serendipitynj.com
info@serendipitynj.com

Serendipity is AAA and Mobil approved seashore inn with private baths and cable TV with VCR's-just ½ block to the beach and fun-filled boardwalk. Year-round, outdoor spa/hot tub, garden veranda and sitting room fireplace. A full breakfast is served with a choice of five entrees daily including vegetarian and high protein options. Special gluten-free menu offers fingers of French toast, eggs and sausage, scrambled tofu, pumpkin pancakes, hot quinoa cereal and bowls of fresh fruit.

New Mexico

Black Mesa Bed & Breakfast
505.583.2545
34328 U.S. Highway 28
Ojo Caliente, NM 87549
www.blackmesabnb.com

At the Black Mesa Bed & Breakfast, you can enjoy the pleasures of Northern New Mexico in an intimate natural setting with great gourmet cuisine. We are often referred to as 'a little oasis in the high desert', our Inn offers welcoming rooms, a wide porch and hammock for relaxing or reading a book from our library. Guests feel special and pampered in our own natural spring hot pool, with gourmet breakfasts that can accommodate food preferences and allergies with advance notice. We are just 10 minutes from a natural spring and one hour from Santa Fe or Taos.

New York

Greenwoods Bed & Breakfast Inn
800.914.3559
8136 Quayle Rd
Honeoye, NY 14471
www.greenwoodsinn.com

Ohio

College and Grove Bed & Breakfast
866.473.2113
93 West College Ave
Westerville, OH 43081

Oregon

Harrison House Bed & Breakfast
800.233.6248
2310 NW Harrison Blvd
Corvallis, OR 97330
www.corvallis-lodging.com

Pennsylvania

Artist's Inn and Gallery, The
(in beautiful Lancaster County)
888.999.4479
117 East Main St.
Terre Hill, PA 17581
www.artistinn.com
stay@artistinn.com

Make your getaway picture perfect…spend the night in an art gallery!

The Artist's Inn and Gallery is a feast for the eyes, soul and appetites. Set in Lancaster County, the heart of Pennsylvania Dutch Country, you can hear the clip-clop of buggies as they pass the inn. Enjoy Jacuzzi baths, fireplaces, wireless internet, cable TV with DVD, gourmet breakfasts (and of course, wheat-gluten-free!) the innkeeper's artwork, and views of rich Amish farmland.

Keystone Inn Bed & Breakfast
717.337.388
231 Hanover St
Gettysburg, PA 17325
www.bboline/com/pa/keystone

Tennessee

Christopher Place
423.623.6555
1500 Pinnacles Way
Newport, TN 37821
www.christopherplace.com

Iron Mountain Inn Bed & Breakfast
888.781.2399
Also Creekside Chalet and Lakeside Cottage
138 Moreland Dr
Butler, TN 37640
www.ironmountaininn.com
www.cottageonwataugalake.com

We are high in the mountains of beautiful northeastern Tennessee. Looking over the Blue Ridge Mountains, the Iron Mountain Inn Bed & Breakfast offers guests 'Pampering Perfected' service at the Inn. Fresh food is served in a relaxing atmosphere. Advance notice necessary for special dietary needs. Or make breakfast yourself in the Chalet. And now, Lakefront Cottage, a disability accessible luxury cottage right on Watauga Lake!

Texas

Blair House Inn
877.549.5450
100 Spoke Hill Rd
Wimberley, TX 78676
www.blairhouseinn.com

Texas, continued

Chicken Paradise
210.340.0648
annebarfield@satx.rr.com
www.chickenparadise.com

We offer a large room that sleeps 2 or 3, small kitchen and bath detached from the main house, with separate entrance. The setting is a small farm in the center of the city. Ten minutes to downtown or the airport. We have chickens, guineas, and peacocks that free range the property. There is a large pool and private outdoor hot water shower. Breakfast arrangements custom designed to suit your needs. No gluten on the premises. Call for more information.

Inn at Craig Place
877.427.2447
117 West Craig Place
San Antonio, TX 78212
www.craigplace.com

Katy House Bed & Breakfast
800.843.5289
201 Romona St
Smithville, TX 78957
www.katyhouse.com

Oge Inn Bed & Breakfast
800.242.2770
209 Washington St
San Antonio, TX 78204
www.ogeinn.com

Virginia

Grey Horse Inn, The
540.253.7000
4350 Fauquier Ave
The Plains, VA 20198
www.greyhorseinn.com

River's Edge
888.786.9418
6208 Little Camp Rd
Riner, VA 24149
www.river-edge.com

Sweet Thyme Inn
304.456.5535
Route 92/28
P.O. Box 85
Green Bank, West VA 24944
www.sweetthymeinn.com

Washington

Kangaroo House Bed & Breakfast
888.371.2175
1459 North Beach Rd
Eastsound-Orcas Island, WA 98245
www.kangaroohouse.com

Wisconsin

Arbor House
608.238.2981
3402 Monroe St
Madison, WI 53711
www.arbor-house.com

Wyoming

A. Drummond's Ranch Bed & Breakfast
307.634.6042
399 Happy Jack Rd
Cheyenne-Laramie, WY 82007
www.cruising-america.com/drum6.html

Canadian Friendly Bed & Breakfast

Alberta

Bear Necessities Bed & Breakfast
403.609.0838
514 Grotto Rd
Canmore, Alberta T1W 1J2
www.bearnecessitiesbb.com

British Columbia

Butternut Ridge Bed & Breakfast
250.490.3640
1086 Three Mile Rd
Penticton, British Columbia V2A 8T7
www.bbcanada.com/butternutridge

Earle Clarke House Bed & Breakfast
866.595.0941
1461 Pembroke St
Victoria, British Columbia V8R 1V7
www.earleclarkehouse.com

Ontario

Alexander House Bed & Breakfast
613.797.5355
542 Besserer St
Ottawa, Ontario K1N 6C7
www.ottawabandb.com

Angels Hideaway
905.354.1119
4360 Simcoe St
Niagara Falls, Ontario L2E 1T6
Reservations@angelshideaway.net

Arbour Breeze Bed & Breakfast
905.468.050
Four Mile Creek Rd., R.R. #3
Niagara-On-The-Lake, Ontario L0S 1J0
www.arbourbreeze.com

Waterlot Restaurant & Inn
519.662.2020
17 Huron St
New Hamburg, Ontario N3A 1K1
www.waterlot.com

Camps

GIG® Kid's Camping Program USA

Contact GIG® at (206)246-6652

www.gluten.net

The Gluten Intolerance Group's Kids Camps are very popular.

GIG staff and volunteers go to camp to cook! We are there to see that the kids have wonderful gluten-free meals and snacks, while enjoying a summer camp experience they might otherwise not be able to do. The camps offer a mainstream program for our children. GIG kids are part of the regular camping programs provided by wonderful camps, getting the opportunity to 'just be a kid.' Our GF menus mimic the regular camp fare. The food preparation is overseen by a registered dietitian knowledgeable in Gluten-free cooking and other allergen restrictions. In 2004 there were two different camp locations. Call or visit our website for more information

Camp Celiac, USA

Tanis Collard at 508.399.6229

csgc@ix.netcom.com

www.csaceliacs.org

Children ages 7–16 with celiac disease are invited. Camp includes canoeing, swimming, outdoor adventures, campfires and completely gluten-free meals. Registration forms and more information are available by e-mailing or calling.

Camp Courage, Twin Cities of St. Paul/ Minneapolis, USA

Katie at kweidner@cvtel.net

www.twincitiesrock.org

The Twin Cities ROCK Group of St. Paul/Minneapolis, Minnesota sponsors an annual Gluten-Free Fun Camp at Camp Courage in Maple Lake, Minnesota. This is a special summer camp focusing on kids with celiac disease as well as many other food allergies. The focus is to provide a well-monitored situation where children with celiac and their siblings, ages 8 – 17 can enjoy a gluten-free summer camp experience. Contact us for more information or visit our website.

Calgary Camp, Canada

The Calgary Chapter of the Canadian Celiac Association organizes the Calgary Alberta Kids Camp each year. The Camp is open to Calgary members only. Camp fills up quickly. For more information on this camp and other gluten-free camps for children in Canada, visit the Canadian Celiac Association at www.celiac.ca.

Ontario Camp, eastern Canada

Kingston Chapter of the Canadian Celiac Association organizes a six-day sleepover camp in Eastern Ontario for celiac children and siblings. Contact the Kingston Chapter of the Canadian Celiac Association for information on future eastern Ontario camps. Information is also available on the Canadian Celiac Association website at www.celiac.ca

Cruise Lines and Riverboats

American Cruise Lines
800.814.6880
Cruise the Chesapeake Bay
www.americancruiselines.com

Can accommodate special diets if arrangements are made in advance by e-mail lubrano@americancruiselines.com or telephone

Carnival Cruise Lines
800.327.9501
305.406.8666 fax
3655 NW 87th Avenue
Miami, FL 33178
www.carnival.com
email: guestinfo@carnival.com

After reservations are made, ask for the Special Services Department and give them the booked cruise confirmation number. Provide them with your special diet information.

Celebrity Cruises
800.446.6620 or 800.437.3111
1050 Caribbean Way
Miami, Fl 33132
www.celebrity.com
email: cruisecommentscci@celebritycruises.com

"We went on a Celebrity Cruise and they couldn't have been more accommodating. I did have to send them a letter requesting gluten-free food but they made every effort to accommodate me. They served gluten-free bread and if there was nothing on the menu I felt I could eat they would make a steak or grill a chicken breast for me. Breakfast was fine because I could eat most things at the buffet. Lunch was a little dicier, but I really never asked at the buffet if they had gluten-free food." Elinor, NJ

"As for cruises, we have been on three since I was diagnosed with CD. We go on Celebrity Cruise Lines. It is not as crowded or noisy as some other cruise lines. The Celebrity Cruise Lines Maitre D' said they get about 8–10 people with food allergies or intolerances on each cruise. They put special gluten-free bread out at dinner every night. There was more than enough to eat. Since I also have diabetes, I didn't wait for the gluten- free pancakes they would make for me. Instead, I ate gluten-free cereal every day." —Charlie

Coral Princess Cruises
S.H. Enterprises
U.S.A. and Canada Offices: 800.441.6880
245-M Mt. Hermon Road #B
Scotts Valley, CA 05066
www.coralprincess.com.au
Email: coralpss@aol.com
Australian cruise line. Well versed in gluten-free.

Costa Cruises
800.462.6782
200 South Park Road
Hollywood, FL 33021
www.costacruises.com
email: info@us.costa.it
Contact the Special Services Department at 954.266.5600. Special dietary needs accommodated upon request, dependent upon specific date, itinerary and vessel.

Crystal Cruises

800.446.6620
2121 Avenue of the Stars
Los Angeles, CA 90067
www.crystalcruises.com

"We love Crystal. We have cruised on their line twice. Evidently they have a dedicated chef/area for dietary restrictions. They take it very seriously. Every evening the head waiter brings the menus for the next day for my husband to make selections from. They also bring plates of gluten-free cookies at the end of the meal as well as occasionally gluten-free breads and rolls." —Jo

Disney Cruise Line

888.325.2500
Fax: 407.566.7417
210 Celebration Place, Suite 400
Celebrations, FL 34747
www.disneycruise.com
email: dcl.guest.communications@disney.com

Advise of any food allergy or food intolerance upon booking. Special Services Department will fill out a medical clearance form to be signed by your doctor. Return form to Special Services Department and they will forward it to onboard ship doctor. This will also alert the wait staff and cooks of the passenger's needs and allow the ships doctor to treat you if needed.

"I went on a Disney cruise and it was wonderful. You have to have a paper signed by your doctor to say you have a gluten-free restriction. No big deal. When you get there the head server comes over. On my cruise he went out of his way to make me happy and make my food safe. If there was a buffet, I never had to eat from it. They got my food from the kitchen. At regular dinners, they made me gluten-free pasta. It was so good." Linda

Holland America Line
877.724.5425
Fax: 206.281.7110
300 Elliott Avenue West
Seattle, WA 98119
www.hollandamerica.com

Ask for a Gluten-Free Request Form when booking reservations. Complete the form (ordering of items for meals) and fax to 800.207.3547 or mail to Ship Services at above address no later than 60 days prior to sailing or 90 days for International travel.

"My husband and I cruised on Holland America to the eastern Caribbean. We contacted the ship before going. They sent by computer a list of the foods that would be available and how many I would be able to have in a day. The only confusion was the first morning. The rest of the trip went okay. Each morning I found a chef and he pointed out what I could eat. Dinners went very well. The maitre d' would take my order the night before and it would be brought to me the next evening meal. Cruising can be done, but bring some snacks." —Nancy

"Holland America offers many more gluten-free items than other cruise lines that I have traveled on. The Indonesian wait staff really doesn't 'get it'. I had to switch tables on my trip to South American to find a head waiter who could accommodate me." —May

Hurtigruten Lines
800.334.6544
www.cruisenorway.com
info@cruisenorway.com

"I took a wonderful trip on a Hurtigruten Line ship that traveled the coast of Norway, from Bergen to above the Arctic Circle, frequently stopping at towns along the way. The trip is advertised as "The world's most beautiful sea voyage" and I agree – the scenery was awesome. As for celiac, it was the easiest trip I've taken. Norwegians understand celiac. I notified the ship ahead of time and was provided with three gluten-free meals a day. The best thing was trust, as everyone understood about celiac. In Bergen, the local pizza chain offers gluten-free pizza, McDonalds offers gluten-free buns, and if you ask for gluten-free in a restaurant your server responds "of course". Even the small towns along the coast often had at least one shop that carried some gluten-free packaged food." Evelyn

Norwegian Cruise Lines
800.327.9020
7665 Corporate Center Drive
Miami, FL 33126
www.ncl.com
email: reservations@ncl.com

"I went on NCL around Hawaii and could not have been more pleased. Once I let them know about my problem they took over. They said what I could eat from the menu and what not. They came out with gluten-free bread. The buffet was a different situation. I was on my own and had to figure out what to eat myself." —Ralph

"My husband and I went on Norwegian cruise lines, the Wind. They do not necessarily cater to wheat-free or gluten-free, but it worked out. My waiter and Maitre'd were exceptional. They made sure I ate gluten-free. They both were on top of things." —Susan

Princess Cruises
800.421.1700 or 800.774.6237
24305 Town Center Drive
Santa Clarita, CA 91355
www.princess.com

Fax special dietary needs request to Onboard Services Department with your Cruise Reservation number. Fax number: 661.259.3108

"My wife and I cruised aboard the Golden Princess for 7 days on the southern Caribbean cruise. What a blast—the level of personal attention was nearly embarrassing, but much appreciated." —Dan

"I went on the Island Princess to Panama Canal. The head waiter was very helpful and obtained gluten-free bread for me. He gave me the menu each evening and had me select which food I wanted for the next day. If it was not gluten-free he would have the cooks make it gluten-free. It was a good experience." —Natalie

"I just returned from a Princess Cruise—the Tahitian Princess, and had a wonderful experience. They bent over backwards to make sure I was taken care of." —Faye

"We chose Princess because it has a gluten-free menu and since my son is 5, they would accommodate his dietary needs along with the kids club activities." —Janine

Royal Caribbean Cruises International

800.327.6700

1050 Caribbean Way

Miami, FL 33132

www.royalcaribbean.com

Contact Special Services Department at 800.722.5472 about special dietary needs.

"Royal Caribbean, on a Mexican Riviera cruise, more than satisfied my needs. They met with me each night asking what I wanted for the next evening meal. I could order anything (within reason) even if it was not on the menu. They baked me corn bread every day and a flourless chocolate cake. I took pasta on board and did not need to use it." —Lynda

"I had a fantastic experience on Royal Caribbean's Mariner of the Seas cruising the western Caribbean for a week. It was the best food week for me since my diagnosis! The first day on board, the head waiter was stationed near the dining room to discuss special dietary needs with anyone who needed his help. As soon as I told him I had celiac disease, he assured me that gluten-free food would be available at every meal. He helped me make menu selections for that evening, and I had no trouble. I would highly recommend Royal Caribbean to anyone with special dietary needs of any kind!" —Louise

"We have organized and enjoyed family cruises with ages ranging from 1 year old to 82. The children had celiac. We have been very happy with RCCL. The food is delicious and they were very careful with cross contamination issues."

Vantage Travel Riverboats
800.322.6677
Fax: 617.878.6141
90 Canal St.
Boston, MA 02114-2031
www.vantagetravel.com

"We travel Vantage Travel. You must be over 50! On their riverboats they offer gluten-free dining. We have been on two cruises with them, and after the second day, I never questioned anything they put before me. They were absolutely fantastic!! On one occasion, they served me something that looked questionable. I looked up only to see the head waiter standing next to me nodding his head yes! They were so careful. Even when we were in town for lunches, they spoke to the staff to assure that I got a gluten-free meal." —Ms. May

"We really have liked the Vantage river boat tours better than the bigger ships because we get to meet more people." —Janet

Viking River Cruises
800.668.4546
21820 Burbank Blvd, Suite 300
Woodland Hills, CA 91367
www.vikingrivers.com

Special thanks to everyone who contributed their cruising stories. And to Debbie Hagglund and Dorian Travel Services specialists in cruise line travel, 708.448.2047 for contributing information.

Hospital Travel

Many of us would prefer not to think of a hospital trip as a form of travel. But it does happen, and sometimes unexpectedly.

When we randomly asked 25 hospitals if they had a written gluten-free menu, only four answered "Yes."

Now is the time to question if your chosen hospital has gluten-free menus or menus to serve your dietary need. If they do have menus, ask if they will send you a copy for your review and files.

What if your hospital does not have a special diet or gluten-free menu they can show you?

Before an emergency occurs, ask a member of your family or support group if they will talk to the dietitian, the floor nurses and the kitchen to verify your meals are properly presented. Perhaps your own dietitian will write up menu options to present to the hospital staff.

If you are gluten-free **The Gluten Intolerance Group® (GIG) publishes a loose leaf Hospital Guide** that is available for sale. It is written specifically for hospital admittance and provides individual pages for each department that should be involved in your hospital care. Order by phone or mail.

Gluten Intolerance Group® (GIG)
206.246.6652
15110 10th Ave SW, Suite A
Seattle, WA 98166-1820
www.gluten.net

National Parks with Friendly Restaurants in Lodging Facilities

Remember to always call ahead; holidays are extremely busy times making it more difficult for restaurants to accommodate special diets; all restaurants contacted above confirmed they do their best to accommodate special diets. There is no guarantee of a meal 100% free of gluten or allergen per restaurants contacted.

More information on these and other Parks may be viewed at www.nps.gov

Arizona

Grand Canyon National Park

Mail: Grand Canyon National Park
Back Country Info Center
PO Box 129
Grand Canyon, AZ
928.638.7875

Call Xanterra Park & Resort Reservations 888.297.2757 if you do not have special dietary needs and to book room reservations.

Reservations may also be made on line at:
www.grandcanyonlodges.com for north and south rim

Phantom Ranch—at the bottom of the canyon. Call Transport at 928.638.3283 to book reservations.

Two meals are served. Breakfast is usually bacon and eggs, a steak and potato for dinner or vegetarian. No meal adaptations available. Verify your dietary needs can be met with these meals.

El Tovar Hotel—South Rim—The Arizona Dining Room Reservations: 928.638.2526. Ask for Food & Beverage to discuss your dietary needs when making reservations.

Bright Angel, Kachina Lodge and Thunderbird Lodge South rim—all have restaurants. Ask for the Food & Beverage Director when booking reservations through Xanterra Parks & Resorts at 888.297.2757 or notify Xanterra by fax 303.297.3175. These lodges request a list of suggestions on what you CAN eat.

The **Grand Canyon Lodge**—north rim—Lodge direct number is 928.638.2611 for special dietary needs. Send a list of food suggestions to: reserve-gcsr@xanterra.com after making reservations.

California

Death Valley National Park

Furnace Creek Inn & Ranch Resort
Call 760.786.2345 for reservations and to speak to Food and Beverage. This location is most apt to be able to handle special diets with plenty of advance notice and during non-holidays.

Florida

Everglades National Park
Mail: 40001 State Road 9336
Homestead, FL 33034
305.242.7700
Park fax: 305.242.7728

Flamingo Lodge, Marina and Outpost Resort
800.600.3813 Reservations
When making reservations, verify chef on duty will be able to handle your dietary needs, or rent any of the 24 cottages that have kitchen facilities.

Hawaii

Hawai'i Volcanoes National Park
Island of Hawaii
Mail: PO BX 52
Hawai'i National Park, HI 96718
808.985.6000

Volcano House
Call 808.967.7321 before making reservations to make certain can handle dietary needs.

Kentucky

Mammoth Cave National Park
P.O. Box 7
Mammoth Cave, Kentucky 42259
270.758.2180

Mammoth Café Hotel
Call Culinary Manager at 270.758.2225 or fax dietary needs ahead of time to 270.758.2301

South Dakota

Mount Rushmore National Memorial

13000 Hwy 244
Keystone, SD 57751

800.827.9323 connects to the dining room. Some items may be available for special dietary needs. Call to confirm.

Utah

Bryce Canyon National Park

Mail: P.O. Box 170001
Bryce Canyon, UT 84717

Call Xanterra Park & Resort Reservations 888.297.2757 if you do not have special dietary needs and to book room reservations.

Bryce Canyon Lodges

For special dietary needs, call 435.834.5361. Ask for Food and Beverage Manager

Zion National Park

Call Xanterra Park & Resort Reservations 307.344.7311 if you do not have special dietary needs and to book room reservations at the Lodge.

Zion Lodge

Call 435.772.3213 and ask for Food and Beverage at the Red Rock Grill to verify they can accommodate diet. Grilled items are usually not marinated, most items cooked from scratch. If extended stay, may bring in unopened box of allergen-free pasta.

Washington

Olympic National Park
Port Angeles, Washington

Lake Crescent Lodge & Hurricane Ridge
Near Port Angeles, WA
360.928.3041 x 20 Office. Ask for Food and Beverage
Director
360.928.3253 fax
Familiar with handling special dietary requests

Wyoming

Grand Teton National Park
Northwest Wyoming
Mail: PO Drawer 170
Moose, WY 83012-0170
307.739.3438 fax

Jackson Lake Lodge
Lodge Switchboard Line: 307.543.1911 Ask for Food
and Beverage.

Call in advance. If possible send recommendations on
what you CAN eat.

Yellowstone National Park
307.344.7311
Call Xanterra Park & Resort Reservations 307.344.7311
if you do not have special dietary needs and to book room
reservations
All of the Ala Carte Restaurants are familiar with special
dietary needs. Know what ingredients you can and cannot
eat; ask specific questions or provide guidance regarding
your meal.

Yellowstone, continued

Soy oil is frequently used. Peanut oil is not used in cooking. Peanuts are an ingredient or garnish in some meals.

There is always the risk of cross contamination when plates 'pass over' other plates.

Advise these Ala Carte Restaurants of your special dietary needs when making reservations:

Old Faithful Inn

Requires reservations at 307.545.4999

Grant Village Hotel

Requires reservations at 307.242.3499

Lake Yellowstone Hotel & Cabins

Requires reservations at 307.242.3899

The restaurants at **Mammoth Hot Springs Hotel** and **Snow Lodge** do not need reservations.

For those who are extremely sensitive, Refrigerators and microwaves can be made available in many of the hotel rooms. After you have made your reservation, call Chris at Food & Beverage 307.344.5202. Give her your reservation number, dates and refrigerator and/or microwave needs. This must be done in advance.

Theme Parks

Always call ahead to book reservations, confirm special diet services are available, and obtain permission to bring own food into the park, if so desired. Be prepared with a copy of a physician's prescription identifying your special dietary needs.

Almost every theme park stated the visitor must be aware of what they can and cannot eat on their own diet and their level of sensitivity. Theme parks contacted cannot offer a 100% guarantee that all foods will be free of specific food allergens or intolerances. Some parks do have specific procedures established to avoid as much cross contamination or error as possible.

Name	Suggested Places to Dine
Celebration City www.silverdollarcity.com Branson, MO 800.225.0222	
How to Handle: Call Celebration City Food and Beverage office at 417.266.7320. Verify they can accommodate your special diet and where appropriate food may be available within Celebration City.	
Branson Belle Showboat Celebration City Branson, MO www.silverdollarcity.com 800.225.0222	
How to Handle: Call 800.225.0222. Ask for the Branson Belle Showboat Food Department. Give them list of what you CAN eat at least two weeks in advance of trip. They will go through the menu and make arrangements for your meal.	

Name	Suggested Places to Dine
Disneyland PO BX 3232 1313 S Harbor Blvd Anaheim, CA 92803 714.781.3463 www.disneyland.com	In the Park, Red Rocket Pizza has rice noodles, hamburgers and hot dogs are gluten-free. French Fries at McDonald carts and in the hamburger locations are gluten-free, unless a dedicated fryer breaks down. All suggestions are subject to change.

How to Handle: Disneyland does its best to accommodate special diets. Generally, look on the menu board for what you believe you can eat. Ask to see the manager or 'lead' person for specific questions. They either have an ingredient book on hand or will bring out the container so you may read the ingredients. The guest is the expert on ingredients they may or may not be able to enjoy. Chef Chris 714.781.3569 is available to provide the most up-to-date information on where to dine when calling ahead.

The Storyteller's Café in Disney's Grand Californian Hotel located at 1600 S. Disneyland Drive, 714.635.2300 is well versed on special dietary needs. Advise them either ahead of time or when arriving and the chef will visit your table for specifics.

Disney World **(Walt Disney World)** Orlando, Florida www.disneyworld.com **The Epcot Center** Food is handled through Disneyworld. Call 407.939.3463 to make meal reservations, or e-mail Sharon.Schifano@disney.com Magic Kingdom meal reservations may be made through Brenda.Bennett@disney.com	Fine Dining Restaurants in the Disney hotels and resorts in the theme park. Information may also be obtained through www.allearsnet.com, an unofficial guide to Disney World.

How to Handle: Call 407.939.3463 at least 7 days prior to arrival. Book Priority Seating reservations at any of the fine dining restaurants. They are all aware of the top 8 major food allergies as well as the wheat/gluten-free diet.

When the reservation is confirmed with the customer service representative, they will give you a phone number to call to discuss your specific dietary and intolerance needs with the chef at each of the booked restaurants.

Name	Suggested Places to Dine
DisneyWorld, Cont. Using the buffets throughout the park are not recommended for special dietary needs since they are unable to make any changes, according to Executive Chef. However, the chef at Cinderella's Royal Table Buffet in Grand Floridian Hotel may prepare special items for dietary needs.	
Dorney Park & Wildwater Kingdom 3830 Dorney Park Road Allentown, PA 18104 www.dorneypark.com 610.395.3724	The Park
How to Handle: Gluten-Free Foods are available throughout the park. Fresh cut French fries in dedicated fryers at Center Stage Fries and Smuggler's Snacks Fresh Kut Fries only. The Park serves grilled chicken breasts, grilled hamburgers and Hershey's Ice Cream. French fries are cooked in peanut oil.	
Dollywood 1020 Dollywood Lane Pigeon Forge, TN 37863 www.dollywood.com 865.428.9488	Aunt Granny's Miss Lillians
How to Handle: Hamburger and hot dogs are 100% beef. Vegetarian menu selections are available as well as salad bars No food or drink is allowed into the park Call 865.428.9428 corporate number for more information and ask if they will give permission to bring dietary foods into the park.	

Name	Suggested Places to Dine
Hershey Park www.hersheypa.com 800.hershey 800.437.7439 **Dining Inside the Park** 717.534.3900	
The Hotel Hershey P.O. Box 400 Hotel Road Hershey, PA 17033 www.Dininginhershey.com 717.534.8800	The Hotel Hershey Fountain Cafe

How to Handle: For information on Dining Inside the Park: Call 717.534.3900

The Hotel Hershey: Call 717.534.8800 and ask to speak to the Chef regarding your special dietary needs. Tell him/her your dates and specific restrictions.

The Chefs at Hotel Hershey are familiar with food allergies and intolerances. Gluten-free pastas are available. Other items may be available as well, depending on how far in advance you advise the restaurant.

When arriving at the Fountain Café in Hotel Hershey, ask for the Front House Manager and identify yourself. They will review your dietary needs and information you sent them.

Knott's Berry Farm 8039 Beach Boulevard Buena Park, CA 90620 714.220.5200	Ghost Town Grill or Mrs. Knott Chicken Dinner Restaurant

How to Handle: According to customer service, most sit down restaurants have a chef available to talk to you. Otherwise, salads are available throughout the park.

Name	Suggested Places to Dine
Legoland One Legoland Drive Carlsbad, CA 92008 www.lego.com 760.918.5346	Ristorante Brickoli

How to Handle: Call 760.918.5346, listen to messages, and then press 0 for representative who will forward you to Executive Chef in Food and Beverage Dept.

Advise how they can help you (what you can eat) when making dining reservations. Inquire on which fast food locations have special diet options.

SeaWorld 8738 International Drive Orlando, FL 32819 www.seaworldvacations.com 800.327.2420	Sharks Underwater Grill Order off menu

How to Handle: Call 800.237.2420. Follow the prompts to dining and then to Sharks Underwater Grill. When make dinner reservations, ask for priority seating and go over dietary restrictions with person answering the phone. S/he will mark your reservation with the dietary needs which gets sent to the chef.

They are familiar with gluten-free and allergen-free meals. Chef will come out if necessary.

SeaWorld San Antonio, Texas www.seaworld.com 800.700.7786	None can be suggested

How to Handle: No dietary arrangements for wheat or peanut allergies or gluten intolerance can be made for dining at SeaWorld in Texas according to customer service. A lunch may be brought into SeaWorld Texas with pre-approval only through the Administration Department at 210.523.3123. Get approval in advance. It is necessary to show approval slip to the gate upon entering.

Name	Suggested Places to Dine
SeaWorld Adventure Park 500 SeaWorld Drive San Diego, CA www.seaworld.com 800.380.3203	Dine with Shamu Shipwreck Reef Café Mama Stella's Hospitality Deli The Calypso Bay Smokehouse

How to Handle: Guests with special dietary requests, including gluten-free foods, will find a variety of options at SeaWorld dining facilities. We encourage any guest seeking gluten-free foods to speak with a restaurant manager or supervisor at restaurants noted or any other park restaurant prior to dining.

Should a guest have a specific request for information prior to their visit to SeaWorld, we encourage them to contact us at SWC.GuestRelations@SeaWorld.com

Stone Mountain Park 5525 Bramm Road Stone Mountain, GA 30007 www.stonemountainpark.com 770.498.5621	

How to Handle: Stone Mountain Park strongly encourages visitors with special diets to give notice prior to visiting and to provide a list of acceptable and not acceptable food items for allergies and food intolerances.

Call the main number and leave a message for Chef Patrick or call him at 404.909.1203. Or visit their website and e-mail him as to what you CAN eat!

Sesame Place 100 Sesame Road Langhorne, PA 19047 www.sesameplace.com 215.752.7070	Breakfast or Dinner with Big Bird & Friends

How to Handle: Breakfast or Dinner with Big Bird & Friends
Special diets may be accommodated, but not guaranteed, by calling 215.752.7070 Culinary Department at extension 387.

They will check with the Purchaser who handles food items to determine if special diet may be accommodated.

Name	Suggested Places to Dine
Silver Dollar City 399 Indian Point Road Branson, MO 65616 www.silverdollarcity.com 800.475.9370 Ask for Food Division	Wagon Works Grill has unmarinated kebobs of beef and chicken. Spring House has fresh salads made to order.

How to Handle: Per the Food Division: When first enter Silver Dollar City, there is a Salad Bar. In the Square is Wagon Works Grill that offers unmarinated kebobs of beef and chicken.

The hamburgers are not gluten-free due to seasonings. In the Spring House are fresh salads made to order.

You may bring in food due to medical reasons. Suggestion is to bring note from doctor as back up.

Peanut oil is not used to cook food, but many food items may contain peanuts or traces of peanuts.

Trains

Alaska Railroad

800.544.0552
411 W. 1st Ave
Anchorage, AK 9950
www.alaskarailroad.com

The Alaska Railroad uses the same catering company as Amtrak. See information under Amtrak.

Amtrak – USA

800.872.7245
Press '0' for an Agent
877.yes.rail for Amtrak Vacations
877.937.7245
www.amtrak.com

Local trains offer snacks from vending machines. A few special diets are available on some Long Distance Dining Cars. Different trains use different vendors. Some Long Distance Dining Cars make all the meals from scratch, while others bring on prepared or semi-prepared foods. Check with your local station. A brief example of food that may be offered on a Long Distance Dining Car is: Breakfast of eggs, potatoes, bacon, fruit and yogurt. Lunch is burgers, grilled chicken breast salad and asparagus. Dinner may be salmon, pork medallions, chicken breast salad and vegetables. When making reservations, ask if your special diet may be accommodated.

Venice Simplon-Orient Express
London – Paris – Venice
800.524.2420 for information and reservations
www.orient-express.com

Special meals must be ordered with a detailed request at the time of booking through the Reservations Manager. Special meals include, but are not limited to vegan, vegetarian, gluten-free. All meals are freshly prepared on board by French chefs. Different travel venues may change the meal offerings and availability.

VIA RAIL – Canada
888.842.7245
www.viarail.ca

Trains in southern Quebec and southern Ontario offer special dietary meals with a minimum of two day advance notice and in first class only (not economy-comfort class).

Allergen-free, Diabetic, Gluten-free, Vegetarian, Low calorie, low-sodium and low-cholesterol

When booking reservations, verify your special dietary needs may be met.

Vacations

Canada

The Hills Health Spa
250.791.5225
108 Mile House, Box 26
British Columbia, Canada V0K 2Z0
www.spabc.com
    Experienced in special diets

France

La Belle Demeure
0870.760.5042
www.glutenfreeinfrance.com
email: clare@glutenfreeinfrance.com
    At La Belle Demeure you can relax in the knowledge
that all our food is completely gluten-free. Coeliac or not,
'La Belle Demeure' provides a warm welcome for your stay
in France.

Italy

Country House Montali Hotel, The
+39.075.8350680
Via Montali 23
06068 Tavernelle di Panicale
(Perugia) Italy
www.montalionline.com
    The Country House Montali caters to tailor made diets.

Italy, continued

Take a truly special luxury villa holiday in lovely Italy with:
Buona Forchetta, Ltd
0044 (0)161.928.8857
33 Rivington Road
Hale, Altrincham
Cheshire WA15 9PJ
England
www.buonaforchetta.co.uk

During June, stay in a breathtakingly beautiful and luxurious hilltop villa with private pool, in the glorious Tuscan countryside between Florence & Siena, complete with all gourmet wheat and gluten-free meals and drinks. Tasting visits to local olive oil & wine producers, and trips to the lovely historic cities of San Gimignano, Siena and Florence. Golf and riding available nearby. Transfers to and from Pisa airport included. Call or e-mail for a brochure or more details on this villa holiday in Italy.

USA

Glutenfreeda San Juan Island Vacations
360.378.3675
Mailing Address: 181 Shooting Star Lane
Friday Harbor, WA 98250
www.glutenfreedavacations.com

Five day, gourmet, gluten-free vacations on beautiful San Juan Island, Washington. Vacation with your own personal chef. Other food intolerances accommodated. Vacations include lodging, all meals and island activities.

Gluten-Free Cooking School, The
602.485.8751
Mailing Address: 4757 E Greenway Road
Suite 107B - #91
Phoenix, AZ 85032
www.glutenfreecookingclub.com

Experienced Gluten-free Baker/Chef, with scheduled guest chefs, authors and nutritionists present valuable information and techniques for the novice as well as the gluten-free gourmet. Many people plan their vacations around our classes, while others attend from various neighborhoods. Whether or not you plan to recreate the delicious freshly prepared items at home, you will enjoy the information, relaxation and camaraderie of others in this gluten-free environment.

Ruby Range, The
970.577.0888
1231 Willow Lane
Estes Park, CO 80517
www.therubyrange.com

The Ruby Range hosts a cooking and life style school at the base of Rocky Mountain National Park in Estes Park, Colorado. Bring the family for a great vacation while learning to enjoy your gluten-free life.

Bob & Ruth's Gluten-Free Travel Club
410.486.0292
22 Breton Hill Rd, Suite 1B
Baltimore, MD 21208
www.bobandruths.com

"We took Bob Levy's Travel Club Mediterranean cruise. The ship had a dedicated gluten-free kitchen. We also took his Orient tour. I don't think we could easily go to that part of the world without his advance gluten-free food work." —Janet R.

Diane Schaefer – Joy In Travel
504.348.3099
504.454.6606
2901 Independence St, Ste 105
Metairie, LA 70006
Email: schfrpd@aol.com

Being a celiac who travels has its advantages! If you have wanderlust, let this fellow celiac travel counselor put you at ease...and on the vacation of your life. Fly anywhere in the world, sign up for a tour, or take a leisurely cruise. You say when and where. I'll make sure they care!

"We have worked with Diane Schaefer of Joy In Travel in the past. Her role as a celiac leader of the local New Orleans Support Group put her expertise in use helping celiacs travel, especially on cruises. Diane has experience in planning conferences and now is planning cruise(s) for the American Celiac Society in cooperation with CSA/USA." —Annette Bentley, Executive Director of the American Celiac Society

International Travel Stories

Five Continents

In 1999 I was diagnosed with celiac disease. This meant going on a gluten-free diet. After my diagnosis I cried for about two weeks and was sure I would never travel again. But I was not about to let my special diet restrict me from doing what I love best. So within six months I was off on a three week trip to Australia and New Zealand.

Within the next five years, I traveled on five continents, sometimes alone, with a friend or with a tour group. My favorite places are Australia, Peru, Egypt, Italy and the Czech Republic.

Here is my suggested routine:

- **Notify everyone who could possibly influence your dining** when you make your travel reservations. I have written a letter explaining celiac disease and what I can and cannot eat. My travel agent has a copy of the letter. If I am going on an organized tour, the tour company gets a copy of it with instructions to forward it to the tour director. If I'm staying at all-inclusive accommodations (such as a spa or a jungle camp—I've stayed in both), the restaurant's chef gets a copy.

- **Call the airline and book a gluten-free meal when making reservations.** One week later, call them again and verify they have it on the records. Sometimes this works! Call them again a few days prior to the flight. When checking in at the airport, ask if there is gluten-free food on board for you. There usually is if you have requested it twice before. Your meal will probably be served just prior to general meal service. Bring along a power bar or two in case in case a mistake is made. At least you'll have something safe to eat if worse comes to worse.

- **Carry a restaurant card explaining your diet in the language of the country you are visiting.** If you do not have a card, get a list of translators from the Consulate of the country. These are located in the nearest large city. For a fee, one of the translators will be able to help you out. Give him the card in English and voila! In the return mail you will receive a copy in the language of the country. Initiate this process six weeks prior to your departure. Dinner is the time to whip out the gluten-free dining card. I have never found a meal to be a problem. Hint: Bring with a couple of copies of the translated card.

- **Bring food with you.** I carry a little food with me. Mostly for the flights, airports and in case I get hungry when I'm not close to a restaurant. I don't bring a lot of food with because I never check a bag. I only travel with a carry-on bag.

While traveling overseas, I found most people to be extremely helpful. In Italy I stumbled into a restaurant with a gluten-free menu and gluten-free pasta. Had I called ahead I could have had pizza!

On a Nile River cruise, my tour director brought out the head chef prior to each meal. With the tour director interpreting, the Arabic-speaking chef described what was on the upcoming menu. If I couldn't eat something, he easily made substitutions.

In Prague and the Czech Republic, I had no problems. The breakfast at the hotel where we stayed was great. The delicious European yogurt, eggs, rice, veggies, fruit, tea, juices, etc. was great. Lunch was a salad. The Czech people are warm, friendly, helpful and very nice. I used a Czech gluten-free dining card and handed it to the waiter who shared it with the chef. They always came up with something I could eat. They don't add a lot of strange things to the food there the way we do here, so there are lots of things I could eat. Traveling is really not a problem. I wish other people on special diets would realize it. When dining back at home, I need to ask a lot more questions than when overseas. I even ask questions when there is a gluten-free menu. We adulterate our food here, adding ingredients and chemicals that are not really necessary. Our food industry workers are not educated about special diets. I worry more about eating in the USA more than I do in other countries!

Barb Strudwick, The International Traveler

Just Choose Anything on the Menu

I have traveled abroad and found very accommodating gluten-free menus in London, England and Oslo, Norway. In Oslo, we stayed at a hotel. While there we ate at the hotel restaurant. When I mentioned to the waiter that I needed a gluten-free dinner, he said, "Of course. Just choose anything on the menu and we'll make it gluten-free." He didn't look at me like I had two heads! He knew exactly what was meant by a 'gluten-free' menu selection. He took my order, and shortly after he brought out our drinks, he also brought out two plates of fresh bread...one for my husband and another for me. It was a wonderful small loaf of gluten-free bread. I was so happy. I ate every morsel, even though I didn't need it. The McDonald's in Norway offers gluten-free buns. Europe is so far ahead of the USA. Maybe one day we'll get there.

Betty Barfield, Texas

Only in the USA

I have traveled to New Zealand and Australia and hands down, they are so aware of the gluten-free diet, that it is pure luxury.

In Vancouver Canada I live within walking distance of two stores that carry gluten-free products, two rice bakeries and one quejo bakery. Many restaurants are aware of the gluten-free diet and I am not afraid of eating out anywhere I wish.

I travel for business and have dined out throughout Canada and the United States. Twice in the United States the hotel chef has refused to cook me a meal unless I signed a napkin releasing him of liability—only in America would that happen!

Lynda

High Tea

My mother and I went to London to celebrate her birthday. Her dream was to take High Tea at the Ritz Hotel. Reservations were set months in advance. A few days before leaving for London, I sent an email inquiring if they could accommodate a gluten-free diet. Since I did not receive a response, I assumed there would be absolutely nothing for me to eat. I resigned myself to simply drinking tea and enjoying the room. When we arrived at the hotel and looked at the reservation book, there in large black print with bright yellow magic marker were the words 'gluten-free.' We were led to a beautiful table and presented with two trays, one with the regular sandwiches and tarts for my mother and another especially for me. I was so overcome with gratitude, I began to cry.

Angela, CA

Dining Out Ingredient Cards

Dining Cards

A dining card lists prohibited ingredients and foods. The card is handed to the server or given to the chef prior to ordering your meal.

Some people never use a dining card. Other people always use a dining card.

The same is true with chefs and kitchen staff. Some like the card approach and others do not.

For those who would like to use a card, you can make your own card on the computer by visiting various websites for appropriate wordage.

A basic card with Italian and German translations is presented at the bottom of this section.

Attractive laminated cards with more detailed information are available through any of the following:

Food Allergy & Anaphylaxis Network (FAAN)
800.929.4040
703.691.3179
10400 Eaton Place, Suite 107
Fairfax, VA 22030-5647
www.foodallergy.org

The Food Allergy & Anaphylaxis Network (FAAN) offers Ingredient Wallet-sized cards that are plastic laminated and easy to read. Allergen cards include: Egg, Milk, Peanut, Tree Nuts, Soy, Fish, Shellfish and Wheat. Order by phone, mail or on their website.

The Gluten-Intolerance Group® (GIG)
206.246.6652
15110-10th Ave., SW, Suite A
Seattle, WA 98166-1820
www.gluten.net

The Gluten Intolerance Group offers plastic restaurant wallet-sized cards in English and in several foreign languages. Quick reference ingredient cards are also available. Order by phone, mail or on their website.

Celiac Sprue Association® (CSA)
877.272.4272
P.O. Box 31700
Omaha, NE 68131-0700
www.csaceliacs.org

The Celiac Sprue Association offers restaurant cards and Helpful Hints for the Kitchen Staff. Order by phone, mail or on their website.

Canadian Celiac Association (CCA)
905.507.6208
5170 Dixie Road, Suite 207
Mississauga, Ontario, Canada L4W 1E3
www.celiac.ca

The Canadian Celiac Association offers wallet-sized gluten-free diet restaurant cards. Visit their website for more information.

Living Without, Inc.
847.480.8810
P.O. Box 2126
Northbrook, IL 60065
www.livingwithout.com

Living Without, publishers of *Living Without* magazine, offers plastic restaurant wallet-sized cards in English for both gluten-free and casein-free.

A Basic Card with Translations

Information presented with the permission of Graeme of New Zealand. English version translated into Italian and German by the New Zealand Department of Internal Affairs.

English

I have a medical condition called Coeliac Disease.

I cannot eat foods containing even the smallest trace of wheat, rye, barley or oats as ingredients. Do you have items on your menu I can safely eat?

Rice and corn are safe. Fresh vegetables are safe. Fresh meat and fish must be cooked in a separate clean pan or in a microwave.

Please do not put sauce on my food.

Thank you.

Italian

Soffro di una malattia che si chiama "morbo celiaco". Non posso mangiare cibi che contengano negli ingredienti neppure una traccia minuscola di frumento (grano), segale, orzo o avena. Avete nel vostro menú dei piatti che posso mangiare senza correre alcun pericolo?

Posso mangiare tranquillamente riso e granturco (mais). Posso mangiare anche qualsiasi tipo di verdura fresca. La carne e il pesce fresco devono essere cucinati a parte in una pentola pulita o in un forno a microonde.

Per favore, non mettete salse sul mio cibo.

Grazie mille.

German

Ich leide an einer Gesundheitsstörung, die als Zöliakie bezeichnet wird.

Darum darf ich nichts essen, was auch nur die kleinsten Spuren von Weizen, Roggen, Gerste oder Hafer enthält. Gibt es auf Ihrer Speisekarte Gerichte, die ich bedenkenlos essen kann?

Reis und Mais sind unbedenklich. Frisches Gemüse ist unbedenklich. Frisches Fleisch und Fisch müssen in getrennten, sauberen Gefäßen oder in der Mikrowelle zubereitet werden.

Bitte keine Sauce auf mein Essen.

Vielen Dank.

Sponsors

Amazing Grains (Montina)
877.278.6585
405 Main Street SW
Ronan, MT 59864
www.amazinggrains.com

Have you ever been disappointed that your gluten-free baking doesn't have the texture and flavor you were looking for? Add 15% to 20% Montina™ Pure Baking Supplement to your standard flour mixture or try Montina™ All Purpose Baking Flour Blend as a cup for cup exchange in your favorite recipe. For more information about Montina™ checkout our website or call the number above. It is toll free.

Amy's Kitchen, Inc.
707.578.7188
P.O. Box 7868
Santa Rosa, CA 95407
www.amys.com

Remember Mac & Cheese and Lasagna? Now you can enjoy then again. Amy's, the producer of the most popular natural and organic convenience foods, offers a wide selection of frozen meals such as Rice Mac & Cheese and Rice Pasta Lasagna that are free from wheat, oats, barely and rye. Amy's also makes gluten-free canned soup, beans, bottled pasta sauces and salsas. Items are available in natural food stores, independent grocery stores, supermarkets and select stores in the USA and Canada, as well as on hundreds of college and university campuses.

Aspire Markets, Inc.

480.348.9124

16455 N Scottsdale Rd., Suite 107

Scottsdale, AZ 85254

www.aspiremarkets.com

At Aspire Markets, we believe that it's not what you can't eat that counts, it's what you can. We carry freshly prepared gourmet meals and bakery items for all dietary needs, as well as an international selection of foods and ingredients to tempt the most discerning palate. Our philosophy of catering to you, whatever diet you are on, is seen in everything we do. At Aspire Markets diet means delicious.

Authentic Foods

800.806.4737

310.366.7612

1850 W 169th St., Suite B

Gardena, CA 90247

www.authenticfoods.com

Authentic Foods is dedicated to providing you all natural gluten-free products without artificial flavors and preservatives. Our flours are superfine which prevents gritty texture and taste in your baked goods, where, upon your first bite; you realize that now you can bake smooth, light and fluffy breads, muffins and cakes. Authentic Foods gluten-free products are the best and the healthiest baking products available. We developed the first bean flour blend called Garfava Flour, a mixture of garbanzo and fava beans, for adding more protein and fiber to your diet. Visit our website for free recipe ideas and browse our storefront for the best products around!

Bob's Red Mill Natural Foods, Inc

5209 SE International Way
Milwaukie, OR 97222
www.bobsredmill.com
800.349.2173

Makers of whole grain, gluten-free flours, cereals and baking mixes.

Bumble Bar

888.453.3369
509.924.2080
3808 N Sullivan Rd
Building 12 Ste 3
Spokane Valley, WA 99216
www.bumblebar.com

Bumble Bar is the first available certified organic energy snack bar! Unlike most candy bars, Bumble Bars are full of ingredients that actually nourish you and are good for your health. There are 8 different bar flavors. All are gluten-free, wheat-free and dairy-free.

'Cause You're Special!

866.NO WHEAT
866.669.4328
715.339.6959
PO Box 316
Phillips, WI 54555
www.CauseYoureSpecial.com
www.GlutenFreeGourmet.com

We make exceptional gluten-free casein-free Gourmet Mixes for Cakes, Breads, Pizza, Pie Crust, Biscuits, Pancakes, Muffins and Cookies.

Chebe Bread Products (Prima Provisions)
800.217.9510
PO Box 991
Newport, VT 05855
www.chebe.com

We offer a choice of dry mixes and oven-ready frozen dough. Our original gluten-free Chebe Bread dry mix is available in individual and food service package sizes. Our Chebe dry mixes for Pizza Crust, Garlic-Onion Breadsticks and Cinnamon Roll-ups are both lactose and gluten-free. Chebe Bread Oven-Ready Frozen Dough Products are available as Bread Sticks, Sandwich Buns, Pizza and Tomato-Basil Rolls.

Chef Aaron, Inc.
714.397.5455
aefteb@sbcglobal.net
www.chefaaron.biz

Chef Aaron Flores is an experienced Special Diet Consultant to restaurants and food manufacturers. His specialized services include developing kitchen and food procurement systems, identifying trouble areas within the operation, guiding and training staff on food allergens and intolerances. He is a consultant for The Gluten-Free Cooking School and supporter of the Gluten Intolerance Group and other national support organization programs and activities. Chef Aaron is dedicated to creating tasty meals for those with food intolerances and food allergies.

Dietary Specialties
888.640.2800
10 Leslie Court
Whippany, NJ 07981
www.dietspec.com

We have been providing gluten-free foods for over 40 years with a wide selection of foods including baking mixes, pastas, fast foods and desserts. Our frozen product line includes fully prepared entrees such as lasagna and chicken nuggets. For the dessert lover, our Pound Cake and Cheesecake will satisfy any sweet tooth! With Dietary Specialties you can enjoy great tasting foods and be confident that your dietary needs are being met.

Dowd and Rogers, Inc.
916.451.6480
1641 49th Street
Sacramento, CA 95819
www.dowdandrogers.com

Manufacturer of premium gluten-free cake mixes made with imported Italian chestnut flour. Direct importer of Italian chestnut flour.

EcoNatural Solutions, Inc.
877.684.5195
303.527.1554
6235 Lookout Rd Ste A
Boulder, CO 80301
www.econaturalsolutions.com

Purely delicious! Enjoy our Organic Sweets, Organic Tarts, Organic Aromatherapy Pastilles Tummy Soothers, Licorice Sweets, Winter Mints, Lemon Drops and more. All are free of GMOs, casein, gluten, dairy, wheat, nuts, eggs, corn and soy.

Edward & Sons Trading Co., Inc.
805.684.8500
Mail: PO Box 1326
Carpinteria, CA 93014
www.edwardandsons.com

Gluten-free, casein-free, dairy-free, soy-free and egg-free products.

Ener-G Foods, Inc.
800.331.5222
5960 First Avenue S
Seattle, WA 98108
www.ener-g.com
A full line of gluten-free products.

Enjoy Life Foods
888.50.ENJOY
773.889.5070
1601 N Natchez Ave
Chicago, IL 60707
www.enjoylifefoods.com

Enjoy Life Foods, is a manufacturer of nutritious ready-made and easy-to-prepare foods that are free of all common allergens. All of our products contain no: gluten, wheat, dairy, casein, egg, soy, peanut, tree nuts, potato, GMOs, hydrogenated oil, or additives. In addition, our foods are vegetarian, and certified kosher by the CRC. We produce everything in a dedicated gluten-free, nut-free facility. Our products include breads, bagels, cereals, cookies, pastas, chocolate chips and snack bars.

Everybody Eats, Inc.
212.491.0020
Mailing: 736 Riverside Dr, 2-G
New York City, NY 10031
Email: everybodyeats@hotmail.com
www.everybodyeats-inc.com

We specialize in foods for those who require a gluten-free diet and wish to savor the same well-loved food combinations and the same tastes and textures that everyone else enjoys. Beautifully prepared, balanced, delicious gluten-free foods are now available for everybody with delivery throughout New York City and also via express mail. Choose and order from our menu of classic standards, children's favorites, and specialty items for daily meals, birthdays, and other occasions. Special party cakes and gluten-free hors d'oeuvres are also available. Please note: there is no retail location at present. All food is delivered or shipped.

Food for Life Baking Company
800.797.5090
951.279.5090
P.O. Box 1434
Corona, CA 92879
www.foodforlife.com

Food For Life offers a wide variety of Wheat & Gluten-Free baked goods including: White Rice Bread, Brown Rice Bread, Rice Almond Bread, Rice Pecan Bread, Raisin Pecan Bread, Bhutanese Red Rice Bread and China Black Rice Bread. All Food For Life products are specifically developed to be moist, flavorful and easy-to use. Food For Life Wheat and Gluten Free breads contain no corn, milk, eggs, preservatives or artificial flavors. Our most recent addition to the Food For Life family is Wheat & Gluten-Free Brown Rice Tortillas—try them served warm with your favorite filling and roll up for a tasty burrito. With just one bite, you'll know they're a food for life! Food For Life products are sold in natural food stores and better supermarkets in The U.S. and Canada.

Fresh & Natural Foods
651.203.3663
1075 West Hwy 96
Shoreview, MN 55126
www.freshnaturalfoods.com

We stock a large assortment of allergen-free and gluten-free items. We also offer freshly made gluten-free Swedish meatballs, meatloaf and sandwiches, as well as frozen foods and cakes. Fresh baked goods by Bittersweet Bakery and Madwoman Foods. Hours: Mon-Sat.9-9pm and Sun. 9-7pm.

Gluten-Free Baking and More
518.279.3884
PO Box 94
Cropseyville, NY 12052
www.glutenfreebaking.com

Gluten-Free Baking and More is <u>The</u> Monthly Ad-Free Newsletter devoted to great tasting gluten-free baking and cooking. Each month new, from-scratch, recipes for breads, muffins, pastries, pasta dishes and more are published in our newsletter. All recipes are tested to ensure your success in the kitchen.

Gluten-Free Cooking Club and School

602.485.8751

Mailing: 4757 E Greenway Rd Ste 107B-#91

Phoenix, AZ 85032

www.glutenfreecookingclub.com

You will enjoy the great recipes, foods and cooking techniques in this gluten-free kitchen. Experienced gluten-free chefs, bakers, and cookbook authors all share their expertise and skills in demonstration or hands-on classes.

Gluten-Free Consulting Services (GFCS)

602.485.8751

www.lynnrae.com

Gluten-Free Consulting Services provides marketing assistance, product line development, representation, menu assistance, column and brochure articles, specialized presentations and speaking engagements to businesses and services catering to the special diet communities.

We also provide individuals with lifestyle coaching, dietary assistance and personal cheffing through our network of service providers.

Gluten-Free Living

914.741.5420

19A Broadway

Hawthorne, NY 10532

info@glutenfreeliving.com

www.glutenfreeliving.com

Gluten-Free Living is the national magazine for people who have celiac disease and follow a gluten-free diet. The writers and editors live with celiac disease and understand the challenges of the gluten-free lifestyle. *Gluten-Free Living*'s pages are all devoted to celiac disease. You will find articles that help you really understand the gluten-free diet and keep you up-to-date on the latest news about people, products, medicine, research, legislation and lifestyle related to celiac disease.

Gluten-Free Mall, The
Your Special Diet Superstore!
www.glutenfreemall.com

A huge selection of the best quality, top selling gluten-free products which can be shipped anywhere in the United States in a single, convenient delivery. www.celiac.com – A celiac disease and gluten-free diet resource since 1995.

Gluten-Free Pantry
800.291.8386
860.633.3826
82 Oakwood Drive
Glastonbury, CT 06033
www.glutenfreepantry.com

We carry a wide array of delicious gluten-free and wheat-free gourmet baking mixes, prepared rolls, breads and baguettes, cookies, snacks, cakes, pasta, vitamins, convenience and prepared meals, baking supplies, 'baking from scratch' ingredients, condiments, cookbooks, reference books, gluten-free skin care products, gluten-free recipes and much more. You can order on line or by calling. Our Order desk is happy to help you.

Gluten Solutions
888.845.8836
www.glutensolutions.com

We offer over 300 gluten-free wheat-free and many casein-free foods, and specialize in hard to find products that taste great. Gluten Solutions—wheat-free groceries at your doorstep.

Grainaissance, Inc.
800.472.4697
1580 62nd Street
Emeryville, CA 94608
www.grainaissance.com

Healthy and delicious dairy-free gluten-free shakes. All natural wheat-free and gluten-free Mochi, a bake and serve rice snack. Smooth and creamy non-dairy and gluten-free pudding with no added sweeteners.

Grassroots Baking Company
503.293.6025
Portland, OR 97219
www.grassrootsbakingcompany.com

Special orders accepted for fresh baked items made in a gluten-free environment. Our products may be found in Portland at the Corbett Fish House, Bob's Redmill Kitchen and Market of Choice. Look for freshly baked cookies, mini pies, bars, breads and the best cheesecake. Fresh baked gluten-free pizza using our crust is available at Talarico's Mercado. A complete listing of our special order items is available on our web or by calling us.

Madwoman Foods
612.728.2679
P.O. Box 14900
Minneapolis, MN 55414
www.madwomanfoods.com

Gourmet Tea Cakes and frozen pizzas in several delectable varieties, hand made in our gluten-free kitchens. We use only the finest natural ingredients, organic and locally produced whenever possible, and all our products are naturally high in nutrition and low in carbohydrates. Visit our website for more information and how to order.

Manna from Anna
Gluten Evolution, LLC
319-354-3886
612 Hwy 1 West
Iowa City, IA 52246
www.glutenevolution.com

"This tastes and feels like wheat bread!" That's what most people say after they have baked up a loaf of Manna from Anna™ bread mix. Order on line, by phone or find our mixes at your local store. If they do not carry the Manna from Anna™ gluten-free bread mixes, either the dairy-free or regular, ask them to order it in for you.

Marlene's Mixes
903.839.3892
PO Box 182
Whitehouse, TX 75791
www.marlenesmixes.com

Marlene's Mixes is a company that produces wheat-free, gluten-free, and potato-free mixes. Everyone raves about our stuffing, hush puppies, bread, muffins and dessert mixes. Order mixes by e-mail or on-line. Mixes are available in a variety of stores.

Masuya (USA) Inc.
916.979.7872
3550 Watt Ave Ste 140
Sacramento, CA 95821
www.masuyanaturally.com

Masuya Rice Sembei Snacks ® Flavors include: Dijon Mustard, Sun Dried Tomato and Cheese, Tamari and Original (lightly salted).

Matter of Flax, LLC
888.541.3529
888.541.FLAX
P.O. Box 12170
Prescott, AZ 86304
www.mattcrofflax.com

Matter of Flax, LLC produces handmade all organic, wheat-free, gluten-free, sprouted raw food snacks. We use the finest whole and ground flaxseed as the foundation for our savory and fruity Whole Life Flax Krisps, making it high in Omega 3 Essential Fatty Acids. Our simple and effective production methods create a healthy new whole food snack that is "Alive with Wellness."

Miss Roben's, Inc.
800.891.0083
301.665.9580
91 Western Maryland Pkwy #7
Hagerstown, MD 21740
www.allergygrocer.com

Miss Roben's, Inc. is known for our customer service, baking and technical support network. Our products and experience cater to multiple food issues as well as the less common ones. At Miss Roben's, our favorite words are, "How can we help you?"

Namaste Foods
866.258.9493
208.676.9632
PO Box 3133
Coeur d'Alene, ID 83816
www.namastefoods.com

Easy to make mixes for: Brownies, blondies, waffles, pancakes (sugar free), muffins, chocolate cake, vanilla cake, pizza crust (sugar and yeast free), cookies spice/carrot cake, sugar-free muffins.

Nature's Hilights, Inc.
800.313.6454
1608-A West 5th St
PO Box 3526
Chico, CA 95927

Gluten-free frozen pizza made in dedicated facility. Look for us in natural food stores.

Nu-World Amaranth, Inc.
877.692.8899
630.369.6819
PO Box 2202
Naperville, IL 60567
www.nuworldfamily.com

Nu-World Amaranth, Inc. under its brand name Nu-World Foods, features nutritious and delicious organic and all natural amaranth food products, free of all common food allergens for gluten-free, casein-free, allergenic and health conscious folks. We offer Puffed Amaranth, Amaranth Bread Crumbs, Toasted Amaranth Bran Flour, Amaranth Seeds, Amaranth Cereals and Snacks.

Nutrition Studio
602.569.3509
Phoenix, AZ
Email: stephanie@nutritionstudio.com
www.nutritionstudio.com

Nutrition Studio offers a full menu of consulting services including culinary and wellness programs, speaking engagements, and recipe development and testing.

P.F. Chang's China Bistro
866.PFCHANG
866.732.4264
www.pfchangs.com

For locations call us or visit our website. Locations also listed in the back of this book.

Serving lunch and dinner daily from 11 am. Gluten-free friendly menu on website and in restaurants.

Menu features traditional Chinese cuisine.

Inform your server about any food allergens or intolerances prior to ordering.

Pam's Celiac Kitchen
201.230.9292
61 Roosevelt St
Pequannock, NJ 07440
www.celiackitchen.com

"Delicious gluten-free meals delivered right to your door!" Pam's Celiac Kitchen offers a wide variety of gluten-free meals, desserts and snacks that are great for any occasion. Whether you are buying for yourself or purchasing a gift, we pride ourselves on providing the freshest, highest quality product possible. The best part about our meals is that you'll never know the gluten is missing!

Pamela's Products, Inc.
707.462.6605
200 Clara Ave
Ukiah, CA 95482
www.pamelasproducts.com
info@pamelasproducts.com

Pamela's Products is known for our decadent gourmet cookies, biscotti, and baking mixes. Everything is wheat-free, most are gluten-free and many are organic. Items are available in grocery and natural food stores nationwide in the USA, Canada and on line. Check our website for listings.

Pei Wei Asian Diner
For locations visit
www.peiwei.com

Gluten-free menu on website and in restaurants. Locations also in the back of this book. Dine in or Take Away Pei Wei serves great tasting Asian dishes made-to-order and served hot from the wok to the table.

Rizopia Food Products
866.749.6742
4490 Sheppard Ave E, Unit 13
Toronto, Ontario, Canada M1S 4J9
www.rizopia.com
Rizopia Rice Pastas are ideal foods for everyone, everywhere. They are nutritious, easy to digest and tasty. Add variety in your meals using our 8 different styles of brown, white or wild rice spaghetti, fettuccine, fusilli, spirals, shells, elbows, penne or radiatore.

Saz's BBQ Products and State House Restaurant
414.453.2410
5539 West State St
Milwaukee, WI 53208
www.sazs.com
Our delicious barbeque sauces are gluten-free: Saz's BBQ Sauce (Original, Sassy and Vidalia Onion.) Our pre-prepared gluten-free meals include Saz's BBQ Pork, Saz's BBQ Chicken and Saz's BBQ Ribs.

Sylvan Border Farm
707.459.1854
P.O. Box 277
Willits, CA 95490
www.sylvanborderfarm.com
Sylvan Border Farm mixes are a blend of light and nutritious flours with excellent baking properties. We market a General Purpose Flour, Pancake & Waffle Mix, Lemon Cake Mix, and three Bread mixes—White Bread, Classic Dark Bread, and a Non-Dairy Bread Mix.

Thaifoon Restaurants

Neighborhood restaurants in Arizona, California and Utah
www.thaifoon.com

Thaifoon serves fresh Asian cuisine in a vibrant yet casual atmosphere. The moderately priced menu features cuisines from all over Asia, with distinctive signature entrees such as Lettuce Wraps, Sizzling Beef, Evil Jungle Princess and Mango Chicken. Thaifoon is also the winner of the 2004 Hot Concepts Award from *Nation's Restaurant News*.

The Garden of Eating

602.840.4556
PO Box 97040
Phoenix, AZ 85060-7040
ChefRachel@thegardenofeatingdiet.com
www.thegardenofeatingdiet.com

Chef Rachel Albert-Matesz is a food and health writer, cooking instructor, cooking coach, personal chef, and co-author of *THE GARDEN OF EATING: A Produce-Dominated Diet & Cookbook*. Her cheffing services, classes, and recipes cater to the needs of people who want healthy food or need to avoid wheat, gluten, dairy, corn, soy, eggs, peanuts, or other common allergens. For more information about her book or services visit her website.

Trigone, Inc.

418.259.7414
93 Aqueduc St
St-Francois, Quebec Canada GOR 3A0

Our major gluten-free products include Hulled Buckwheat Groats, Buckwheat Porridge, Buckwheat Flour and Hemp Nuts (shelled hemp seeds).

U.S. Mills, Inc.
800.422.1125
200 Reservoir Street
Needham, MA 02494
www.usmillsinc.com

We believe it is important for people with gluten sensitivity to be able to find great tasting food products that fit their dietary needs. That is why we work hard to offer a variety of great tasting gluten-free cereals that appeal to both adults and children.

Van's International Foods
310.320.8611
20318 Gramercy Place
Torrance, CA 90501
www.vansintl.com

Our wheat-free waffles combine a delicious blend of brown rice flour, potato starch flour and sweet rice flour. They are great tasting, as well as light and crisp, gluten-free, vegan (eggless and dairy-free), yeast-free and fruit-juice sweetened. Find them in your local Natural Food Store and Supermarkets.

Water To Go Diet & Nutrition Center
Corporate Headquarters
800.976.9283
702.895.9350
702.895.9306 fax
5160 S. Valley View Blvd Ste 100
Las Vegas, NV 89118
www.watertogo.com

Water To Go Diet & Nutritional Centers are the industry leader in offering purified water sold by the gallon, vitamins and wellness resources in a one-stop shop. Our Diet & Nutrition Centers supply products that are low-carb, gluten-free, sugar-free, lactose-free, and cholesterol-free. Today we have more than 100 stores in the United States and Canada. We are proud to offer specialty products to meet the needs of those who live a gluten-free lifestyle.

Z'Tejas Southwestern Grill
www.ztejas.com
11 restaurants in the United States

Z' Tejas sets itself apart by being a chef-and-food driven restaurant company committed to creating bold new combinations with traditional ingredients originating from the south, southwest and West Coast, and takes pride in its Southwestern cuisine influenced by these areas as a true culinary experience.

Special Sponsors

- Aspire Markets
- Authentic Foods
- Chēbē Bread
- Enjoy Life Foods
- Food for Life
- Gluten-Free Living
- U.S. Mills
- Water To Go Diet & Nutrition Center
- Biaggi's
- P.F. Chang's China Bistro
- Pei Wei Asian Diner

Aspire Markets, Inc.
16455 N. Scottsdale Rd, Suite 107
Scottsdale, AZ 85254
www.aspiremarkets.com
info@aspiremarkets.com
480.348.9124

At **Aspire Markets**, we believe that it's not what you can't eat that counts, it's what you can.

We carry freshly prepared gourmet meals and bakery items for all dietary needs, as well as an international selection of foods and ingredients to tempt the most discerning palate. Our philosophy of catering to you, whatever diet your on, is seen in everything we do…

You'll Never Have To Read Another Label…

Or consult another chart. We've done it for you. In fact, we've scoured the world for the best and most delicious foods on your diet and then assembled them all in one store. What's more, each diet gets its own symbol. So, you know instantly what's right for you.

Or Cook Another Meal.

In addition to our international selection of gourmet products, we offer prepared meals so delicious they would tempt people who aren't on a diet. From a snack to an entire meal, we cater to your needs.

Diets Are No Excuse For Eating Bad Food.

Don't think we've neglected dessert. In our Sweet Indulgences Department, you'll find the perfect end to a meal or the beginning of a life-long passion for our freshly baked pastries and confections.

Food For Thought:

Every **Aspire Market** has a concierge. These friendly, knowledgeable people are there to help you. They may even be on the same diet. So, whether you want to lose weight or manage your health, they can answer your questions and direct you to the right foods.

Enjoy…

Think of **Aspire Markets** as a theme park for your taste buds—and the theme is diets. Any diet. Imagine enjoying great food and still being able to stay on your program. Including:

*Low Calorie * Gluten Free * Low Carb * Lactose Free * High Fiber
Sugar Free * Low Fat * Low Sodium * Diabetic * And more*

Remember, it's not what you can't eat, it's what you can.
Follow your diet to **ASPIRE MARKETS**

Authentic Foods

Manufacturer of Gluten-Free & Wheat Free Products

For Your Health,
All Products at Authentic Foods
are Manufactured
in a Gluten-Free Environment!

Authentic Foods specializes in all your Gluten-free baking needs. Our facilities blend only the freshest, gluten-free ingredients to ensure the best products for our customers. Our flours are ground to a superfine texture for a light delicious cakes and breads.

At Authentic Foods we produce an assortment of flours and baking mixes for your enjoyment and convenience. Our line of cake mixes are made from our special Garfava Flour (specialty processed and blended garbanzo and fava beans) and brown rice flour for a delicious and protein-rich diet—beans area natural aid in the protection fo liver function as well as controlling diabetes

We also feature flour blends created by Bette Hagmar, author of the Gluten-Free Gourmet series. Recreate Bette's recipes or try your own with Bette's Flour Flour Blend ard Bette's Featherlight Rice Flour Blend. Be good to yourself and pick up an Authentic Foods product today!

Product List

Baking Supplies

Bette's Gourmet Four Flour Blend
Bette's Gourmet Featherlight Rice Flour
Garfava Flour
Garbanzo Flour
Brown Rice Flour-Superfine
White Rice Flour-Superfine
Sweet Rice Flour-Superfine
White Corn Flour
Corn Starch
Tapioca Flour
Potato Flour
Potato Starch
Sorghum Flour
Arrowroot Flour
Xanthan Gum
Guar Gum
Dough Enhancer (Dairy Free)
Vanilla Powder
Maple Sugar
Almond Meal

Baking Mixes

Pancake & Baking Mix
Bread Mix (Homestyle)
Cinnamon Bread Mix
Chocolate Cake Mix
Vanilla Cake Mix
Lemon Cake Mix
Blueberry Muffin Mix
Pie Crust Mix
Pizza Crust Mix
Falafel Mix

For more information: toll free: 1-800-806-4737 or 310-366-7612 Fax: 310-966-6938
Web site: www.authenticfoods.com Email: sales@authenticfoods.com

How much
do you
know
about the
gluten-free
diet?

Gluten-Free Living
will keep you informed!

Subscribe today!
19A Broadway, Hawthorne, NY 10532
(914) 741-5420
info@glutenfreeliving.com
www.glutenfreeliving.com

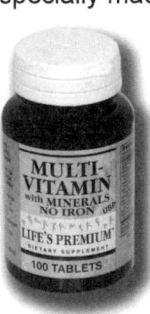

Biaggi's Locations

Colorado

1805 Briargate Parkway
Colorado Springs, CO 80920
719.262.9500

Illinois

1501 N Veterans Pkwy
Bloomington, IL 61704
309.661.8322

2235 S Neil Street
Champaign, IL 61820
217.356.4300

20560 North Rand Road
Deer Park, IL 60010
847.438.1850

Indiana

16401 E Lloyd Expressway
Suite #3
Evansville, IN 47715
812.421.0800
4010 W Jefferson Blvd
Fort Wayne, IN 46804
260.459.6700

Iowa

320 Collins Rd NE
Cedar Rapids, IA 52402
319.393.6594

5195 Utica Ridge Road
Davenport, IA 52807
563.344.2103

5990 University Avenue
West Des Moines, IA 50266
515.221.9900

Minnesota

8251 Flying Cloud Dr #3010
Eden Prairie, MN 55344
952.942.8555

12051 Elm Creek Blvd
Maple Grove, MN 55369
763.416.2225

Nebraska

13655 California St
Omaha, NE 68154
402.965.9800

New York

818 Eastview Mall
Victor, NY 14564
585.223.2290

North Carolina

1060 Darrington Drive
Cary, NC 27513
919.468.7229

Utah

194 South 400 West
Salt Lake City, UT 84101
801.596.7222

Wisconsin

601 Junction Road
Madison, WI 53717
608.664.9288

RECOMMENDATIONS FOR GLUTEN INTOLERANT DIETS

ASK YOUR SERVER FOR THESE SUBSTITUTIONS

CHANG'S CHICKEN IN SOOTHING LETTUCE WRAPS
With our Gluten Free Sauce.

SHANGHAI CUCUMBERS 素
With wheat free soy sauce.

ORIENTAL CHICKEN SALAD
Without wonton strips.

GINGER CHICKEN AND BROCCOLI - STEAMED
With our Gluten Free Sauce.

CANTONESE SHRIMP OR SCALLOPS

PHILIP'S BETTER LEMON CHICKEN

火 CHANG'S SPICY CHICKEN OR SHRIMP

CHANG'S LEMON SCALLOPS

MOO GOO GAI PAN

SHRIMP WITH LOBSTER SAUCE

火 MANGO CHICKEN

STEAMED FISH OF THE DAY
With wheat free soy sauce.

CANTONESE CHOW FUN*
Substitute in rice "stick" noodles and our Gluten Free Sauce.

火 SINGAPORE STREET NOODLES*
Substitute our Gluten Free Sauce for the Singapore sauce.

SPINACH STIR-FRIED WITH GARLIC* 素

GARLIC SNAP PEAS* 素

BUDDHA'S FEAST - STEAMED* 素

P.F. Chang's Gluten Free Sauce contains garlic, ginger, rice wine, chicken stock, Sichuan pepper, salt, sugar and wheat free soy sauce.

---

*Marinated chicken, shrimp, scallops or calamari can be added to these dishes. These marinades contain cornstarch.

火 *Spicy* 素 *Vegetarian*   *Products containing gluten are prepared in our kitchens.*

Waiter, Is there Wheat in My Soup? 331

P.F. Chang's China Bistro Locations

Alabama

233 Summit Blvd
Birmingham
205.967.0040

Arizona

3255 W Chandler Blvd
Chandler
480.899.0472

16170 N. 83rd Ave
Peoria
623.412.3335

7014 E Camelback Rd
Scottsdale
480.949.2610

7132 E Greenway Pkwy
Scottsdale
480.367.2999

740 S Mill Ave
Tempe
480.731.4600

1805 E. River Rd
Tucson
520.615.8788

California

201 E. Magnolia Blvd
Burbank
818.391.1070

2041 Rosecrans Ave
El Segundo
310.607.9062

61 Fortune Dr
Irvine
949.453.1211

340 S Pine Ave
Long Beach
562.308.1025

121 N. La Cienega Blvd
Los Angeles
310.854.6467

800 the Shops at Mission Viejo
Mission Viejo
949.364.6661

1145 Newport Ctr Dr
Newport Beach
949.759.9007

900 Stanford Shopping Ctr
Palo Alto
650.330.1782

260 E. Colorado Blvd
Pasadena
626.356.9760

71800 Highway 111
Rancho Mirage
760.776.4912

1180 Galleria Blvd
Roseville
916.788.2800

1530 J. Street
Sacramento
916.288.0970

7077 Friars Rd
San Diego
619.260.8484

4540 La Jolla Village Dr
San Diego
858.458.9007

98 S. Second St
San Jose
408.961.5250

326 Wilshire Blvd
Santa Monica
310.395.1912

15301 Ventura Blvd
Sherman Oaks
818.784.1694

390 W El Camino Real
Sunnyvale
408.991.9078

1205 Broadway Plaza
Walnut Creek
925.979.9070

21821 Oxnard St
Woodland Hills
818.340.0491

5633 Bay St
Emeryville
510.879.0990

Colorado

1 W Flatiron Circle
Broomfield
720.887.6200

1725 Briargate Pkwy
Colorado Springs
719.593.8580

1415 15th Street
Denver
303.260.7222

7210 W. Alameda Ave.
Lakewood
303.922.5800

8315 S. Park Meadows Ctr Dr
Littleton
303.790.7744

Florida

1400 Glades Rd
Boca Raton
561.393.3722

8888 SW 136th Street
Miami
305.234.2338

17455 Biscayne Blvd
N. Miami Beach
305.957.1966

10840 Tamiami Trail North
Naples
239.596.2174

4200 Conroy Rd
Orlando
407.345.2888

3101 PGA Boulevard
Palm Beach Gardens
561.691.1610

219 Westshore Plaza
Tampa
813.289.8400

436 N Orlando Ave
Winter Park
407.622.0188

Georgia
7925 N. Point Pkway
Alpharetta
770.992.3070

500 Ashwood Pkwy
Atlanta
770.352.0500

3333 Buford Drive
Buford
678.546.9005

Iowa
110 S. Jordan Creek Pkwy
West Des Moines
515.457.7772

Illinois
530 N. Wabash Ave
Chicago
312.828.9977

2361 Fountain Square Dr
Lombard
630.652.9977

1819 Lake Cook Rd
Northbrook
847.509.8844

Indiana
49 W Maryland St
Indianapolis
317.974.5747

8601 Keystone Crossing
Indianapolis
317.815.8773

Kansas
1401 Waterfront Pkwy
Wichita
316.634.2211

Louisiana
3301 Veterans Memorial Blvd
Metairie
504.828.5288

Massachusetts
8 Park Plaza
Boston
617.573.0821

Maryland
11301 Rockville Pike
N. Bethesda
301.230.6933

10300 Little Patuxent Pkwy
Columbia
410.730.5344

Michigan
2425 Lake Lansing Rd
Lansing
517.267.3833

17905 Haggerty Rd
Northville Township
248.675.0066

2801 W. Big Beaver Rd
Troy
248.816.8000

Minnesota
2700 S Southdale Center
Edina
952.926.1713

12071 Elm Creek Blvd
Maple Grove
763.493.9377

Missouri
1295 Chesterfield Pkwy E
Chesterfield
636.532.0215

102 W. 47th St
Kansas City
816.931.9988

North Carolina
6809–F Phillips Place Court
Charlotte
704.552.6644

6801 Fayetteville Rd
Durham
919.294.3131

4325 Glenwood Ave
Raleigh
919.787.7754

Nebraska
10150 California St
Omaha
402.390.6021

New Jersey
2801 N. Pacific Ave #101
Atlantic City
609.348.4600

500 Rte 73 South
Marlton
856.396.0818

10 Port Imperial Blvd
West NY
201.866.7790

New Mexico
4440 The 25th Way, NE
Albuquerque
505.344.8282

Nevada
101 So Green Valley Pkwy
Henderson
702.361.3065

4165 S. Paradise Rd
Las Vegas
702.792.2207

1095 So Rampart Blvd
Las Vegas
702.968.8885

3667 Las Vegas Blvd
South Las Vegas
702.836.0955

5180 S. Kietzke Lane
Reno
775.825.9800

New York

820 Eastview Mall
Victor
585.223.2410

1504 Old Country Rd
Westbury
516.222.9200

125 Westchester Ave
White Plains
914.997.6100

Ohio

26001 Chagrin Blvd
Beachwood
216.292.1411

4040 Townsfair Way
Columbus
614.416.4100

6135 Parkcenter Circle
Dublin
614.726.0070

2633 Edmondson Rd
Norwood
513.531.4567

9435 Civic Center Blvd
West Chester
513.779.5555

Oklahoma

1978 Utica Square
Tulsa
918.747.6555

Oregon

19320 NW Emma Way
Hillsboro
503.533.4580

1139 NW Couch St
Portland
503.432.4000

Pennsylvania

983 Baltimore Pike
Glen Mills
610.545.3030

148 W Bridge St
West Homestead
412.464.0640

Tennessee

439 Cool Springs Blvd
Franklin
615.503.9640

6741 Kingston Pike
Knoxville
865.212.5514

1181 Ridgeway Rd
Memphis
901.818.3889

2525 West End
Nashville
615.329.8901

Texas

10114 Jollyville Rd
Austin
512.231.0208

201 San Jacinto Blvd
Austin
512.457.8300

18323 No Dallas Pkwy
Dallas
972.818.3336

225 NorthPark Center
Dallas
214.265.8669

760 Sunland Park Dr
El Paso
915.845.0166

400 Throckmorton
Ft. Worth
817.840.2450

650 Highway 114
Grapevine
817.421.6658

4094 Westheimer Rd
Houston
713.627.7220

11685 Westheimer Rd
Houston
281.920.3553

255 E Basse Rd
San Antonio
210.507.1000

2120 Lone Star Dr
Sugarland
281.313.8650

1201 Lake Woodlands Dr
The Woodlands
281.203.6350

Utah

575 E University Parkway
Orem
801.426.0900

174 W 300 South
Salt Lake City
801.539.0500

Virginia

4250 Fairfax Corner Ave
Fairfax
703.266.2414

1716M International Dr
McLean
703.734.8996

9212 Stony Point
Richmond
804.253.0492

4551 Virginia Beach Blvd
Virginia Beach
757.473.9028

Washington

525 Bellevue Square
Bellevue
425.637.3582

3000 184th St.
Lynnwood
425.921.2100

400 Pine Street
Seattle
206.393.0070

Wisconsin

2500 N Mayfair Rd
Wauwatosa
414.607.1029

Pei Wei Asian Diner Locations

www.peiwei.com

Arizona

7131 W Ray Rd
Chandler
480.940.3800

1085 W. Queen Creek Rd
Chandler
480.812.2230

14835 E Shea Blvd
Fountain Hills
480.837.0926

1084 So Gilbert
Gilbert
480.926.9749

20022 N 67th Ave
Glendale
623.825.9949

3426 E Baseline Rd
Mesa
480.539.4454

4340 E. Indian School Rd
Phoenix
602.956.2300

742 E Glendale
Phoenix
602.707.0049

8787 N Scottsdale Rd
Scottsdale
480.365.6000

20851 N Scottsdale Rd
Scottsdale
480.365.6002

32607 N. Scottsdale Rd
Scottsdale
480.488.8630

845 E University Blvd
Tucson
520.884.7413

5285 E Broadway Blvd
Tucson
520.514.7004

California

1560-A Leucadia Blvd
Encinitas
760.635.2888

5781 Alton Pkwy
Irvine
949.857.8700

1302 Bison Ave
Newport Beach
949.629.1000

3455 E Foothill Blvd
Pasadena
626.325.9020

10341 Fairway Dr
Roseville
916.724.0080

24250 Valencia Blvd
Santa Clarita
661.600.0132

2777 Pacific Coast Hwy
Torrance
310.517.9366

Colorado

200 Quebec St
Denver
720.532.5999

University Park
Ranch
303.346.4329

7148 N Academy Blvd
Springs
719.260.9922

New Mexico

2201 Louisiana Blvd NE
Albuquerque
505.883.1570

Nevada
1311 W Sunset Rd
Henderson
702.898.6730

Oklahoma

5954 S Yale Ave
Tulsa
918.497.1015

Texas

4801 Beltline Rd
Addison
972.764.0844

1008 W McDermott Dr
Allen
469.675.2266

4133 E Cooper St
Arlington
817.466.4545

3412 E Hebron Pkwy
Carrollton
972.407.0056

19411-A Gulf Freeway
Clear Lake
281.554.9876

18204 Preston Rd
Dallas
972.985.0090

3001 Knox St
Dallas
214.219.0000

8305 Westchester Dr
Dallas
214.765.9911

11700 Preston Rd
Dallas
214.765.0030

City View Shopping Center
Fort Worth
817.294.0808

5110 Buffalo Speedway
Houston
713.661.0900

5203 FM 1960 West
Houston
281.885.5430

1005 Waugh Street
Houston
713.353.7366

7600 N Mac Arthur Blvd
Irving
972.373.8000

1590 S Mason Rd
Katy
281.392.1410

702 Kingwood Dr
Kingwood
281.318.2877

713 Hebron Pkwy
Lewisville
469.948.9000

1802 N. Loop, 1604 East
San Antonio
210.507.9160

19075 I.H. 45 S
Shenandoah
936.321.1153

1582 E Southlake Blvd
Southlake
817.722.0070

16101 Kensington Dr
Sugar Land
281.240.1931

Utah

1028 E 2100 So
Salt Lake City
801.907.2030

Contributors

Contributors

Annotated Bibliography

The information for this book was compiled from numerous interviews, conversations, internet searches, books, magazines and newspapers. From the hundreds of books reviewed, below are some of my favorites.

Trang, Corinne. *Authentic Vietnamese Cooking*. New York: Simon & Schuster, 1999

Pham, Mai. *Pleasures of the Vietnamese Table*. New York: HarperCollins Publishers, 2001

Sterling, Richard. *World Food Vietnam*. Australia: Lonely Planet Publications, 2000

The Food of Vietnam. Periplus World Cookbooks

My Tran, Diana. *The Vietnamese Cookbook*. Virginia: Capital Books, Inc., 2000

Solomon, Charmaine. *Encyclopedia of Asian Food*. Massachusetts: Periplus Editions Ltd, 1998

Brennan, Jennifer. *The Cuisines of Asia*. New York: St. Martin's Press, 1984

Morgan, Lane. *The Ethnic Market Food Guide*. New York: Berkeley Publishing Group, 1997

Herbst, Sharon. *Food Lover's Companion*. New York, Barron's Educational Series, 1995

Von Welanetz, Diana and Paul. *The Von Welanetz Guide to Ethnic Ingredients*. New York, Warner Books, 1982

Mariani, John. *The Encyclopedia of American Food & Drink*. New York, Lebhar-Friedman Books, 1999

Jue, Joyce. *Savoring Southeast Asia*. California, Weldon Owen, 2000

McDermott, Nancie. *Real Thai.* San Francisco, Chronicle Books, 1999

Cummings, Joe. *World Food Thailand.* Australia: Lonely Planet Publications, 2000

Labensky, Sarah R. *On Cooking: Techniques from Expert Chefs.* New Jersey, Pearson Education, Inc. 2003

Ingram, Christine. *Cooking Ingredients.* New York, Hermes House, 2002

Clements, Carole. *Cook's Companion.* New York, Hermes House, 2001

Gissen, Wayne. *Professional Cooking,* New York, John Wiley & Sons, 2003

Batmanglij, Najmieh. *A Taste of Persia.* Mage Publications, 2003

Bladholm, Linda. *Latin & Caribbean Grocery Stores Demystified.* Los Angeles, Renaissance Books, 2001

Cost, Bruce. *Asian Ingredients.* New York, Harper Collins Publishers, 2000

Dorrenburg, Andres. *Becoming a Chef.* New York John Wiley & Sons, 2003

Resources

American Dietetic Association (ADA)
800.877.1600
120 South Riverside Plaza
Suite 2000
Chicago, IL 60606
www.eatright.org

Food Allergy & Anaphylaxis Network
800-929-4040
Fax: 703-691-2713
11781 Lee Jackson Hwy,
Suite 160
Fairfax, VA 22033
www.foodallergy.org

American Celiac Society (ACS)
504.737.3293
PO Box 23455
New Orleans, LA 70183
Email:
Amerceliacsoc@onebox.com

Canadian Celiac Association (CCA)
800.363.7296
Fax: 905.507.4673
5170 Dixie Rd, Ste 104
Mississauga, ON,
Canada L4W 1E3
www.celiac.ca

Celiac Disease Foundation (CDF)
818.990.2354
Fax: 818.990.2379
13251 Ventura Blvd Ste 1
Studio City, CA 91604-1838
www.celiac.org

Celiac Sprue Association/USA, Inc. (CSA)
877.242.4272
Fax: 402.558.1347
P.O. Box 31700
Omaha, NE 68131
www.csaceliacs.org

Gluten Intolerance Group of North America (GIG)
206.246.6652
Fax: 206.246.6531
15110-10th Ave. SW, Suite A
Seattle, WA 98166
www.gluten.net

Additional Resources

Living Without Magazine focuses on living with allergies and other sensitivities. It may be found in many natural food stores, and is available for ordering on line or phone

Living Without Inc.

847.480.8810   www.livingwithout.com

Gluten-Free Living is a national magazine for people who have celiac disease and follow a gluten-free diet. It is available by ordering on line, by mail or fax. See Sponsors page.

Gluten-Free Living Magazine

Fax: 914.747.4344   www.glutenfreeliving.com

The Clan Thompson website offers pocket guides and databases for gluten-free food lists, prescriptions and over the counter drugs. Visit them at www.clanthompson.com.

Internet: The internet is a wonderful tool. When viewing or discussing a health issue—or any issue on the internet, it is to your benefit to always consider how up to date the information is, the source and if personal opinion or verifiable information is being presented. Many of the sites are available through the National Support Organizations, the magazines listed above or by typing gluten-free or casein-free in a search engine.

Books: Whether you are at a library, a bookstore or on the internet, you will find a large array of books on your special dietary need. Type key words into the search engines or ask at the Reference Desk.

References for Gluten Intolerant Medical Conditions

Fasano, A., *Celiac disease: the past, the present, the future.* Pediatrics, 2001. **107**: p. 769-770.

Pietzak, M.M., Catassi, C. , Drago, S., Fornaroli, F., Fasano, A., *Celiac disease: going against the grains.* Nutrition in Clinical Practice, 2001. **16**(6): p. 335-44.

Cook, M.L., & Tutwiler, H.L., *Common errors in diagnosing celiac disease in adults.* Physician Assistant, 2001. **25**(3): p. 45-8, 51-2.

Fasano, A., Catassi, C., *Current approaches to diagnosis and treatment of celiac disease: An evolving spectrum.* Gastroenterology, 2001. **120**(3): p. 636-651.

Fasano, A., Berti, I., Gerarduzzi, T., Not, T., Colletti, R.B., Drago, S., Elitsur, Y., Green, R.H.R., Guandalin, S., Hill, I.D., Pietzak, M., Ventura, A., Thorpe, M., Kryszak, D., Fornaroli, F., Wasserman, S.S., Murray, J.A., Horvath, K., *Prevalence of Celiac Disease in At-Risk and Not-At-Risk Groups in the United States: A Large Multicenter Study.* Archives of Internal Medicine, 2003. **163**(3): p. 286-292.

Farrell, R.J., Kelly, C.P., *Current Concepts: Celiac Sprue.* The New England Journal of Medicine, 2002. **346**(3): p. 180-88.

Biagi, F., Corazza, G., *Clinical features of coeliac disease.* Digestive and Liver Disease, 2002. **34**(3): p. 225-8.

Ryan BM, K.D., *Refractory celiac disease.* Gastroenterology, 2000. **119**: p. 243-251.

Cellier C, D.E., Helmer C, et al, *Refractory sprue, coeliac disease, and enteropathy-associated T-cell lymphoma.* Lancet, 2000. **356**: p. 203-208.

Hallert, C., Grant, C., Grehn, S., Granno, C., Hulten, S, Midhagen, G., Strom, S., Svensson, H., Valdimarsson, T., *Evidence of poor vitamin status in coeliac patients on a gluten-free diet for 10 years.* Alimentary Pharmacology & Therapeutics, 2002. **16**(7): p. 1333-9.

References for The Gluten-Casein Free Diet

White, JF. Intestinal Pathophysiology in Autism. Experimental Biology and Medicine 228:639-649, 2003.

Millward C, Ferriter M, Calver S, Connell-Jones, G. Gluten- and Casein free diets for autistic spectrum disorder. Cochran Database Syst Rev. 2004 (2): CD003498, 2004.

Understanding and Implementing a Gluten; Casein Free Diet. Autism Research Unit of the University of Sunderland (Great Britain). 1994. www.enabling.org/ia/celiac/aut/autintro.html Accessed Oct 7, 2004

Arnold GL, Hyman SL, Mooney RA, Kirby RS. Plasma amino acids profiles in children with autism: potential nutritional deficiencies. J Autism Dev Disorder. 33(4):449-54.

Manual of Clinical Dietetics: Sixth Edition. (Chicago, IL, American Dietetic Association, 2000).

Common Food Allergens. May 12, 2004 The Food and Allergy Anaphylaxis Network. Accessed Oct 6, 2004.

Personalized Dining Out Notes

Dining Out Notes for (name) _____
Intolerances/Allergens_____

Dining Out Notes

Restaurant name: _____

Address: _____

Hours:_____

Phone Number: _____

Web site: _____

Type of food: _____

Item(s) ordered:_____

_____

Changes made: _____

_____

Comments: For instance, waitperson name, how pleased you were with the meal, reminders to yourself on how you would change your order next time: _____

_____

If you would like to share this information with others through the update or next edition of this book, please complete the Submittal form or send above information to What No Wheat Publishing, 4757 E. Greenway Road, Ste 107B-#91, Phoenix, AZ 85032.

We look forward to building a network of 'Friendly Restaurants' with you.

LynnRae Ries

Personalized Dining Out Notes

Dining Out Notes for (name) _____
Intolerances/Allergens_____

Restaurant name: _____

Address: _____

Hours:_____

Phone Number: _____

Web site: _____

Type of food: _____

Item(s) ordered:_____

_____

Changes made: _____

_____

Comments: For instance, waitperson name, how pleased you were with the meal, reminders to yourself on how you would change your order next time: _____

_____

If you would like to share this information with others through the update or next edition of this book, please complete the Submittal form or send above information to What No Wheat Publishing, 4757 E. Greenway Road, Ste 107B - #91, Phoenix, AZ 85032.

We look forward to building a network of 'Friendly Restaurants' with you.

LynnRae Ries

Personalized Dining Out Notes

Dining Out Notes for (name) _____
Intolerances/Allergens_____

Restaurant name: _____

Address: _____

Hours:_____

Phone Number: _____

Web site: _____

Type of food: _____

Item(s) ordered:_____

_____

Changes made: _____

_____

Comments: For instance, waitperson name, how pleased you were with the meal, reminders to yourself on how you would change your order next time: _____

_____

If you would like to share this information with others through the update or next edition of this book, please complete the Submittal form or send above information to What No Wheat Publishing, 4757 E. Greenway Road, Ste 107B - #91, Phoenix, AZ 85032.

We look forward to building a network of 'Friendly Restaurants' with you.

LynnRae Ries

Personalized Dining Out Notes

Dining Out Notes for (name) _____
Intolerances/Allergens_____

Restaurant name: _____

Address: _____

Hours:_____

Phone Number: _____

Web site: _____

Type of food: _____

Item(s) ordered:_____

_____

Changes made: _____

_____

Comments: For instance, waitperson name, how pleased you were with the meal, reminders to yourself on how you would change your order next time: _____

_____

If you would like to share this information with others through the update or next edition of this book, please complete the Submittal form or send above information to What No Wheat Publishing, 4757 E. Greenway Road, Ste 107B - #91, Phoenix, AZ 85032.

We look forward to building a network of 'Friendly Restaurants' with you.

LynnRae Ries

Shopping List

How many times have you wondered where you purchased an item, or if you called one of our sponsors for an order! This section of the book is to help you keep a record of which stores carry your favorite items and the items you enjoy from certain mail order businesses.

It is also an excellent spot to record names of brands you have verified are gluten-free or suit your dietary needs.

Favorite Item or Verified Brand	Store or mail order company Manufacturer	Notes

Shopping List

How many times have you wondered where you purchased an item, or if you called one of our sponsors for an order! This section of the book is to help you keep a record of which stores carry your favorite items and the items you enjoy from certain mail order businesses.

It is also an excellent spot to record names of brands you have verified are gluten-free or suit your dietary needs.

Favorite Item or Verified Brand	Store or mail order company Manufacturer	Notes

Submittal Form

For Restaurants, Stores, Bakeries, Bed & Breakfasts

Please use this form for submitting information to help others. Complete this form if either you or your company answers "Yes" to any of the following:

■ Provides a walk in service for the gluten-free and allergen-free community (restaurant, store, bakery, Bed & Breakfast, vacation or get-away)

■ Would like to be a Sponsor because you provide a manufactured product or service that was developed to meet the needs of those on the gluten-free allergen-free diet.

■ Wants to recommend any of the above to be included in the next issue of this book or its update. When sending the submittal form, please include your name, phone number or e-mail so we may let the company know of the recommendation.

■ Would like to make a comment or recommendation for the next issue of this book or its update.

Submittal Form

For Restaurants, Stores, Bakeries, Bed & Breakfasts

Date: _____

Contact Person:_____

Business (or your) Name:_____

Business Address:_____

City, State, Zip:_____

Phone Numbers:_____

Fax:_____

Website:_____

E-mail:_____

Description of the business, service or sponsor. Your comment or recommendations:

_____

_____

_____

_____

Please send this form to: What No Wheat Publishing, 4757 E. Greenway Road, Suite 107B - #91, Phoenix, AZ 85032 OR email information to glutenfreenews@cox.net

Submittal Form

For Restaurants, Stores, Bakeries, Bed & Breakfasts

Date: _____

Contact Person:_____

Business (or your) Name:_____

Business Address:_____

City, State, Zip:_____

Phone Numbers:_____

Fax:_____

Website:_____

E-mail:_____

Description of the business, service or sponsor. Your comment or recommendations:

_____

_____

_____

_____

Please send this form to: What No Wheat Publishing, 4757 E. Greenway Road, Suite 107B - #91, Phoenix, AZ 85032 OR email information to glutenfreenews@cox.net

Submittal Form

For Restaurants, Stores, Bakeries, Bed & Breakfasts

Date: _____

Contact Person:_____

Business (or your) Name:_____

Business Address:_____

City, State, Zip:_____

Phone Numbers:_____

Fax:_____

Website:_____

E-mail:_____

Description of the business, service or sponsor. Your comment or recommendations:

_____

_____

_____

_____

Please send this form to: What No Wheat Publishing, 4757 E. Greenway Road, Suite 107B - #91, Phoenix, AZ 85032 OR email information to glutenfreenews@cox.net

Submittal Form

For Restaurants, Stores, Bakeries, Bed & Breakfasts

Date: _____

Contact Person:_____

Business (or your) Name:_____

Business Address:_____

City, State, Zip:_____

Phone Numbers:_____

Fax:_____

Website:_____

E-mail:_____

Description of the business, service or sponsor. Your comment or recommendations:

_____

_____

_____

_____

Please send this form to: What No Wheat Publishing, 4757 E. Greenway Road, Suite 107B - #91, Phoenix, AZ 85032 OR email information to glutenfreenews@cox.net

Submittal Form

For Restaurants, Stores, Bakeries, Bed & Breakfasts

Date: _____

Contact Person:_____

Business (or your) Name:_____

Business Address:_____

City, State, Zip:_____

Phone Numbers:_____

Fax:_____

Website:_____

E-mail:_____

Description of the business, service or sponsor. Your comment or recommendations:

_____

_____

_____

_____

Please send this form to: What No Wheat Publishing, 4757 E. Greenway Road, Suite 107B - #91, Phoenix, AZ 85032 OR email information to glutenfreenews@cox.net

About This Book

After many years of being gluten-free and helping others live the gluten-free lifestyle, I began to feel isolated from a world that offers fabulous foods. I also longed for the freedom of being able to dine out and travel wherever I chose—as safely as possible.

When I spoke with other people across the country, the vast majority said they felt the same way.

Out of this combined desire to venture beyond our front doors, *Waiter, Is there Wheat in My Soup?* was born.

Over the next year the book grew to include food allergens. It grew again to include services, businesses and Sponsors that welcome and cater to people on specialized diets.

Consequently, *Waiter, Is there Wheat in My Soup?* became my mission…

….and the mission of others in the gluten-free and allergen-free communities as they submitted information, helped with research, offered their stories and sponsored this book.

I enjoyed every minute of researching and writing this book, even though it was not always easy.

Not every place of business or service wants to deal with special diets. I was amazed at some remarks made by people. But the sting of being turned away was soothed each time a store, restaurant, bed & breakfast or park said, "Yes, we can do that. Include us in your book."

Each time I was told about or discovered a new restaurant that would commit to being in print, I was joyous to think another nugget of gold would be shared with you, my friends.

Naturally, *Waiter, Is there Wheat in My Soup?* does not provide all the answers

It simply is not possible—yet. But with the changing of food labeling, more recommendations being submitted, and the increasing diagnosis of celiac, gluten intolerance and food allergens, this book will grow to twice its size at its next publication.

We request stores, bakeries, restaurants, Bed & Breakfasts, etc who are not included, to take the steps necessary to become part of the next edition of *Waiter, Is there Wheat in My Soup?* and if you already are servicing people on medically prescribed diets, please submit your information to us so you may be included in the update. See Submittal form

We also welcome suggestions for the next edition of this book, and comments on how this book has helped you. See Submittal form.

Thank You to everyone who helped to make this book possible.

And to you, the reader, may this book improve your life, especially when you venture beyond your front door.

LynnRae Ries

About the Author

LynnRae Ries is a well-known and experienced business-woman, author, speaker and supporter in the gluten-free and allergen-free communities. In addition to this book, her publications include *What? No Wheat? A primer to living the gluten-free wheat-free life; Delicious Gluten-Free Wheat-Free Breads;* and *No Cook No Bake Gluten-Free Appetizers, Snacks and Finger Food.*

LynnRae was diagnosed with celiac gluten-intolerance in 1999. Since that time she has written books, reviewed restaurants, developed gluten-free-friendly menus, represented manufacturers, consulted with businesses, and helped others to live the gluten-free life through local and national support organizations.

She is Executive Director of the Gluten-Free Cooking Club/ School; Advisor to the Gluten-Free Group of Arizona, a GIG Branch and consults with others in the development of their businesses.

LynnRae Ries graduated Magna Cum Laude from the University of Minnesota with a degree in Business and Communication and has created a number of successful start up businesses. Visit her website at www.whatnowheat.com.